HSC
Health & Safety Commission
Printing Industry Advisory Committee

THE PRINTER'S GUIDE
TO HEALTH AND SAFETY

PRINTING HEALTH & SAFETY

Second edition

WHAT IS PIAC?

The Printing Industry Advisory Committee (PIAC) was formed in July 1979 to advise the Health and Safety Commission (HSC) on matters concerning the printing industry. The members of PIAC are nominated by the CBI and the TUC and appointed by HSC to work together with the Health and Safety Executive (HSE) to advise the industry on health and safety.

Why does PIAC exist?

Every year people working in the printing industry are seriously injured. Many others suffer ill health which prevents them from doing their normal work. Almost all of these cases could be prevented.

PIAC is determined to take action to improve health and safety performance in the printing industry. As part of this process PIAC has produced this guidance book to help those responsible for health and safety in the industry understand their responsibilities and take the necessary action.

ACKNOWLEDGEMENTS

Assistance from the following in providing photographs is gratefully acknowledged:

Matthews the Printers

Harmsworth Quays Printing Ltd

Delta Displays

Heidelberg Graphic Equipment

Printo Wrappings

Goss Graphic Systems Ltd

Palamatic Handling Systems Ltd

Strategic Safety Systems

Health and Safety Laboratory

News International Newspapers Ltd

MEMBERS OF THE PRINTING INDUSTRY ADVISORY COMMITTEE

Mr A D Porter	Chair, Health and Safety Executive
Mr I Wilcock	British Printing Industries Federation
Mr R A Hudspith	Graphical, Paper and Media Union
Mr D Barker	Graphical, Paper and Media Union
Mr A Clarke	Graphical, Paper and Media Union
Mr G Mcintyre	National Union of Journalists
Mr G Cooper	Newspaper Society
Mr G McNab	Scottish Print Employers Federation
Mr B Purkis	Newspaper Publishers Association
Mr W Stothard	British Printing Industries Federation
Ms S Whittaker	Newspaper Publishers Association
Mr M Griffiths	Graphical, Paper and Media Union
Mr M D Wilcock	Secretary, Health and Safety Executive

MEMBERS OF PIAC SAFETY AND HUMAN FACTORS SUB-COMMITTEE

Mr M D Wilcock	Chair, Health and Safety Executive
Mr R A Hudspith	Graphical, Paper and Media Union
Ms Z Denmark	Jarrard Printing Ltd
Mr P Chambers	Strategic Safety Systems
Mr D Wallis	Goss Graphic Systems Ltd
Mr P Bryant	Goss Graphic Systems Ltd
Mr M McGilly	West Ferry Printers

The assistance provided by S Peace, S Huggans, J Hardy, K Marriott and T Stonley is gratefully acknowledged.

CONTENTS

Contents

INTRODUCTION

Every year people in the printing industry are injured and become ill through work. The aim of this booklet, and others produced by PIAC, is to help all those involved in printing, including employers, employees and suppliers, to identify the main causes of accidents and ill health and to explain how to eliminate the hazards and control the risks. If you are a manager, it will help you manage health, safety and welfare in your company and comply with your legal responsibilities. If you are an employee or safety representative in the industry, it should provide you with some useful information about what standards to expect and how accidents and ill health might be prevented.

What is in this book for me?

This book is a 'one-stop shop' giving health and safety advice to printers. All printers, large and small, should find something of interest in it. Chapters 1, 2, 3, 6, 7 and 8 cover general health and safety issues and will be useful to everyone, from newspaper producers to high-street copiers or digital printers. Chapters 4 and 5 are more specialised and cover specific hazards arising from substances or processes used by printers. To help you find your way around the book, each chapter is colour coded and a comprehensive index can be found at the back.

As printing is a wide-ranging activity, this book does not deal with every hazard which may arise or every precaution that can be taken. It does, however, outline some of the more serious and frequent hazards and ways of dealing with them.

There are 'Relevant legislation' sections at the start of each chapter which list the Acts, regulations etc which apply and may also contain summaries of the main legal requirements. These sections have a blue background.

You may find this book tells you all you need to know, but if not, the 'References' section will help you find out more. This is structured in chapter order to make it easier to use. See the 'Further information' section for useful addresses.

Looking at your business in the way this book suggests will help you stay safe. Following the advice in it will mean that you are going a long way to satisfying the law.

The law and guidance

The term 'reasonably practicable' is used in much of UK health and safety law and will be found in this book. This means that the degree of risk in a particular job or workplace needs to be balanced against the time, trouble, cost and physical difficulty of taking measures to avoid or reduce the risk. In other words, it would have to be shown that a particular risk is insignificant in relation to the sacrifice needed to reduce it. This book will help you decide what is reasonably practicable for your company.

The word 'must' indicates a definite legal requirement. 'Do's and don'ts', 'shoulds' and 'should nots' and other recommendations represent best and good practice which will lead to compliance with what is reasonably practicable. However, there may be other legally acceptable ways of achieving the

same objective. The requirements of an
Approved Code of Practice (ACOP) have a
special status in law; a court will find fault if
you have not followed the Code or done
something equally effective.

'Think about', 'consider' and similar phrases
contain a tip or hint which may not amount to
a precise legal requirement but indicate an
approach to a health and safety problem
which ought to be considered.

A 'safeguard' is a means of reducing risk to
health and/or safety.

Chapter 1
MANAGING HEALTH AND SAFETY

■ ■ ■ ■ ■ ■ ■ ■ ■ ■ ■ ■

See the 'References' section at the back of the book for details of publications which relate to MANAGING HEALTH AND SAFETY

Relevant legislation

The Health and Safety at Work etc Act 1974 (HSW Act) and the Management of Health and Safety at Work Regulations 1999 place duties on companies and individuals to ensure that adequate provisions are made for health and safety at work. Directors, managers and other responsible people all have duties under the Act. Commitment to the effective management of health and safety should come from the top.

You must ensure, so far as is reasonably practicable, the health, safety and welfare of your employees and any others who may be affected by what you do. This will include those who work for you as casual workers, part-timers, trainees and others who visit your premises, eg customers or contractors. It will also include those who may be affected by what you do, eg neighbours, clients, sales people, members of the public and those who use products or equipment you make, supply or import.

In addition, employers must:

● identify the measures they need to take by carrying out a risk assessment (and if you employ five or more you will need to record the main findings);

● have a written health and safety policy (if you employ five or more people);

● have adequate arrangements for health and safety and, in particular, for the effective planning, organisation, control, monitoring and review of the preventive measures required under health and safety law;

● provide employees with any necessary information and training in safe practices;

● appoint one or more competent persons to help them take the measures necessary to comply with their legal duties. This includes requirements imposed by the Fire Precautions (Workplace) Regulations 1997. A competent person is regarded as a person who has had enough training, experience or knowledge and other qualities to enable them to provide effective help. Employers should appoint their own employees for this role if possible.

Health and safety in the printing industry

The printing industry is a significant employer in the United Kingdom. There are approximately 340 000 workers employed in over 15 000 companies, making the industry one of the largest employers in the country.

According to HSE's annual statistics, the printing sector has a lower accident rate than associated industries such as paper and board production. However, there are aspects of the printing sector's health and safety record which cause concern, in particular a high rate of machinery-related accidents (five times higher than in other industries) and the number of contractors involved in accidents. There are also significant health risks, such as dermatitis and other problems associated with the use of solvents that need to be considered.

Detailed analysis of the pattern of accidents in the printing industry shows many similarities to industry in general, but there are key sector-specific differences. Particular parts of the manufacturing process - printing itself, and warehousing, yard and waste disposal activities, consistently emerge as the main areas where accidents occur.

The proportion of accidents attributable to finishing varies considerably from 13% in the newspaper sector to 40% in book binding and finishing. Almost a quarter of all accidents result from manual handling, usually lifting. Many are also caused by contact with moving machinery.

For accidents directly involving some form of machinery, almost three-fifths occur while the injured person is cleaning or preparing the printing machinery, ie 'make-ready'. One in five such accidents occur as the injured person is attempting to free a blockage in their machine. Cuts, strains and pinch injuries are the most common type across the industry. Many of these accidents can be easily prevented.

Most warehouse accidents involve workplace transport or result from manual handling.

Employers in the printing sector need to look carefully at their risk assessments and the control measures they use such as physical safeguards, safe systems of work and training. Compare where you are now with the benchmark standards for the industry described in this book. This publication gives you a good starting point for all your health and safety needs.

Setting your policy

If you employ five or more people, you must have a written statement of your health and safety policy. It needs to be a carefully prepared, well-thought-out and up-to-date document based on commitment at senior management level.

The statement should be specific to your firm, setting out your general policy for protecting the health and safety of your employees at work and specifying the organisation and arrangements for putting the policy into practice. The primary purpose of this document is to set out your basic action plan on health and safety and it should lead to better standards in the workplace.

The policy needs to:

- state what your general aims are with regard to your employees' health and safety. The statement should be signed and dated by senior management to make the firm's commitment to the policy clear;

- clearly show where the duties for health and safety lie. Responsibility for health and safety rests at the highest management level, however, individuals at every level will have to contribute and accept some responsibility for carrying out the policy;

- describe the systems and procedures in place for ensuring the health and safety of your employees. You can link this to other documents such as risk assessments, fire precautions and your COSHH assessment (see Chapter 4), in which you will have considered the risks that arise in your workplace and the action to control them. Your policy should be clearly set out;

- be brought to the notice of your employees, eg by giving them a copy;

- be reviewed and if necessary revised if the organisation changes or new hazards arise;

- be supported by sufficient resources, eg enough finance, people and time to translate the policy into action.

Organising your staff

The four 'Cs' of a positive health and safety culture are:

- competence - in recruitment, training and advisory support;

- control - by allocating responsibilities and securing commitment;

- co-operation - between individuals and groups;

- communication - including oral, written and visible forms.

Ask yourself:

- Do people know what they should be doing and how to do it?

- Do you consult and involve your staff and the safety representatives effectively? (See 'Consulting employees on health and safety' later in this chapter.)

- Do your staff have enough information about the risks they may be exposed to, the controls provided and how to use them?

- Do you have the right levels of expertise? Are your people properly trained? (See Chapter 2.)

- Do you need specialist advice from outside the organisation and have you arranged to obtain it?

Planning and risk assessment

Systematic planning for health and safety is needed so that hazards can be identified, risks assessed, control measures and priorities determined and the necessary resources allocated. Ask yourself:

- Do you have a health and safety plan?

- Is health and safety always considered before any new work is started?

- Have you identified hazards and assessed risks to your staff and the public, and set control standards for premises, plant, substances, procedures, people and products?

- Do you have a plan to deal with serious or imminent dangers, eg fires, or chemical spills?

- Are the standards implemented and risks effectively controlled?

The Management of Health and Safety at Work Regulations 1999 set out broad general duties aimed at improving health and safety management. Among other things, they require precautions to be identified by means of risk assessments carried out in the workplace and a competent person to be appointed to help employers carry out their duties.

Risk assessment

The purpose of risk assessment is to help employers or self-employed people determine what measures should be taken to comply with legal duties. This includes general duties under the HSW Act and the more specific duties in other Acts and regulations. Once determined, action will need to be taken to put the necessary preventive and protective measures in place.

For most common chemicals, PIAC has already done most of the work for you. (See *COSHH essentials for printers* and Chapter 4 for details.)

The risk assessment needs to consider:

● the level of risk;

● who might be harmed;

● whether significant risks are being adequately controlled.

A hazard is anything with the potential to cause harm, and risk is the chance of harm actually being done. For example, a can of highly flammable liquid stored in a closed metal cabinet in a workroom may be a flammable hazard because of its nature but there is little risk as it is stored safely. The risk increases if the liquid is poured into an open container because there is then a danger of spillage. The risk significantly increases if people are smoking in the area.

The following five steps need to be followed when carrying out a risk assessment:

Step 1 Identify the hazards

● Take a careful look at what you do and how you do it. Remember to include everything like transport, solvent storage, housekeeping and work equipment. You will identify numerous health and safety hazards with the help of this book.

● Think about what can go wrong, how people can be harmed and where it might happen. For example people being hit by a vehicle, trapped in a machine or exposed to hazardous chemicals.

● Consider the worst. Could they be killed, will they lose a limb or simply be bruised? This will help you later when you need to work out what action you need to take first.

Step 2 Decide who might be harmed and how

● Consider who could be hurt if things go wrong. Include your employees, contractors and new untrained, unskilled operatives and other vulnerable groups such as the young.

● Do not forget visitors, maintenance staff and members of the public.

Step 3 Evaluate the risks arising from the hazards and take the necessary remedial action

● Ask whether existing precautions are enough to protect people and, if they are not, what more needs to be done. Do not assume people can concentrate all of the time. Check existing safeguards do what they're intended to do. Remember, badly designed guards can be defeated and, if not properly maintained, will fail. (See Chapter 5 for more detail.)

● Use recognised industry standards, such as publications from the Health and Safety Executive (HSE), PIAC, the British Printing Industries Federation (BPIF) or other trade associations as a benchmark.

● For chemicals refer to *COSHH essentials for printers* and manufacturers' data sheets. For further advice, see Chapter 4. You need to keep up to date with developments such as safer solvents or new types of machinery guarding. Refer to suppliers' instructions and data sheets. Ask yourself whether the precautions you have in place comply with the law, represent good practice and reduce risk so far as is reasonably practicable.

- Prioritise your actions.

- Allocate necessary resources.

- Implement procedures to ensure the necessary work will be done.

Step 4 Record your findings

- If you have five or more employees you must record the significant findings of your assessment. (An example risk assessment form is given in Appendix 2. A schematic diagram of hazards to consider in an overall assessment of a small printing premises is given in Appendix 3.)

Step 5 Review your assessment

- You will also need to revise your assessment when necessary. You may find that you need to make changes to your arrangements after you have investigated the causes of an accident. Once improvements have been made, remember that things change and you need to check regularly that precautions remain in place and are effective.

Monitoring

Monitoring is a management responsibility and should take place at all levels. Your safety policy should include arrangements for monitoring and it is a requirement under the Management of Health and Safety at Work Regulations 1999. Monitoring should include spot checks and more detailed inspections. Reports of all accidents, near misses and ill health caused by work should be studied to identify emerging trends or patterns. Information from monitoring helps you to decide:

- what needs improvement;

- what progress is necessary and reasonable in the circumstances;

- how that progress might be achieved against particular restraints (eg resources or time).

Inspection and checks

Monitoring can be carried out by several different methods, eg:

- routine checks by managers, supervisors and maintenance staff, eg tours of inspection;

- statutory tests and examinations by competent persons, eg of lift truck chains, lifting equipment, and pressure systems by engineering surveyors;

- reporting of defects by employees, eg operator daily/weekly inspection of machinery safeguards;

- health surveillance by a responsible person, eg inspecting hands of printers who work with UV-cured inks for signs of dermatitis;

- investigation of incidents and monitoring of reports to identify reasons for failures in controls and the steps needed to prevent a recurrence.

Evaluation of accidents, ill health and near misses

An effective system for recording all relevant incidents is important. Records of accidents/ill health and near misses can be used to identify problem areas and take relevant action. A lack of accidents does not necessarily mean all is well - good luck may have been playing a role.

Detailed investigation of incidents will help you identify the underlying causes of all incidents. It will help you highlight weaknesses or omissions in your policy or management systems. The findings can be used to help prevent recurrence and initiate the necessary remedial action (which should be carried out promptly). See 'Accidents and emergencies'.

Auditing and review

Health and safety auditing aims to provide a comprehensive, independent check of work activities. It will review existing arrangements for managing and monitoring health and safety and identify any shortcomings. It provides feedback to managers on how well risks are being controlled. Auditing is usually most effective when it is carried out by people independent of the areas being audited, eg from another department or site.

Auditing schemes can be developed in-house or commercially available schemes can be used. A number of consultants operate schemes but printing firms need to satisfy themselves that a consultant is appropriate, sufficiently qualified and competent to help in their particular operation.

The information obtained from measuring safety performance and auditing can be used to review how well you are doing and what might need improvement.

Home working

Health and safety legislation also applies to those employees who work at home. If you have employees who do this, you still need to ensure they are not exposed to risks from the work they do. See the leaflet *Homeworking: Guidance for employers and employees on health and safety* (INDG226) for further advice.

Lone working

Solitary workers may face particular problems. Without supervisors or co-workers present, they are vulnerable to the normal workplace hazards and do not have access to the assistance they can normally call on. In certain circumstances they may be more exposed. For example, staff leaving later than normal may be unable to get help if threatened in the car park. Solitary workers should not be exposed to significantly more risk than employees who work together. Precautions should take account of normal working conditions and foreseeable emergencies including, fire, illness and accident. For further advice see the leaflet *Working alone in safety: Controlling the risks of solitary work* (INDG73).

Accidents and emergencies

As an employer you need to put in place suitable arrangements for identifying, recording and investigating all relevant accidents and incidents. Certain accidents, dangerous occurrences and incidences of ill health are also reportable.

The law and reporting accidents

The Reporting of Injuries, Diseases and Dangerous Occurrences Regulations 1995 (RIDDOR) require you to report certain accidents, incidents and occupational diseases to your enforcing authority. From 1 April 2001 there has been an Incident Contact Centre (ICC) to record the details you supply. Reports no longer need to be made to your HSE or local authority office.

RIDDOR requires you to do the following:

- Keep details of the incident (eg in your accident book).

- Notify the enforcing authority immediately (via the ICC) if any of the following happen as a result of work:

  - anybody dies;
  - an employee receives a major injury (such as a broken arm or leg or an amputation injury) or any other

person is taken to hospital immediately as a result of an injury caused by your work activities;

- anyone is seriously affected by an electric shock or poisoning;
- if there is a dangerous occurrence, eg a fire or explosion which stops work for more than 24 hours, or a crane overturns.

- Report within ten days accidents at work which result in an employee being absent from work (or unable to do their normal job) for more than three days.

- Report certain diseases suffered by workers who do specified types of work as soon as possible on receiving a written diagnosis about the illness from a medical practitioner.

You can report incidents by telephone (0845 300 9923), fax (0845 300 9924), e-mail (riddor@natbrit.com) or by post to ICC, Caerphilly Business Park, Caerphilly CF83 3GG.

Investigating accidents and emergencies

At the time of writing, the Health and Safety Commission was consulting on a new legal duty to investigate accidents. Whatever the outcome, investigation of accidents and incidents in-house is important to establish the causes and preventive measures needed to minimise the risk of further accidents. You should also look at near misses, minor accidents and property damage. It is often only by good fortune that someone is not injured. Employers need to put procedures in place to ensure the following stages are followed if there is an accident or dangerous occurrence:

- Take any action required to deal with the immediate risks, eg provide first aid, put out the fire, isolate any danger, fence off the area, call the emergency services.

- If the incident is one that must be immediately notified to your enforcing authority, consult them before disturbing the site. Even if the incident

is not reportable, it is sensible to take photographs and measurements before disturbing the site.

- Obtain basic facts, eg witness names, plant condition, substances in use, place, time, extent of injury.

- Establish the circumstances, eg what was being done at the time.

- Try to understand the sequence of events leading up to, during and immediately following the accident.

- From the accident sequence write down the immediate causes of the accident.

- From this list identify the underlying causes of the accident. (You may have to repeat this step several times to get to the root causes of the accident.) For example if an individual did not follow a procedure, try to identify why they did not - it could be due to lack of training, an unrealistic procedure or lack of supervision.

- For each of the underlying causes identified consider what steps need to be taken to prevent a recurrence. At this point consult the guidance issued by PIAC and HSE for specific information on how to control hazards.

- Think also if the initial response to the accident was adequate, eg whether there was an effective first-aid response or whether correct spillage arrangements were used.

- Consider if any of the lessons learned apply elsewhere within the organisation.

- Consider if the risk assessments need to be reviewed in the light of your findings.

- Throughout the investigation, it is important not to jump to conclusions, and involve your trade union appointed safety representatives or employees as appropriate. Think about each step, and if necessary plan what you are going to do BEFORE it happens. The following investigation checklist may be useful. Although it is not an exhaustive list, it gives examples of questions that might be relevant.

Investigation checklist

FACTORS INVOLVED IN THE ACCIDENT	Why this occurred	Action to be taken
Machinery or equipment failure, eg lack of guards, interlocks or maintenance		
Working practice or procedure, eg lack of supervision, custom and practice or no procedure		
The working environment, eg state of the floor, fumes or noise		
The individual, eg lack of training, poor instructions or badly labelled controls		
Substances used, eg solvents or inks have changed		

AS A RESULT OF THIS ASSESSMENT YOU SHOULD THEN TAKE ACTION TO STOP THE ACCIDENT HAPPENING IN FUTURE

DO YOU NEED TO:	YES	NO
Improve physical safeguards, eg provide an interlocked guard?		
Provide and use local exhaust ventilation?		
Use mechanical handling aids, eg pile turners or mobile lifts?		
Introduce better test and maintenance arrangements?		
Improve work methods?		
Provide and use personal protective equipment?		

DO YOU NEED TO:	YES	NO
Make changes to supervision and training arrangements?		
Review similar risks in other departments?		
Set up systems to risk assess new plant and chemicals before use?		
Review procedures for contractors?		
Update standards and policies?		
Introduce monitoring and auditing systems?		
Give training in manual handling techniques?		
Substitute chemicals with something less hazardous?		
Change make-ready procedures or other systems of work?		
Institute health surveillance, eg for UV ink users?		

Dealing with emergencies

When things go wrong people may be exposed to serious and immediate danger. Special procedures are necessary to deal with emergencies such as serious injuries, explosion, fire, electrocution, power failures and chemical spills.

You should prepare an emergency plan especially if a major incident at your workplace could involve risks to the public, the need to rescue employees or co-ordination of the emergency services.

To do this you should carry out a risk assessment and consider:

- the worst that could happen;

- how people - those in charge and others - are instructed and equipped to deal with the problems;

- how the emergency services should get access onto the site;

- how the alarm will be raised (don't forget night and shift working, weekends and holidays);

- how and when to call the emergency services and how to help them with information when they arrive;

- that you will need to notify the fire authority if you have over 25 tonnes of certain dangerous substances on site;

- where to go to reach a place of safety or to get rescue equipment;

- providing emergency lighting;

- whether you have enough emergency exits to allow everyone to escape quickly (and suitable arrangements to ensure that emergency doors and escape routes are kept unobstructed and clearly marked);

- nominating competent employees to take control;

- pre-planning and practising emergency plant shutdowns or making processes safe. Important items such as shut-off valves, electrical isolators etc should be clearly labelled to avoid confusion;

- ensuring you have adequate first-aid provision and first aiders;

- training people in emergency and evacuation procedures and remembering the needs of people with disabilities.

First aid

The Health and Safety (First-Aid) Regulations 1981 require you to have adequate arrangements for first aid. The minimum first-aid provision for each work site is:

- a person appointed to take charge of first-aid arrangements including looking after the equipment and facilities and calling the emergency services when required. An appointed person will need to be available whenever people are at work;

- a suitably stocked first-aid container (easily accessible in cases of emergency);

- information for employees on first-aid arrangements (including notices telling people where the first-aid equipment, facilities and personnel can be found).

Additional provision will be appropriate in many cases, for example:

- If the risks of injury and ill health arising from the work as identified in your risk assessment are significant, trained first aiders may be needed. They may also be needed where large numbers of people are employed. They must be given the right training and hold a certificate (which will be valid for three years). Refresher courses and re-examination will be required when old certificates expire. Information on training courses and organisations can be obtained from your local Employment Medical Advisory Service (who can be contacted via your local HSE office).

- Where there are specific risks from working with hazardous substances, dangerous machinery and loads, consider specific training for first aiders, extra first-aid equipment, siting of first-aid equipment, informing emergency services and first-aid rooms.

- Where workplaces are remote from emergency medical services, inform local medical services of your location and consider special arrangements with them.

- Where you have inexperienced workers, disabled workers or personnel with special health problems, consider the needs for special equipment and local siting of equipment.

- For mobile people, eg sales staff, a first-aid kit needs to be provided.

If you have a small company with few employees it may be more appropriate to have a person trained in emergency first aid. As your company grows you will need to make sure your first-aid provision remains adequate.

Permits to work

Some high-risk activities such as entry into confined spaces or working large machinery will require a permit to work. This is a formal written system used to control certain types of potentially hazardous work. The permit details the work to be done and the necessary precautions to be taken, and forms an essential part of many safe systems of work for maintenance activities. See Chapter 8 for more details.

Working time

The main aim of the Working Time Regulations (WTR) is to ensure that workers are protected against adverse effects on their health and safety caused by working excessively long hours or having inadequate rest. At the time of publication, proposals for changes were under consideration, however further guidance can be found in the booklet *Your guide to the Working Time Regulations* and *A short guide to the Working Time Regulations* (available from DTI, Tel: 08456 000925 or from the DTI website: www.dti.gov.uk).

The problem

Working long hours can have a major effect on the health and safety of employees - those who are tired are more prone to make mistakes, which could result in accidents - or they could develop long-term adverse health effects. For historical or production reasons there is a culture of long hours in some parts of the printing industry, but in many companies careful management of production pressures and planned preventive maintenance programmes can resolve most of the problems that can arise.

Application of WTR

If you employ workers, night workers or young people you are covered by the Working Time Regulations. You need to take particular care to know the rules about young people (between school leaving age and 18 years old) and people who work at night, since special requirements apply to them. Most people working in printing are covered by the law.

Working time limits

For adult workers the limit is 48 hours per week averaged over a 17 week 'reference period'. The average can be calculated over different periods depending on the circumstances. Where a trade union is recognised, employers who want to extend the reference period will need to make an agreement with that trade union. Workforce agreements apply in the absence of a recognised trade union.

Current provisions which allow for individual 'opt-out' from the average 48 hours limit are expected to end within the next two years. Companies will need to take account of the ending of the 'opt-out' and make arrangements to cover this.

Nobody should work for long periods without a break. These are needed to break up monotonous or continuous processes and there are special entitlements for young workers.

Health assessment

Working long hours, especially at night, can disrupt the 'body clock'. Workers who are to work at night must be offered a free health assessment by their company before they start night work and then at suitable intervals, for example before the introduction of a new shift pattern. Take advice from an occupational health professional when you design the assessment.

Night shift risk assessment

The WTR require a risk assessment for the special risks associated with night work which is in addition to the requirements laid down by the Management of Health and Safety at Work Regulations for a general risk assessment and the Control of Substances Hazardous to Health Regulations (COSHH) for a risk assessment for harmful substances. For advice on making these assessments see earlier in this chapter and *COSHH essentials for printers*.

A WTR risk assessment is needed because tasks may become more difficult:

- when performed at night in darkness;

- when the full range of daytime services may not be available;

- where workers find difficulty adjusting to different working patterns;

- where there is increased risk of violence to staff;

- where workers are subject to increased stress because of reduced supervision or management.

The assessment may, for example, identify the need for emergency or supplementary lighting to be installed. Act on the assessment and provide whatever control measures might be needed such as more lighting, additional training in first aid, additional security measures, or perhaps adjust the frequency of breaks.

Records

You do not need to keep special records. Most companies find that the records they already keep of hours worked for other purposes, like pay, are more than adequate for WTR. However, if you have not previously kept records of any sort then WTR does require you to keep sufficient records of the hours your employees work.

People with more than one job

Some people have two or even three jobs, for example working at night in a pub. Where this is the case then the total hours worked should be added together when calculating working time. It is up to you to make reasonable enquiries about any second jobs done by your staff and to co-operate with other employers to calculate total working time.

Good time management is good business

Promotion of good time management results in better health and safety management. It allows employers to plan properly for peaks and troughs, workers to plan a proper regime of work and family life and results in a workforce that is 'happy, healthy and here', increasing production efficiencies.

Figure 1 Contracted work can be small- or large-scale

Control of contractors

Contractors are employed to work in the printing industry for machinery or buildings maintenance and modifications, installation of plant and other equipment. However, nowadays contractors can also be found throughout the industry, as freelance designers, cleaners, caterers and in logistics, doing a range of tasks that were previously done by employees. Everyone working on your premises or for you needs to know what health and safety standards they have to achieve, including notionally self-employed labour-only contractors.

The law and managing contractors

The HSW Act places duties on you and your contractor to protect, so far as is reasonably practicable, the health and safety of employees and other people who may be affected by your work activities. All parties will need to co-operate with each other and co-ordinate their work to ensure everyone is complying with their legal duties.

In addition to the HSW Act and the Management of Health and Safety at Work Regulations 1999, you should be aware of the Construction (Design and Management) Regulations 1994. These Regulations place duties on clients, clients' agents, designers and contractors to plan their approach and take health and safety into account. Health and safety needs to be co-ordinated and managed effectively throughout all stages of a construction project, from conception through to subsequent maintenance and repair arrangements.

Clients must be reasonably satisfied that they only use competent people as planning supervisors, designers and principal contractors. They need to be satisfied that enough resources, including time, have been or will be allocated to enable the project to be carried out. They also require clients to provide relevant information - good examples are the location of services and asbestos-containing products within buildings. (See Chapters 3 and 4 for further information on managing asbestos in workplace buildings.)

The Construction Design and Management Regulations apply where construction work is expected to last more than 30 days or involve five or more people on-site at any one time. This will include the installation of fixed plant where people are liable to fall more than 2 m, such as installation of larger web-fed presses. Where demolition or dismantling of a structure is taking place, the Regulations apply regardless of the length of time or the number of people carrying out the work.

For further information see *A guide to the Construction (Health, Safety and Welfare) Regulations 1996* (INDG220) and the Approved Code of Practice on the Construction (Design and Management) Regulations 1994 (HSG224).

If you have people working under your control and direction who are self-employed for tax and/or NI purposes, they are likely to be treated as your employees for health and safety purposes. You may therefore need to take appropriate action to protect them. If you are in any doubt about who is responsible for the health and safety of a person working for you this could be clarified and included in the terms of the contract. However, remember, you cannot pass on a legal duty that falls to you under the HSW Act by means of a contract and you will still retain duties towards others by virtue of section 3 of the Act.

Five practical stages for working with contractors

As with all things a few simple precautions will save time and prevent accidents in the future. Just like managing your own employees, working with contractors will be made so much easier (and safer) if you follow these five practical stages:

Stage 1: Plan before you start

Decide a few ground rules before you even start to use contractors. If the contractors are going to be working with you for a long time it is especially important to make plans about what you are asking them to do and how your own staff will be working with them.

- Ensure that you have a good planning framework to pull together all the separate elements of what you are asking the contractor to do. Write plans down, meet and consult everyone involved.

- Define the job.

- Identify the hazards. Consider the individual elements of the job and the effect of each piece of contracted work on the whole project.

- Assess the risks.

- Eliminate and reduce the risks that you control.

- Specify the health and safety conditions that you want the contractor to follow.

- Discuss these with the contractor/s.

Stage 2: Choosing a contractor

Contractors should be chosen carefully. Before you choose a contractor:

- Decide what are your criteria for selecting contractors and placing them on an Approved List? Assess their competence in health and safety matters. This applies to senior people as well as those who will be working on your site.

- Decide what safety and technical competence is needed. Has the contractor got it?

- Ask questions about their safety performance. How do they manage their performance? Ask to see the written procedures for similar previous work - their accident record may be a good place to start.

- Get evidence. Examine their training and relevant certificates. Safety passport schemes are a good way of demonstrating the training of individual workers.

- Make contractors aware of your company safety culture.

- Go through information about the job and the site, including site rules and emergency procedures.

- Agree respective responsibilities for risk assessments and precautions.

- Ask for a safety method statement, risk assessment or safety policy.

- Decide whether subcontracting is acceptable and use the information gathered to help you make your decision. If it is, how will health and safety be ensured?

- If you haven't used the contractor before, ask to talk to some of their previous clients.

- Consider how you will monitor their health and safety performance.

Stage 3: Contractors working on site

When they arrive on site you need to have the ground rules in place. These should be agreed BEFORE the contractor starts work. They can include the following:

- How do you control access to your site? Does everyone sign in and out?

- Name a site contact for day-to-day communication - don't just wait for site meetings to discuss and resolve problems. Make sure the person appointed is competent and trained.

- Reinforce health and safety information and site rules with a simple induction course or a safety check card setting out your rules for every visitor. Make sure emergency procedures are covered.

- Implement safe systems of work, such as for hot work or work on fragile roofs.

- How will your own operations affect the contractor's work?

- What tools, plant, substances and equipment will be used?

- What will the arrangements for proper supervision be?

- Check that everyone understands the job before you allow work to begin.

- Don't forget to provide facilities for contractors, ie washroom, toilets, canteen etc.

Stage 4: Keeping a check

Don't just leave the contractor to it. Not only can costs spiral out of control, but safety can too.

- Decide how often you or your managers need to make contact with your contractors.

- Is the job going as planned? Is the contractor working safely and in the way that they agreed? Check if there have been any incidents or changes in personnel?

- Are any changes or special arrangements required?

Stage 5: Reviewing the work

Learn lessons from contracting so that everyone, including your employees and the contractor can improve the way they work. Before you start, plan to review.

- How do you plan to review the job and the contractor's performance with all those involved, including the contractor?

- During the review, ask yourself how effective your planning was, how the contractor performed, and how the job went.

- Record the lessons, review and link these to your selection procedures.

Contractors and your employees

At times such as major rebuilding works there may be large numbers of contractors on site, often working in proximity to your own employees and each other and to a tight deadline. You need to think about how their work may affect each other and how they interact with your own maintenance or production activities. The more activities that are going on, the greater the chance there is of something being overlooked. The key is good communication, planning and control. Without these, chaos can result and accidents will happen.

Consulting employees on health and safety

Employers must consult all of their employees on health and safety matters. Where employers have recognised unions, the Safety Representatives and Safety Committees Regulations 1977 will apply. Where employees are not members of a union, or the union is not recognised, the Health and Safety (Consultation with Employees) Regulations 1996 (HSCER) will apply.

Consultation should include:

- any change that may substantially affect their health and safety at work, eg in procedures, equipment or ways of working such as safe systems of work for cleaning printing cylinders;

- the employer's arrangements for getting competent people to help him or her satisfy health and safety laws;

- the information that employees must be given on the likely risks and dangers arising from their work. This would include fire and explosion hazards when using highly flammable inks and measures to reduce or get rid of these risks;

- the planning of health and safety training;

- the health and safety consequences of introducing new technology, for example use of UV inks.

Further information on consulting employees is available in the free leaflet *Consulting employees on health and safety: A guide to the law* (INDG232).

Under the Safety Representatives and Safety Committees Regulations 1977, trade union appointed safety representatives have the right to:

- investigate potential hazards and dangerous occurrences;

- examine the causes of accidents;

- investigate complaints by employees relating to health and safety;

- make representations to their employer on health and safety matters;

- carry out inspections of the workplace;

- receive time off with pay to perform these functions and undergo training.

Employers have a general duty to consult safety representatives on all aspects of health and safety in the workplace, and provide them with the necessary information, facilities and help to allow them to carry out their functions. This is with a view to making and maintaining arrangements for their joint co-operation in the promotion and development of measures to ensure employees' health and safety at work, and to check the effectiveness of such measures.

A safety committee must be established if requested in writing by two safety representatives. The employer should then consult with the safety representatives and establish the safety committee no later than three months after the request was made. A notice should be posted for employees stating the composition of the committee.

Further information can be found in the priced publication *Safety representatives and safety committees* (L87), known as the 'Brown Book'.

Inspectors and enforcement

Enforcement for health and safety at work lies with either inspectors from HSE or from your local authority. Health and safety in printing and many allied trades is normally enforced by HSE inspectors. An inspector's primary function is to ensure relevant legal standards of health and safety in the workplace have been achieved.

To help enforcing authorities carry out their duties, you are required by law to notify your enforcing authority (normally your local HSE office) that you are occupying a factory or office.

Powers of inspectors

Following a visit, inspectors will provide advice and may confirm this in writing. Inspectors have powers of enforcement which might include:

- serving improvement notices that require improvements to be made within a certain time;

- serving prohibition notices that stop a process or the use of a piece of equipment where a risk of serious personal injury exists;

- prosecution of a business, or under certain circumstances an individual, for breaches of health and safety law.

They may visit to inspect the workplace or to investigate accidents or complaints. They often visit workplaces without giving notice but you are entitled to see their identification before letting them in. Their powers include right of entry into your premises, the right to talk to employees and safety representatives and to take photographs and samples. They are entitled to your co-operation and answers to questions.

Inspectors will enforce the law when they judge it necessary, but they are concerned to help you do what is reasonable and practicable to control risks to health and safety. They will give advice and you may turn to them for guidance. They are happy to answer questions and give you information, much of which is free. You can also contact your local HSE office or HSE's website: www.hse.gov.uk or HSE Books: www.hsebooks.co.uk or, for general enquiries, contact HSE's InfoLine Tel: 08701 545500.

Chapter 2

TRANING

. . . .

See the 'References' section at the back of the book for details of publications which relate to TRAINING

Relevant legislation

Training requirements are identified in several Acts and regulations including the following:

- Health and Safety at Work etc Act 1974 (HSW Act)

- Management of Health and Safety at Work Regulations 1999

- Provision and Use of Work Equipment Regulations 1998 (PUWER 98)

- Control of Substances Hazardous to Health Regulations 1999 (COSHH)

- Electricity at Work Regulations 1989

It is crucial that all employees, including supervisors and managers, have adequate health and safety training.

Training methods

These will vary for different people and jobs depending on existing abilities and the risks of the job. Any training provider needs to be competent.

Training can be carried out by one or more of the following:

- in-house training personnel (this might include supervisors);

- external trainers (this can be done on the premises or by sending employees away on short courses or day-release courses);

- distance and open-learning techniques;

- training provided by suppliers and manufacturers following installation of new or refurbished machinery, or the introduction of new consumables such as blanket washes;

- 'sitting with Nellie' - you should be confident that the person giving the training is competent both in the job and its health and safety aspects to avoid passing on bad habits.

Training materials are available from a number of sources including the Printing Industry Advisory Committee (PIAC), trade organisations, safety organisations such as the British Safety Council (BSC) and the Royal Society for the Prevention of Accidents (RoSPA), and independent training and health and safety consultants.

The PIAC *Printing industry: Health and safety training package* published by HSE is a comprehensive open-learning course designed for use in medium and larger print employers and printing colleges. It contains targeted modules covering a range of subjects including noise and risk assessments, assessing machinery guarding and conducting accident investigation.

For each activity a structured training session is provided including subjects for discussion and case studies, supported by hand-outs and visual aids. The package has been designed to be used and delivered by competent in-house staff.

Sector Skills Councils (SSCs)(UK-wide), Learning and Skills Councils (LSCs) in England, Education and Learning Wales (ELWa) in Wales and Local Enterprise Companies (LECs) in Scotland are able to provide practical help on training. They can also provide information on National and Scottish Vocational Qualifications (NVQs and SVQs) which meet standards of competence laid down for particular jobs. Many of these qualifications can be obtained by attendance at various printing colleges around the country.

The Institute of Occupational Safety and Health (IOSH) provides training and examination in technical, legal and health and safety management.

Organisations such as the British Printing Industries Federation (BPIF) and the Graphical, Paper and Media Union (GPMU) also provide a range of print-specific health and safety training courses for all levels within companies.

See the 'Further information' section for the full contact details of these organisations.

Induction training

Induction training for new employees will help them settle into their work. This type of training usually includes information about the company, the organisation for managing health and safety, the hazards of the workplace, the principles of safe working practice and the safety responsibilities of individuals.

Managers and supervisors have a legal responsibility to maintain a safe working environment. They are accountable for the safety of those under their control. They are responsible for spotting hazards or poor working practices and correcting them. They are also responsible for investigating accidents and near misses and may have further specific duties allocated to them under the safety policy.

Senior managers need to know enough about health and safety to determine priorities and to assess the performance of people further down the management line. They should examine the health and safety training needs of individuals at regular intervals. The commitment to training should be spelt out in the company safety policy.

After induction, the health and safety training needs for each individual should be identified and training provided so that no one is asked to perform a task for which they have not been trained.

The following are examples of the topics appropriate for inclusion in induction training at different levels within a company:

Training for all employees - example topics

- Company structure

- Company safety policy

- Safety committees

- Safety representatives

- Occupational health arrangements

- Responsibilities of individuals

- Company rules

- Hazards and safe working standards, including:

    - Safe systems of work
    - Housekeeping
    - Machinery safety

- Visual display units (VDUs)
- Fire
- Chemicals and solvents
- Materials handling
- Electricity
- Noise
- First aid

Training for all supervisors/managers - example topics

- Responsibilities - including their own responsibilities and those of others in the company
- Monitoring of health and safety standards
- Hazard identification
- Accident investigation and reporting
- Risk assessment
- Relevant legal requirements
- Safe systems of work and other methods used to control risk
- Sources of information
- Control of contractors

Training for senior managers - example topics

- Purpose of company health and safety policy
- Causes of accidents/ill health and their costs
- Planning for health and safety
- Monitoring accidents, reports and statistics
- Personal responsibility and accountability
- Functions of safety committees and safety representatives
- Developing a safety culture
- Use of safety audits
- Relevant legal requirements
- Role of safety adviser
- Knowledge of the work of HSE and other authorities
- Role of the Occupational Health Service
- Existence of relevant standards and guidance

Remember there are many hazardous activities in the printing industry where specific job training in safe systems of work etc is essential, eg press cleaning, webbing-up, guillotine operating, maintenance work, lift trucks, and manual handling.

Even experienced employees may need training when they are moved to new areas of work or asked to operate new types of machines. Retraining should be carried out regularly, to reinforce particular safety issues, or when there are changes in the process and equipment. Sometimes accident investigations can reveal the need for retraining.

Training needs should be regularly reviewed to check that the training delivered is adequate. Training needs can also be reviewed when investigating accidents, investigating near misses and as a result of carrying out risk assessment. From time to time it pays to do refresher training. Everyone can get stale and this avoids slipping into bad habits.

Training safety representatives

Trade union appointed safety representatives have two distinct training needs. Firstly, they need to understand their functions as a trade union official and to do this they are entitled to time off with pay to attend a TUC or other approved trade union course.

Secondly, they may need additional training in the particular hazards of the industry - not only the hazards in their own jobs but also the hazards of work done by the people they represent. The employer has duties towards safety representatives (see 'Consulting employees on health and safety' in Chapter 1). Companies should co-operate so that trade union appointed safety representatives in their company can receive adequate training on industry hazards, rules and procedures.

ACCIDENTS

Job specific

The operator of an offset litho printing machine was strangled when his pullover was caught by the inking rollers. He was trying to retrieve misfed paper via the gap beneath the duct keys below the inking rollers guard. The guard was deficient and the operator did not turn the machine off before trying to retrieve the paper. Training should have been given in the safe method of working and the required standard of machinery guarding. Procedures should have been in place to check the condition of guards regularly.

A machine operator in a printing works damaged his spine when he fell from a ladder while carrying out maintenance work at high-level machinery. The ladder was not tied or footed. Operators regularly carried out minor maintenance work but no one had been trained to use ladders.

Training for those moving jobs

An experienced printer had part of his right index finger amputated while changing the blade of a guillotine he had not operated before and had not been trained to use.

Refresher training

A printing shop supervisor trapped two fingers in a folding machine while clearing a creased piece of paper without stopping the machine. He had been fully trained some years previously but had short-circuited the safe work procedures so frequently without incident that he no longer recognised the obvious risk.

Chapter 3
WORKPLACE AND TRANSPORT SAFETY

See the 'References' section at the back of the book for details of publications which relate to WORKPLACE AND TRANSPORT SAFETY

Relevant legislation

General requirements for workplace and transport safety are contained in a number of Acts and regulations such as the Health and Safety at Work etc Act 1974 (HSW Act) and the Management of Health and Safety at Work Regulations 1999.

The Workplace (Health, Safety and Welfare) Regulations 1992 are specifically aimed at protecting the health and safety of everyone in the workplace, and ensuring that adequate welfare facilities are provided for people at work. Employers have duties to ensure that workplaces under their control comply with these Regulations. More detailed information can be found in the publication *Workplace health, safety and welfare. Workplace (Health, Safety and Welfare) Regulations 1992. Approved Code of Practice* (L24).

The Disability Discrimination Act 1995 creates a right of non-discrimination against disabled people in the field of employment, including a duty on employers to provide 'reasonable adjustment' to working conditions or the working environment to overcome the practical effects of disability. Employers are not expected to make any changes which would break health and safety laws.

The employment part of the Disability Discrimination Act does not apply to employers who employ fewer than 20 people. However, they are encouraged to follow good practice guidelines. Further information on the Disability Discrimination Act should be obtained from the Department for Education and Skills.

Fundamentals of workplace health and safety

Some of the basic requirements for employers are:

Safe place of work

You must have:

- buildings in good repair;

- precautions that stop people or materials falling from open edges, eg mezzanine floors, racking areas and running boards;

- space for safe movement and access, eg around reelstands and on mezzanine floors;

- floors, corridors and stairs etc free from obstructions, eg trailing cables and pallets;

- good drainage in wet processes, eg screen cleaning in screen printing or flexographic printing using water-based inks;

- windows that can be opened and cleaned safely including roof lights. You may need to fit anchor points if window cleaners need to use harnesses;

- weather protection for those working outdoors, eg lift truck drivers, security guards, traffic controllers (banksmen) and delivery workers;

- outdoor routes kept safe during icy conditions, eg salted, sanded and swept.

Also think about:

- machinery and furniture being sited so that projecting parts do not cause a risk of injury, eg at buckle-folders;

- not overloading floors - presses, particularly old ones, are very heavy;

- space for storing tools and materials.

Lighting

You must provide:

- enough light. Use natural light where possible but try to avoid glare;

- a good level of local lighting at workstations;

- suitable forms of lighting. Some fluorescent tubes flicker and can be dangerous, giving some rotating machinery the appearance of being stationary;

- well-lit outside areas - this will help security.

You will need special fittings for flammable or explosive atmospheres, eg at heat-set ovens, flexographic and gravure presses (see 'Explosion risks in flexographic and gravure' in Chapter 7).

Light-coloured walls help to make the most of natural and artificial light.

Further guidance about lighting is given in the booklet *Lighting at work* (HSG38).

Moving around the premises

You must have:

- safe passage for pedestrians and vehicles. You may need clearly marked separate routes (see 'Safe movement of vehicles' later in this chapter);

- level, even surfaces without holes or broken boards;

- hand-rails on stairs and ramps where necessary;

- safe doors, eg vision panels in swing doors and sensitive edges on power doors;

- surfaces which are not slippery.

Think about marking steps, kerbs and fixed obstacles, eg by black and yellow diagonal stripes.

Designing workstations

When designing workstations and seating arrangements, consider comfort and safety. Ergonomic principles should be followed and adequate account taken of responsibilities under the Manual Handling Operations Regulations 1992 and the Health and Safety (Display Screen Equipment) Regulations 1992. This advice applies to the hand-working and insertion sectors in particular.

Workstations and seating must suit the worker and the work. Seating must be provided where the work operations (or substantial parts of the operations) can or must be done sitting. Seating should also be provided for employees whose work necessitates them having to stand for long periods.

In some circumstances manual handling risks may be better controlled by people standing up to carry out a task. Other measures to reduce the risks and provide relief from standing, such as regular job rotation, can also be taken. Further information is given in the booklet *Seating at work* (HSG57).

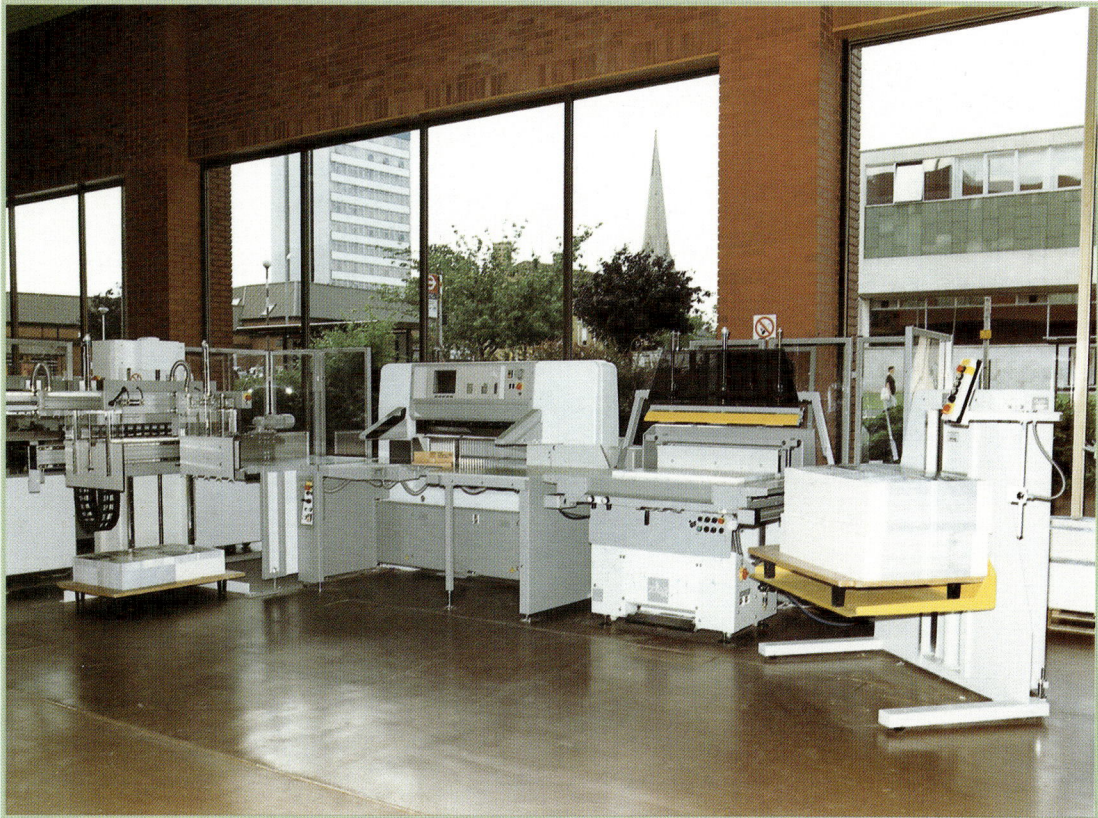

Figure 2 *Modern guillotine and handling system*

Cleanliness

You must:

- provide clean floors and stairs which are not slippery;

- provide clean premises, furniture and fittings (eg lights);

- provide containers for waste materials, eg metal-lidded bins for wash-up cloths;

- remove dirt, refuse and trade waste regularly - remember to notify laundries if they are receiving solvent or uncured UV ink-laden cloths/wipes;

- clear up spillages promptly and arrange proper disposal, eg through a licensed contractor;

- keep internal walls or ceilings clean. They may need painting to help easy cleaning.

Hygiene and welfare

You must provide:

- clean, well-ventilated toilets (separate for men and women unless each toilet has its own lockable door);

- wash basins with hot and cold (or warm) running water;

- soap and towels (or a hand dryer);

- skin cleansers, with nail brushes where necessary;

- pre- or after-work creams and skin conditioning or moisturising creams where necessary;

- drying facilities for wet clothes;

- facilities for workers working away from base;

- lockers or hanging space for clothing;

- changing facilities where special clothing is worn;

- a clean drinking water supply (marked if necessary to distinguish it from the non-drinkable supply);

- rest facilities, such as rest rooms or rest areas, including suitable facilities to eat meals where food eaten in the workplace would otherwise become contaminated. The *Workplace (Health, Safety and Welfare) Regulations 1992. Approved Code of Practice* (L24) outlines additional arrangements, eg for heating food;

- arrangements to protect non-smokers from discomfort caused by tobacco smoke, eg provide separate areas or rooms for smokers and non-smokers or prohibit smoking in rest areas and rest rooms;

- rest facilities for pregnant women and nursing mothers;

- a comfortable temperature and adequate ventilation including fresh air. The *Workplace (Health, Safety and Welfare) Regulations 1992. Approved Code of Practice* (L24) refers to a minimum temperature of 16°C unless the work involves a lot of severe physical effort, in which case the temperature should be at least 13°C.

Safe movement of vehicles

Many accidents each year involve powered vehicles including lorries, vans and lift trucks. Injuries may be severe, and even fatal. Transport movements in and around the workplace need to be controlled to protect pedestrians, and to prevent damage to plant and equipment such as racking systems. Risk assessments need to take account of any contractors who may work on, or visit the site, such as contract loaders in the newspaper industry.

Look at the movement of goods around, into and off the site. For example, check that:

- vehicles and pedestrians are separated as much as possible. Traffic routes used by both need to be wide enough to enable vehicles to pass pedestrians safely. Barriers or rails may be needed in particularly vulnerable places, such as doorways, gateways, tunnels, bridges or other enclosed routes;

- pedestrian access to loading bays and delivery points is controlled;

- the need for vehicles to reverse is kept to a minimum and that, where possible, reversing is restricted to designated areas;

- areas in which vehicles are moved are well lit;

- workstations, vulnerable plant, gas containers and chemical storage facilities are not likely to be struck during vehicle movements;

- traffic routes, roadways and pedestrian routes are clearly marked;

- site speed limits are marked and observed;

- speed control measures, such as humps, are provided where appropriate (gaps may be needed to allow lift trucks to pass safely);

- safe crossing points for pedestrians are marked;

- action is taken to control danger at blind spots, including openings with strip curtains which vehicles travel through or past;

- visiting drivers know and follow your rules;

- if necessary, vehicle movements are directly supervised by properly trained signallers (banksmen), particularly when reversing and near blind corners;

- banksmen are visible to drivers at all times, and are able to stand in a safe position while guiding the reversing vehicle;

- if necessary, high-visibility clothing is provided for and worn by banksmen;

- training in the use of recognised signals is given to drivers and anyone who controls vehicle movements;

- floors and roadways are kept in good condition.

For further information see the free leaflet *Managing vehicle safety at the workplace* (INDG199).

Loading and unloading of vehicles

Accidents frequently happen when people fall from vehicles, or the load moves unexpectedly and they are struck by it. Particular dangers exist where reels of paper are being unloaded as they are heavy and gain momentum once they start to move.

Unloading of reels needs to be done with suitable equipment such as a clamp, boom or pole attachment on a lift truck, and in accordance with a safe system of work. Tilting clamp devices are particularly useful, as they permit reels to be picked up from the horizontal and placed vertically, or vice versa.

A reputable supplier of lift truck attachments will be able to give advice about suitable equipment for your job, and the effect the use of the device will have on the rated capacity of your truck.

Points to check:

- avoid the need to climb on loads by using curtain-sided vehicles, or proprietary sheeting systems;

- provide safe access if work must be done at a height;

- provide and use a gantry system, safety lines and harnesses if work on high loads cannot be avoided;

- eliminate manual handling of reels;

- load and unload in a safe place and keep everyone, including members of the public, well clear of the area during loading and unloading operations;

- avoid manual handling by using pallets, a lift truck or a porter's trolley;

- devise a safe system to deal with mishaps, such as stuck loads. A common mistake is to attempt to free a stuck load by tying a rope to it and pulling with the lift truck - injuries occur when the rope or its fixing breaks and it recoils violently;

- make sure instructions exist for dealing with any vehicle that might arrive on-site with an unsafe load, for example palletised newspaper bundles which have shifted during transit, and that the instructions are followed;

- make arrangements to secure loads before vehicles leave the site, for example using load binders inside curtain-sided vehicles, to prevent dangerous movement of the load in transit.

Figure 3 *Racking should be securely fixed and have aisles wide enough to allow manoeuvring*

Safe stacking and storing

General principles

- Storage areas should be specifically designated, clearly marked and under the control of a responsible person.

- Consider permissible floor loadings.

- Place materials handled by crane or lift truck on battens or other suitable material to ensure that a sling or forks can be inserted under them.

- Good housekeeping is essential at all times.

- Provide sufficient lighting.

- Maintain adequate clearance between rows to ensure safe stacking and withdrawal.

- Maintain adequate headroom for lift trucks. Remember to check that lighting, cabling and heaters are mounted high enough to prevent them being accidentally struck by the mast.

- Position loads capable of being stacked directly on top of each other on a firm, level base.

- Check stacks periodically for stability and take corrective measures where necessary.

- Consider fire precautions at an early stage - stacks which are too high may prevent sprinkler systems from working correctly.

Don't:

- exceed the safe load of racks, shelves or floors;

- allow items to stick out from stacks into gangways;

- climb racks to reach upper shelves - use a ladder or steps;

- lean heavy stacks against walls;

- de-stack by throwing down from the top or pulling out from the bottom.

Racking installations

Racking should:

- be installed and maintained in accordance with the manufacturer's instructions;

- be erected on sound, level floors capable of withstanding the point loading of each base plate;

- be securely fixed to the floor where lift trucks and mechanical handling equipment are used. If racks have to be secured to the building, calculations should confirm the building is fit for this purpose;

- have aisles wide enough to ensure that mechanical handling equipment can be easily manoeuvred;

- have the maximum load clearly stated on them;

- never be altered without consulting the manufacturer first;

- make key components highly visible to help lift truck drivers position their forks correctly.

Use of pallets

Operators should receive instruction on the safe use of pallets. Accidents involving pallets are caused by:

- poor design;

- poor construction;

- using pallets unsuitable for particular loads/racking systems (remember you may receive consignments with different-sized pallets);

- continued use of damaged pallets;

- bad handling.

Precautions to reduce the risk of accidents when working with pallets

- Establish an effective pallet damage inspection scheme at the goods-in stage. If pallets are regularly in a damaged condition, take action with the supplier.

- Inspect all pallets again each time before re-use (damaged ones should be withdrawn).

- Handle empty pallets carefully and make sure they are not dragged or thrown about.

- To avoid damage to pallets, and to lift the loads safely, make sure the forks of any handling device extend into the pallet to at least three-quarters of its depth.

- Forks should not extend beyond the pallet being lifted (eg they could overturn an adjacent load).

- As a general guide, the height of the load should not exceed the longest base dimension of the pallet.

- Avoid stacking of palletised loads capable of being crushed.

Reel storage and stacking

Ideally, pedestrians should be excluded from reel storage areas in which lift trucks are used. This is especially important when stacking or de-stacking operations are taking place.

Stacking reels on end usually requires the use of clamp trucks or similar equipment. The maximum height for any stack will depend on the reel size and will be limited by stability, driver vision and overhead obstructions. There should be good lighting with minimum shadow. Reels should be stacked safely. Pillars should be clearly marked, eg with yellow banding.

Where clamp trucks or other safe means of stacking on end are not available, reels will probably be stored horizontally. It is safest to store reels without stacking but if they are stacked more than one tier high

Correct positioning of wedges

WRONG   RIGHT

                                         Height limited
                                         for this method

Reels must be stacked true and vertical and be of equal diameter in
any one stack, except that a reel with diameter slightly less than the
other may be used as the top reel of a stack

Reels with dished ends or protruding   Reels must not be placed
centres must not be stacked on end   horizontally against a vertical reel

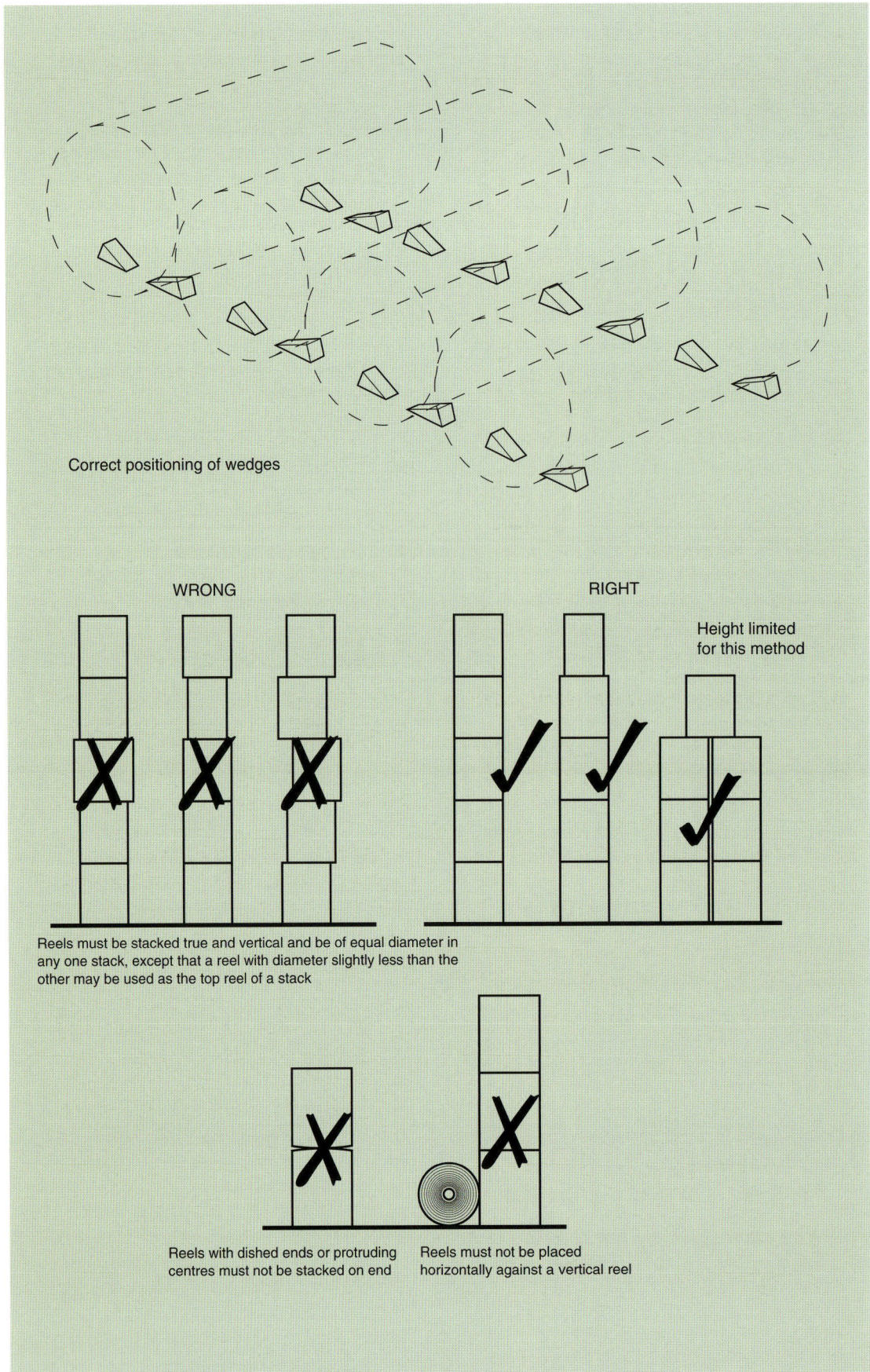

Figure 4 *Correct positioning of wedges and safe stacking of reels*

due to lack of space, it is vital to use proper wedges to prevent accidental breaking down of the stack. If wedges are too small or incorrectly shaped, not only will they be liable to move, but the paper will also be damaged. At least one wedge should be placed at each side of every reel at floor level - large wedges with handles may be best.

Stacking aisles should be wide enough for any vehicles doing the work.

Manual breaking down of pyramid stacks

Reels may be delivered on lorries in pyramid stacks, or be stored that way in the warehouse. Where possible, consider changing the delivery and storage arrangements so reels are stored and delivered on end. It is best to use mechanical methods of handling reels stacked like this, eg by using a lift truck with tilting clamp, lifting boom or tine devices - ask a specialist supplier of lift truck attachments for advice. Mechanical handling devices will help protect your employees and also help prevent damage to the reels.

If manual breaking down of such stacks cannot be eliminated, a safe system of work must be set down and implemented. The system needs to take account of:

- the need to de-stack reels in a predetermined order;

- the need to ensure that people only work from the side of the stack, where they will not be hit by a reel if it moves suddenly;

- the need to adequately and firmly chock all reels on the bottom row of the stack until it is necessary to move them (chock design is important - the height of the chock should be at least one eighth of the diameter of the reel);

- the use of properly designed bats or paddles to control unchocked reels.

Braking chocks may be used, together with a chock paddle and a lever bat;

- the need to provide enough people for the job - unloading should be conducted by a team of at least three adequately trained and supervised people, and this may include the driver of the delivery lorry. One person will drive the lift truck, while the other two work at the side of the stack, barring down the reels;

- the need to provide a safe system of work for dealing with reels delivered in containers where side access may not be possible.

There have been fatal accidents when reels being manually de-stacked have run out of control - mechanical methods should be used if at all possible.

See Chapter 7 for fire precautions relating to stacked reels.

Lift and clamp trucks

Lift and clamp trucks can be used for many material handling operations in the printing industry, particularly in the movement of pallets of paper, paper reels, chemicals and waste materials. Lift truck accidents cause many serious injuries including fatalities every year - suitable operator training, vehicle maintenance and working conditions are essential.

The law and lift trucks

In addition to the general requirements of the HSW Act, thorough examination and testing of the chains of a lift truck by a competent person is required. You will need to obtain and keep a copy of these reports and rectify any safety deficiencies identified in them.

The publication *Rider-operated lift trucks: Operator training. Approved Code of Practice and guidance* (L117) gives practical guidance on complying with the requirements of section 2 of the HSW Act in relation to the basic training of operators of rider-operated lift trucks.

The Approved Code of Practice requires:

- employers to provide basic training for operators by recognised instructors (such instructors may be employees who are competent to carry out this role);

- competence testing of lift truck operators;

- authorisation of, and appropriate records for, all employees permitted to drive lift trucks.

In addition to the above, driver-operated lift trucks used regularly on the road for long periods, and their drivers, must be licensed by the Driving Standards Agency.

Health problems

Lift trucks can create health problems which will need to be considered. These can include:

- breathing problems from using diesel trucks in confined working environments (good maintenance, eg of fuel injectors, can reduce fume problems);

- back and upper limb disorders due to poor seating and/or controls.

Poor roadways can cause excessive truck vibration and back problems.

Figure 5 *Use mechanical methods such as a clamp truck to de-stack and move reels*

COMMON ACCIDENTS

Some common causes of lift truck accidents include:

- unsafe reversing;
- speeding;
- overloading;
- passenger carrying;
- untrained drivers;
- poor or inadequate visibility;
- poor working environment, eg uneven road surfaces or obstacles;
- inadequate separation of pedestrians and lift trucks;
- inadequate separation of highway vehicles and lift trucks;
- poor truck maintenance including maintenance of chains and brakes.

Safety guidelines for lift trucks

- Ensure all operators have received adequate training.

- Ensure enough people have been trained to cover holidays, weekends, overtime and sickness.

- Ensure training instructors are competent in instructional techniques and skills assessment.

- Restrict use of lift trucks to authorised operators only (authorisation should only be given to adequately trained and experienced operators). It may help to post a list of authorised drivers on the truck.

- Provide suitable refresher training for operators.

- Ensure managers and supervisors are trained in safety aspects of lift and clamp trucks.

- Managers should have an appreciation of the risks and the ways to minimise them.

- Supervisors should have enough knowledge to be able to recognise inadequacies in the operation of lift trucks and the training needs of operators.

- Screen operators for fitness, eg eyesight testing.

- Keep floors and roadways in good condition, free from obstacles, obstructions and potholes.

- Allow enough room for lift truck manoeuvres.

- Maintain all lift trucks on a regular basis to ensure they are in good condition (including examination of the mast chains, tyres, brakes and horns). Introduce daily driver checks of the safety equipment.

- Ensure that thorough examination and testing of lifting chains are being carried out by a competent person as required.

- Segregate lift truck routes from pedestrian and working areas as much as possible and mark them with barriers or lines on the floor.

- Ensure gradients are not too steep.

- Keep keys safe when the lift trucks are not being used by authorised drivers.

- Ensure that operators use seatbelts.

- Ensure good visibility when moving loads - where necessary use a banksman to direct traffic safely.

- Remember that the fitting of crane jib attachments is subject to additional legal requirements.

Don't:

- allow anyone to drive a lift truck unless they have been selected, trained and authorised to do so;

- carry reels stacked on top of each other (as the top reels will be unsupported and liable to fall);

- use lift trucks in areas where flammable concentrations of vapours may be present, eg close to gravure or flexographic presses using highly flammable liquids or in ink stores unless the trucks have been specially designed and protected;

- leave keys in the ignition when trucks are parked or left unsupervised;

- allow any operators to consume any alcohol while at work;

- use forks, pallets or bins to lift people to work at heights (use properly designed mobile work platforms);

- pick up loads if someone is standing close to the load;

- allow people to walk under raised loads;

- move unstable loads;

- leave a lift truck unattended on a gradient except in an emergency (if you do have to leave the truck on a slope in an emergency use wheel chocks);

- carry passengers unless the lift truck is designed to do so;

- run over electrical cables or flexible pipes on the floor unless they are suitably protected;

- operate with the load raised except for stacking and de-stacking manoeuvres;

- allow speeding or unsafe reversing practices;

- fit attachments to lift trucks which could affect their lifting capacity without consulting the manufacturer, authorised supplier or qualified lift truck engineer;

- forget to consider the need for beacons, mirrors, horns etc, the protection of drivers from falling objects and lighting where necessary;

- allow other people, such as delivery drivers, to use your lift trucks unless you are certain that they have received appropriate training etc.

ACCIDENT

A print worker was crushed between two full pallets of paper weighing half a tonne each when a lift truck reversed and inadvertently pushed a pallet into her back as she stood at her workstation. Despite having a consultants' report warning that the risk of collision between pedestrians and lift trucks in the cramped premises was high, no attempt had been made to segregate the activities or provide a one-way traffic management system.

Safety guidelines for automatic guided vehicles (AGVs)

These include:

- ensuring that all safety features are operating correctly;

- ensuring that stopping performances are appropriate to the risk and load. Vehicles will need to come to a controlled stop so they do not release their load suddenly;

- ensuring that appropriate maximum speeds are set;

- ensuring that adequate clearances have been left to prevent trapping people between moving vehicles and fixed structures.

Warning light

Beacon

Emergency stop

Trip bumpers

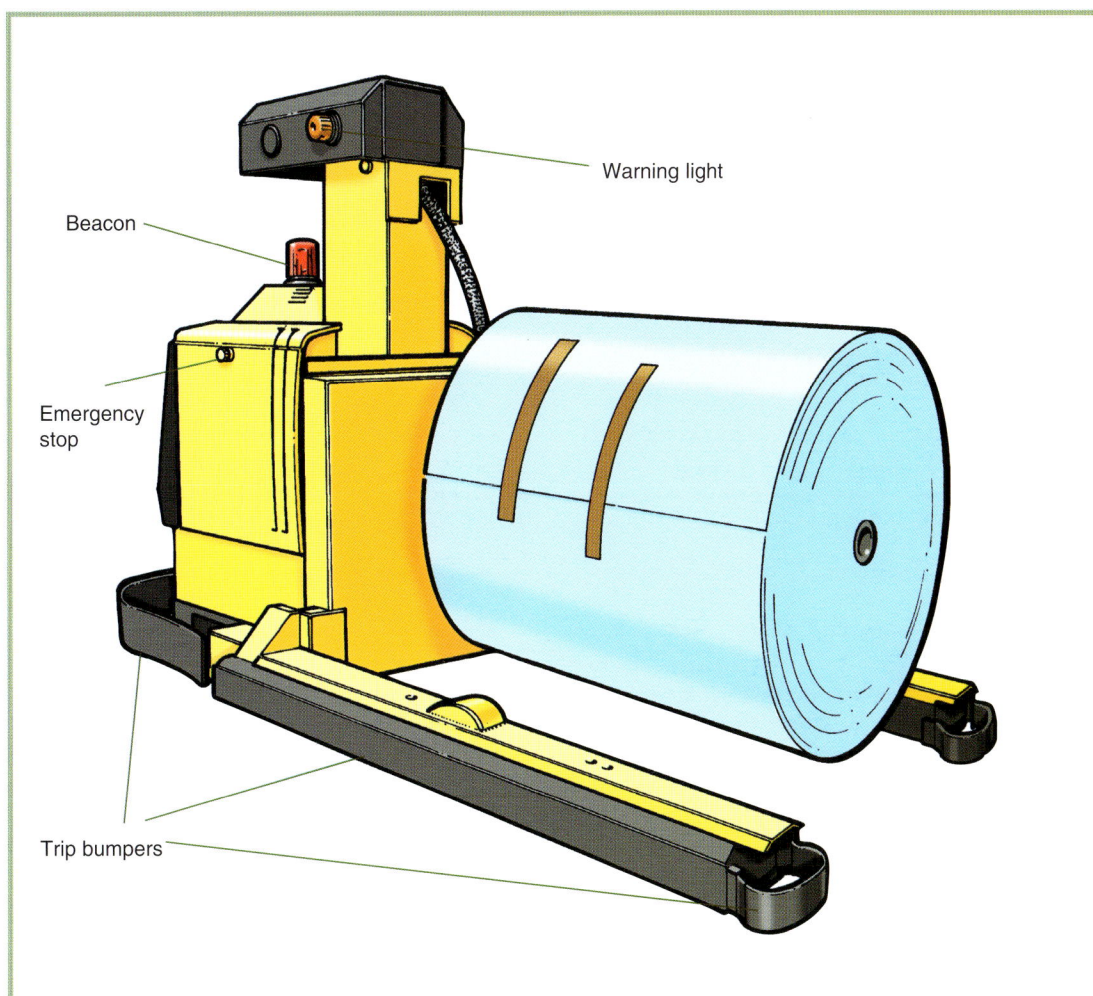

Figure 6 *Safety features of an AGV*

Asbestos in buildings

WARNING CONTAINS ASBESTOS
Breathing asbestos dust is dangerous to health
Follow safety instructions

Asbestos-related diseases kill an estimated 3000 people each year in the UK and this figure is expected to rise. Many of the people now suffering from these diseases worked in the building and maintenance trades - joiners, plumbers, electricians, engineers etc.

As a rough guide, if your building was built before the 1980s and you carry out any type of maintenance, repair or refurbishment work, you could be exposing people to asbestos dust without realising it. Any individual exposure may be small - but these can build up and may result in an asbestos-related disease later on in life. This is particularly relevant to maintenance personnel. At the time of writing (January 2002) the Health and Safety Commission proposes to introduce a new duty to manage asbestos in buildings.

The intention of the 'duty to manage', as currently drafted, is to require employers to:

● take reasonable steps to determine the location of materials likely to contain asbestos;

- presume that materials contain asbestos unless there is a reason to suppose they do not;

- make a written record of the location of asbestos and presumed asbestos material, and keep it up to date;

- keep a check on the condition of asbestos and presumed asbestos materials; and

- assess the risk of exposure from asbestos and presumed asbestos materials and record the action necessary to ensure that:

  - if the material may create a risk of exposure because of its state and location it is repaired or if necessary removed;
  - any such material is maintained in a good state of repair;
  - information about the location and condition of the material is given to anyone likely to disturb it, including maintenance contractors as well as those normally present in the building.

A new Approved Code of Practice will be produced for the duty, together with supporting guidance. Remember your own employees may also be exposed if they work in office or storage areas where asbestos insulation board products have been used which have been damaged by alterations or the movement of materials.

Where is asbestos found in buildings?

The following are areas where asbestos might be found in older buildings:

- in spray coating for fire protection and insulation on steelwork, concrete walls and ceilings;

- in insulation lagging, on pipework, and for boilers and ducts;

- in asbestos insulating board used as wall partitions, fire doors, ceiling tiles etc;

- in asbestos cement products such as sheeting on walls and roofs, tiles, cold water tanks, gutters, pipes and in decorative plaster finishes.

What should you do?

- Identify any asbestos material on site (if you are unsure, have it tested). Keep a record of its location.

- Ensure any relevant employees or contractors know if and where asbestos may be present within your works.

- Ensure any asbestos you do find is in a safe condition, eg undamaged and/or sealed (and will not affect existing employees working in your factory). Carry out regular checks to make sure that it remains safe.

- If work is required on or near the asbestos you may need to call in licensed contractors. You will need to inform anyone carrying out the work of the dangers and ensure they carry out the work safely.

- Ask your local enforcing authority for further information. Free and priced publications are available, eg *Managing asbestos in premises* (INDG223rev2).

Chapter 4

HEALTH RISKS

See the 'References' section at the back of the book for details of publications which relate to HEALTH RISKS

Nationally, over 2 million people a year suffer from ill health caused or made worse by work. Thirteen million working days are lost as people take time off because work has made them ill. The printing industry is no exception. Ill-health problems include musculoskeletal disorders, occupational asthma, deafness, eye damage and dermatitis. Dermatitis is a particular problem in printing - European reports have indicated that it accounts for 65% of all cases of ill health in the industry.

The management of health risks within the workplace is often neglected or fails because, unlike safety issues, health risks tend to be both less obvious and less well understood. Because the onset of ill health is often delayed, the risks can be underestimated until it is too late and permanent damage has occurred.

Employers have just as much responsibility for safeguarding the health as the safety of their employees. Risk assessments need to cover health as well as safety hazards (see the general advice given on risk assessment in Chapter 1).

Relevant legislation

- Health and Safety at Work etc Act 1974 (HSW Act)

- Control of Substances Hazardous to Health (COSHH) Regulations 1999

- Management of Health and Safety at Work Regulations 1999

- Workplace (Health, Safety and Welfare) Regulations 1992

- Noise at Work Regulations 1989

- Control of Lead at Work Regulations 1980 (CLAW)

- Manual Handling Operations Regulations 1992

- Control of Asbestos at Work Regulations 1987 (Consolidated Regulations are due to be made in 2002)

- Ionising Radiations Regulations 1999

Table 1 Examples of health hazards in printing

Hazard	Health effects	Typical processes
Inhalation of solvent vapour (health effects depend on the solvent, its concentration in air and the length of exposure)	Headaches, nausea Effects on the central nervous system	Cleaning litho and letterpress rollers and cylinders Screen, flexo and gravure printing
Contact with and absorption of solvent through the skin	Dermatitis	
Inhalation of vapours and mists from isocyanates or reactive acrylates	Occupational asthma	Use of lacquers, adhesives, inks etc containing isocyanates or reactive acrylates
Skin contact with reactive chemicals (health effects depend on the chemical, its concentration and the length of exposure)	Dermatitis including sensitisation (skin allergy)	Use of UV-cured products Etching, engraving Platemaking Screen reclamation Stereo roller preparation Gravure cylinder preparation
Skin contact with and inhalation of potentially toxic, very toxic additives (eg those with risk phases R40 'Possible irreversible effects', R45 'May cause cancer', R46 'May cause heritable genetic damage', R61 'May cause harm to the unborn child')	Carcinogenic (cancer) Mutagenic (harm to the unborn child)	Screen printing with specialist inks and coatings Screen reclamation General printing and cleaning activity involving the use of, eg font solutions, biocides, formaldehyde, dichloromethane, N-vinyl pyrrolidone (NVP)
Exposure to high levels of noise	Noise-induced deafness Tinnitus	Web printing Print finishing
Unsafe manual handling	Back injuries	Handling of paper reels, sheets and bundles
Awkward or repetitive movements	Upper limb disorders, eg tenosynovitis and carpal tunnel syndrome	Typesetting Print finishing
Exposure to micro-organisms from contaminated water	Humidifier fever Legionnaires' disease	Paper storage or printing where humidifiers are used Any printing process in buildings with cooling towers or other water systems that can become contaminated

Occupational health and rehabilitation

In any business, workers are the most valuable assets and it is important to look after them properly. Employers need to actively manage health. With effective occupational health support and advice, health risks at work can be managed in ways that are not costly or difficult. Many workers who have already been made ill, from whatever cause, can be helped to remain in or return to work.

There are legal duties to prevent ill health caused by work. The main legal framework is the HSW Act, supplemented by regulations which cover particular activities, such as manual handling and exposure to harmful substances. These require you to make assessments of the health risks to workers arising from work activities and to take action to prevent or reduce those risks.

Occupational health services

Employers may need expert and specialist advice on how to help them with issues such as:

- identifying health hazards, assessing risks and choosing the necessary control measures;

- checking the effectiveness of the control measures and, where required, measuring the exposure of employees, for example by atmospheric sampling;

- advising on placement and rehabilitation of employees;

- provision of appropriate on-site first-aid and treatment facilities;

- identification of causes of ill health within the workforce;

- promotion of good general health among employees.

Occupational health services may be able to help with these matters. HSE's Employment Medical Advisory Service can advise you and the leaflet *Need help on health and safety?* (INDG322) provides more information. (See also NHS Plus: www.nhsplus.nhs.uk)

Health surveillance

Health surveillance is one component of the overall management of health risks. It involves obtaining information about an employee's health and helps to protect that employee from health risks at work. It may be necessary:

- under the Control of Substances Hazardous to Health (COSHH) Regulations 1999, for example to protect against dermatitis or occupational asthma;

- under the Management of Health and Safety at Work Regulations 1999, where people work in noisy processes;

- where there is significant exposure to lead in premises such as traditional craft printers and the Control of Lead at Work Regulations 1980 apply.

The need for health surveillance should be decided as part of the assessments required by these Regulations. Health surveillance cannot replace proper control measures but is an essential part of a health conservation programme.

Health surveillance is required where:

- an identifiable disease or adverse effect may be related to exposure;

- there is a reasonable likelihood of that disease or effect occurring under the particular work conditions;

- there are valid techniques for detecting signs of the disease or adverse effect and surveillance is likely to improve the protection of employees' health.

The main objective of health surveillance is to protect the health of individual employees by checking for early signs of work-related illness. It also provides information about and early detection of adverse changes, which may be caused, for example, by exposure to noise or a substance hazardous to health.

Further guidance about health surveillance is given in the HSE booklet *Health surveillance at work* (HSG61).

All employees will need to be given information, instruction and training about any risks to their health that might arise from their work. Where health surveillance is appropriate they also need to know:

● what symptoms and signs to look out for, and where appropriate, how to self-examine (eg for dermatitis);

● how the health surveillance scheme works and who to report to if they are concerned;

● what the arrangements are for seeing their own health records and collective results of the health surveillance programme.

Records must be kept where health surveillance is carried out to comply with the COSHH Regulations. The information that should be held in the records is detailed in the Appendix of the COSHH General Approved Code of Practice (L5). Records should be retained for 40 years.

Rehabilitation

Early detection of illness gives you a chance to deal with the problem promptly, and provides the opportunity for you to help workers remain at work, perhaps by arranging for light duties or modifying work for a limited period. If a worker experiences difficulties in returning to their normal duties within a few weeks then you should speak to a health professional about setting up an active rehabilitation programme.

Larger organisations may have their own specialists and an occupational health service, but all businesses can obtain access to treatment and rehabilitation. Some make arrangements through their

employer's liability insurer, some have 'good neighbours' (larger companies that offer small businesses in their supply chain access to their support services), and others go it alone. Some small businesses find it worthwhile to make local partnership arrangements with health professionals.

A number of people can advise you about what is available to you locally. A trade association, chamber of commerce or trade union representative, if you have one, will probably know if there are any 'good neighbour' businesses you could contact. Your local Health and Safety Executive office might also be able to advise.

Hazardous substances

Many chemical substances can cause harm if they are inhaled or absorbed through the skin. Many also cause dermatitis or damage to the eyes. Exposure can have an immediate effect or may be delayed. Repeated exposure to some substances may cause damage to the lungs, liver or other organs. They can be taken into the body by breathing them in, passing through the skin or by eating food which has been touched by contaminated hands.

Some substances can cause both local and internal effects, for example they might damage the skin and cause liver damage. The most effective way to protect employees from any harmful substance is to see if the use of the substance can be avoided completely, perhaps by finding a safer substitute or by changing the process in some way.

Many of the health hazards listed in Table 1 relate to the use of hazardous substances. With the exceptions of asbestos and lead (for which there are specialised regulations), the use of hazardous substances at work is subject to the Control of Substances Hazardous to Health (COSHH) Regulations 1999. This section summarises the requirements of those

Figure 7 *The use of hazardous substances at work is subject to the COSHH Regulations*

Regulations and gives advice on the control measures for particular printing processes.

For everyday tasks involving commonly used printing chemicals, the Printing Industry Advisory Committee (PIAC) has produced *COSHH essentials for printers*. This guidance gives you a good head start with your COSHH assessments, and comprises a series of summary sheets covering typical tasks, which explain the steps you need to take to control employees' exposure. The first stages of the assessment process have been done for you using information from suppliers.

Under the COSHH Regulations you must:

- assess the risks to health arising from the use of hazardous substances at work (and review your assessment if changes occur);

- prevent or control the risk, eg by using a safer substitute, or by suitable control measures;

- ensure that control measures are used and maintained;

- monitor exposure and carry out health surveillance when necessary;

- inform, instruct and train your employees about the risks and the precautions needed;

- keep records where required.

Exposure limits

For certain substances, where there is a risk of inhalation, occupational exposure limits have been set. There are two kinds - maximum exposure limits (MELs) and occupational exposure standards (OESs). You may need to refer to these when assessing the risks in your workplace. Further information, including an explanation of the difference between the types of exposure limits, is given in the guidance booklet *Occupational exposure limits* (EH40), which is published yearly.

Assessment under COSHH

First gather information on the substances used in your workplace. Use manufacturers' labels and safety data sheets to help you decide which ones are hazardous. Any substance which carries the classification 'very toxic', 'toxic', 'harmful', 'corrosive', or 'irritant', or which has been assigned a maximum exposure limit or occupational exposure standard because of risks following inhalation, is subject to the COSHH Regulations. This also applies to biological agents, substantial quantities of dusts, and other substances which present comparable hazards.

Suppliers of chemicals for use at work are legally obliged to provide safety data sheets containing information under 16 headings, specified in the Chemicals (Hazard Information and Packaging for Supply) Regulations. This information will help you to carry out your COSHH assessment, but simply collecting information is not enough - you need to use the information to decide whether or not there is a risk, and whether or not your own controls and working procedures are sufficient. Contact your supplier for advice if you are in any doubt about the information provided in safety data sheets.

Consider:

- how the substance is used, handled or stored;

- who might be affected;

- the likely routes of exposure - inhalation, ingestion, skin absorption;

- the likelihood and effects of spills or leaks;

- what control measures are currently used;

- any risks during cleaning or maintenance activities.

It is important to find out how substances are actually used in the workplace, and who is exposed to them - don't forget contractors and maintenance workers. Think about the handling of substances from delivery, to use and disposal. Think also about what can go wrong, for example how you would deal with spillage or leaking containers of solvent, or carry out repairs on machines where there is uncured UV ink. Draw conclusions about the risks and decide if you need to take action to reduce them. Specialist help may be required to help you make these decisions, for example from an occupational health professional. Record your conclusions.

Prevention or control of exposure

If your assessment concludes that there are risks to health, then you need to decide what else you need to do to comply with the COSHH Regulations.

If possible, prevent exposure by using a less hazardous substance or a different process. A good example of this is the Printing Solvent Substitution Scheme for the offset and UV-curable sector introduced in this country in October 2000. This is a voluntary scheme, based on a very successful approach in Germany, to reduce volatile organic compounds (VOCs) in the process, by replacing roller and blanket washes with a high boiling point solvent/vegetable cleaning agent (VCA) and taking steps to reduce or eliminate isopropylalcohol (IPA) from the fount solution. The principles of the scheme are shown in the box insert later in this chapter. Another example is the use of water-based inks for flexible packaging. Ask your supplier for alternative products that may be safer to use. Remember if you change your product you will still need to carry out a COSHH assessment for the new substance and ensure that you provide appropriate controls.

Where prevention of exposure is not possible, you need to consider control measures. This usually means a combination of some of the following:

- Enclosing the process.

- Partial enclosure and/or local exhaust ventilation (LEV).

- General ventilation.

- A system of work and handling procedures to minimise leaks and spills.

- If, and only if, you cannot adequately control exposure by a combination of the measures above, then you should also provide personal protective equipment (PPE) such as respiratory protective equipment, gloves and eye protection. See 'Personal protective equipment (PPE)' towards the end of this chapter for further information.

Chemical hazards in printing

Table 2 Printing processes which may give rise to skin or eye contact hazards

Process or activity	Type/name of substance	Potential health hazard
Etching, engraving, platemaking, certain photographic reproduction systems, correction of litho plates (hydrofluoric acid)	Corrosive acids, eg concentrated nitric and sulphuric acids, hydrofluoric acid	Skin burns and blisters Burns with concentrated hydrofluoric acid are very severe Eye damage
Cleaning of screens in screen printing	Strong alkalis, eg concentrated sodium or potassium hydroxide	Corrosive to skin, eyes and mucous membrane
Concentrated photographic developer solutions	Hydroquinone	Irritant to eyes but may cause permanent damage Irritant and sensitising to the skin, may cause dermatitis
UV and electron beam curable inks, varnishes and lacquers	Reactive acrylates or methacrylates	Corrosive to skin, eyes and mucous membranes Potential for skin sensitisation
Photographic fixer solutions	Acetic acid, acidic salt solutions (eg sodium thiosulphate)	Irritant
Hardener added to photographic fixer solutions	Dilute formaldehyde solution	Irritant Frequent contact may lead to skin sensitisation
Litho platemaking, gravure cylinder preparation, photoengraving, photographic bleaches	Dichromates, eg ammonium, potassium and sodium dichromates	Very corrosive In high concentrations can cause deep ulcers Potential for skin sensitisation
Litho printing: fount solution, blanket restorers, cleaning solvents	Isopropylalcohol (IPA), methyl ethyl ketone (MEK), white spirit	Dermatitis
Gravure and flexographic printing: various inks	MEK Alcohols, eg industrial methylated spirits (IMS), IPA Esters, eg ethyl acetate Aromatic hydrocarbons, eg toluene, xylene	Dermatitis
Screen printing: UV-cured inks	N-vinyl pyrrolidone (NVP) and Michler's Ketone	Cancer, harm to the unborn child
Screen printing: inks	Ketones, eg cyclohexanone Aromatic hydrocarbons, eg toluene, xylene	Dermatitis

Note: The examples here are only illustrative and are not exhaustive

Table 3 Printing processes which may give rise to inhalation hazards

Examples of process or activity	Type/name of substance	Potential health hazard
Making flexographic and letterpress plates	Perchloroethylene	Dizziness, drowsiness and other effects on the central nervous system
Cleaning rollers, cylinders and blanket restoring	Chlorinated hydrocarbons, eg dichloromethane Ketones, eg methyl ethyl ketone (MEK)	Dizziness, drowsiness and other effects on the central nervous system Cardiac arrhythmia (high concentration) Affects liver and kidneys on long-term exposure
Litho printing - fount solution	Alcohols such as isopropylalcohol (IPA)	Dizziness, drowsiness and other effects on the central nervous system
Gravure and flexographic printing	Inks containing ketones (eg cyclohexanone), alcohols (as in IMS), esters (eg ethyl acetate, isopropyl acetate) or aromatic hydrocarbons, eg toluene, xylene	As above
Screen printing	Inks containing ketones or aromatic hydrocarbons	As above
Screen printing: UV-cured inks	N-vinyl pyrrolidone (NVP) and Michler's Ketone	Cancer and harm to the unborn child
Adhesive laminating Use of polyurethane lacquers	Isocyanate prepolymers	Irritation of respiratory tract (high concentration) Occupational asthma could occur even at low levels
Handling, cutting, grinding lead type, hot metal work	Lead dust/fume	Lead absorbed in bloodstream leads to headaches, tiredness, stomach pains, constipation and loss of weight
Dyeline printing	Ammonium hydroxide	Irritation of respiratory tract (as ammonia vapour)
High-speed printing using UV ink - leading to ink misting	Reactive acrylates contained in UV inks etc	Irritation of respiratory tract Potential for occupational asthma
Laser engraving (gravure cylinders) Maintenance involving welding	Metal fume	Irritation of respiratory tract, 'flu-like' illness (metal fume fever depending on the metal) Poisoning from substances in the fume

Table 3 Printing processes which may give rise to inhalation hazards (continued)

Examples of process or activity	Type/name of substance	Potential health hazard
Use of UV lamps for photo processing, UV curing, corona discharge	Ozone	Irritation of the upper respiratory tract Headaches and nausea
Digital (ink-jet) printing	Methyl ethyl ketone	Cardiac arrhythmia (high concentration) Affects liver and kidneys on long-term exposure
	Propanol	Dizziness, drowsiness and other effects on the central nervous system

Dusts

Examples of process or activity	Type/name of substance	Potential health hazard
Saw/knife milling in bindery	Paper	Dust of any kind can irritate the respiratory tract and block the nose
Use of anti-set-off powder	Sugar/starch	
Thermography	Plasticisers	
Bronzing machines, mixing aluminium pastes	Metal	
Manufacture of formes	Softwood dust	Respiratory disorders including occupational asthma
Maintenance involving cutting, sawing, drilling etc	Hardwood	Occupational asthma and cancers
Maintenance work, particularly to buildings	Asbestos	Cancers and asbestosis

Specific process health hazards

Design and artwork

Risks to health from design and artwork can be reduced by:

- using non-flammable adhesives - preferably wax;

- removing wax from glass surfaces by scraping rather than using solvent;

- using alternatives to aerosols where these are available and only using aerosols if there is good ventilation;

- not smoking where aerosols are used - many will be flammable.

Graphic reproduction

Darkrooms with automatic film processors need mechanical ventilation to ensure healthy and comfortable working conditions. Ten to fifteen air changes per hour is the standard normally achieved in the industry. A suitable extractor fan mounted in an outside wall will do, but it is important to provide an air inlet. Carefully designed louvre covers will ensure that unwanted light does not enter the room.

Platemaking

Automatic processing effectively reduces the likelihood of skin contact with chemicals during normal operation. Some developers can cause aggressive skin reactions, so nitrile or butyl rubber gauntlets and protective clothing are needed when manipulating the chemical containers. Suitable goggles or face shields should be provided and worn if there is a risk of splashing.

Keep drums of replenisher solution feeding process equipment in shallow trays, so as to contain spillage (and protect the floor).

Deletion fluids

Deletion fluids containing hydrofluoric acid in toxic and corrosive concentrations may be used to make minor alterations to printing plates. These products are particularly harmful if skin or eye contact occurs - the affected area should be washed immediately under running water, and medical advice obtained.

Check the safety data sheets for these products to ensure that appropriate first aid is available. Antidote cream (calcium gluconate gel) will prevent serious burns right down to the bone. If it is needed, keep fresh stock on the premises. Make sure people know why it is needed and how to use it.

Where possible, use deletion pens as an alternative to small jars or pots of deletion fluid to reduce the danger of skin contact. If large-scale deletion work is essential, keep the containers of deletion fluids in secure storage when not in use.

Lithographic printing

Wash-up solvents have commonly included white spirit and similar mixtures of petroleum distillates. Vegetable oil derivatives and high boiling point solvents are now available for use as roller and blanket cleaners, and these products usually reduce risk to health by inhalation. Skin contact may remain a hazard so that a skin care regime may be necessary. Try using these products as part of the substitution approach under COSHH. See the box insert overleaf for details of the UK Printing Solvent Substitution Scheme.

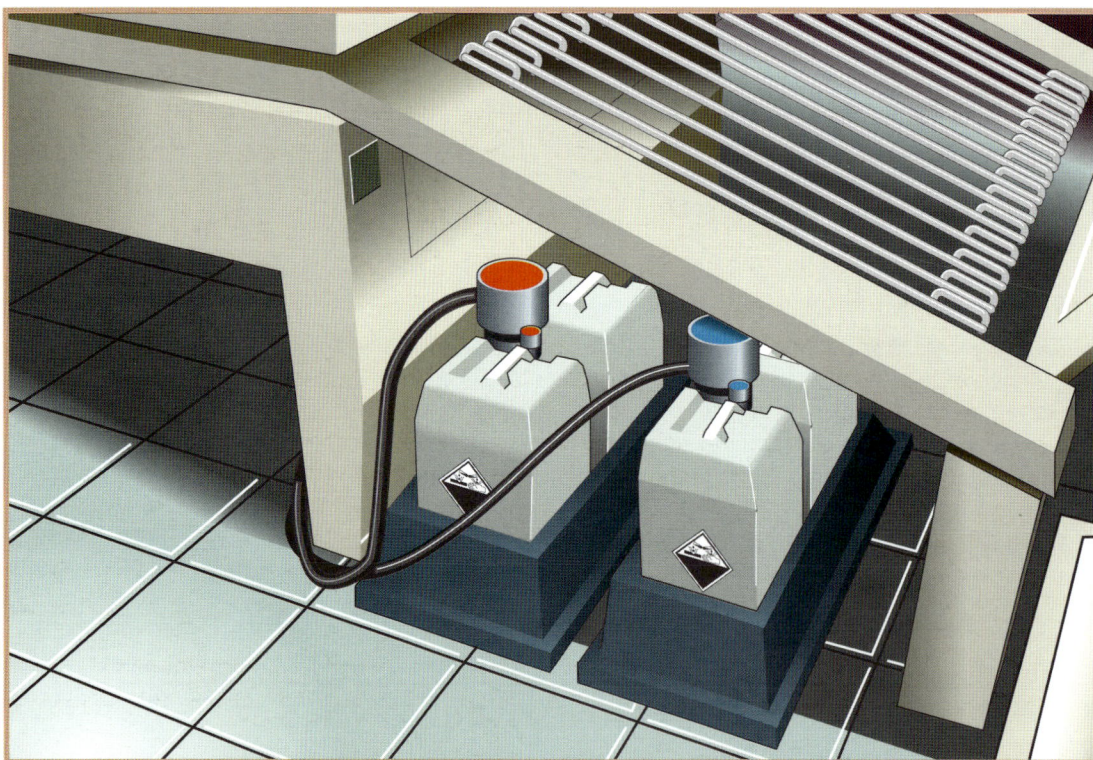

Figure 8 *Use drip trays and automatic pumping to reduce skin contact with chemicals*

UK Printing Solvent Substitution Scheme

Principles of the scheme:

- All 'new' machines (supplied after 11 October 2000) will be capable of being used throughout their normal working life and across the normal range of production capabilities with cleaning solvents having a flashpoint of 55°C or more ('AIII solvents').

- Cleaning solvents with a flashpoint of less than 21°C will not be supplied or used for routine roller and blanket washing ('AI solvents').

- Cleaning solvents with a flashpoint of between 21°C and 55°C will exceptionally be restricted to machines in use before the date of this agreement where, for technical reasons, there is no other possible option. They will not be used on new machines ('AII solvents').

- Manufacturers, suppliers, printers and employees and the authorities will work together to promote the use of alternatives to the above solvents, including high boiling point solvents (flashpoint >100°C) and vegetable cleaning agents.

- Solvents in blanket reviver and ink stripper products which have been intentionally formulated to include halogenated hydrocarbons, terpenes (assigned the risk phrases R38 'Irritating to the skin', R43 'May cause sensitisation by skin contact'), n-hexane and secondary amines or amides will not be supplied or used.

- The benzene content of solvents supplied or used will be less than 0.1%.

- The toluene and xylene content of solvents supplied or used will be less than 1%.

- The aromatic content (C_9) of solvents supplied or used will be less than 10%.

- The percentage of isopropyl alcohol or alternative low boiling organic substances used in fount solutions will be reduced (immediately to 5-10%) and progressively to 5% or less.

- Small amounts of low boiling point materials that are infrequently used - such as blanket revivers or dried ink removers containing methyl ethyl ketone - may continue to be used provided appropriate special precautions are observed and training given to those using them.

Suppliers will indicate conformance with the scheme by insertion of the PIAC symbol (available from the PIAC Secretariat) with the phrase 'UK Printing Solvent Substitution Scheme' - and the AI, AII or AIII designation on the product label. The phrase 'Conforms to UK Printing Solvent Substitution Scheme', the AI/AII/AIII designation together with the words 'It is the aim of the scheme to reduce the use of low boiling point organic solvents in the printing industry in accordance with the principles of the Control of Substances Hazardous to Health (COSHH) Regulations 1999 and promote improved control of solvent exposure in line with the guidance given in the booklet *COSHH essentials for printers'* shall be inserted into Section 16 'Other information' of the material safety data sheet (MSDS).

Press, press component and consumable suppliers and users will work together through PICON, the Association of Printing Machinery Importers, the Screen Printers Association, the Flexible Packaging Association, the Corrugated Packaging Association, the Newspaper Publishers Association, the Newspaper Society, the British Printing Industries Federation, the Scottish Print Employers Federation and the Graphical, Paper and Media Union to provide technical support and training on new cleaning methods to users who make the change to higher boiling point solvents and who, where necessary, replace blankets and inking rollers.

More volatile and aggressive organic solvents are sometimes used for removal of dried ink or to swell low areas of the blanket. Check with the suppliers to make sure that the least hazardous product has been chosen. Whatever solvent is selected, use a safe system of work to control it and reduce exposure. Use of these products should be kept to a minimum.

Isopropylalcohol (IPA) is a major contributor to the total solvent content of press room air. Make sure that the percentage concentration in the fount does not exceed 5% and consider suitable alternatives.

Humidifiers may be used to maintain suitable environmental conditions for litho printing. (See under 'Humidifier fever' in the 'Other health issues' section later in this chapter. This needs to be considered if humidifiers with water reservoirs are used.)

Ultraviolet (UV) curable materials

Particular care is needed when handling ultraviolet (UV) and electron beam curable materials (inks, varnishes and lacquers). They are used in all types of printing and packaging applications where their fast drying and durable film-forming properties allow immediate processing of the print, such as carton printing, labels, plastic substrates, pharmaceutical packaging, printing of the outer surface of food and confectionery wrappers and metal decorating. Clear UV-curable varnishes and lacquers give a protective and high gloss finish and are used for general overprinting work.

UV light cures freshly printed material almost instantaneously by initiating a rapid polymerisation process. Before the ink or varnish is cured the application viscosity is dependent on the mixture of reactive acrylates chosen. Most UV-curable inks can be considered solvent free.

However, the handling and use of uncured material and associated wash-up solvents give rise to a number of risks.

Burns

The initiators and some consituents included in UV-curable inks are powerful UV absorbers and can cause severe burning if ink or vanish contaminates the skin and is then exposed to sunlight. It is important to ensure that ink and varnish does not get onto the skin. You should ensure that appropriate personal protective equipment is provided and used.

Skin irritancy

Polyfunctional acrylates and methacrylates can cause skin irritation and some can also cause skin sensitisation. The first signs of irritation - reddening of the skin and appearance of a rash - may not develop until a day after exposure, and may worsen over the following two to three days. It is generally a temporary effect and disappears once exposure stops.

The UK Printing Industry has agreed a scheme known as Acrylate Preference Criteria, summarised in the box insert, to control the use of acrylates with a high potential to irritate. Reactive acrylates meeting the preference criteria still have the potential for irritancy and sensitisation, but to a lesser extent, and their preferred use should be considered under the COSHH substitution duty.

Acrylate Preference Criteria

Preferred use of acrylates fulfilling the following criteria:

- Skin irritancy rating (OECD test 404) less than 2.

- Organic solvent content less than 0.2%.

- Acrylic acid content less than 0.1%.

- Members of the acrylate suppliers CEFIC UV-curable acrylates sector group will provide information in safety data sheets and skin irritation ratings to ink manufacturers.

- Printing ink members of the BCF will preferentially formulate products with acrylates meeting the criteria and indicate this on safety data sheets.

- Printers advised to use products conforming with the criteria.

- GPMU members advised in general only to use products conforming with the criteria.

- Detailed COSHH assessment and additional control measures needed if non-conforming acrylates used.

- The phrase 'This product conforms to the BCF guidelines on Acrylate Preference Criteria' to be added to Section 16 of the product safety data sheet. The following information on gloves to be added to Section 8 of the product safety data sheet:

'Gloves of a length to overlap the sleeves of overalls should be used. The following is recommended:

- Single-use disposable unpowdered nitrile gloves (short-duration exposure not exceeding 30 minutes or where only splashes are likely). Not to be used where mechanical resistance is required, or where punching or tearing of the gloves is likely to occur. Not to be reused when removed.

- Minimum 0.45 mm thickness, unlined, unpowdered, natural rubber, latex-free, nitrile gloves (longer duration exposure, up to 4 hours, or mechanical handling activities). To be replaced immediately when punctured or degraded or when a change of appearance (colour, elasticity, shape) occurs.

- Heavy duty, unlined, natural rubber, latex-free, nitrile gloves (when using solvents). Note that contact with ketones or chlorinated solvents may accelerate glove deterioration. To be replaced immediately when punctured or degraded or when a change of appearance (colour, elasticity, shape) occurs.'

Some acrylates that are less well used, but may be required to meet the demands of particular applications, do not currently conform to the Acrylate Preference Criteria. Typically, commercial grades of these acrylates have skin irritation ratings of 2 or more. Particular care should be taken in the rare exceptions where it is necessary to use such products.

Skin sensitisation

Skin sensitisation is a powerful allergic reaction that can occur at any time, causing sensitivity to further contact, even at low levels - well below those associated with irritancy. The skin can become red and swollen, not always at the site of contact, for example, around the eyes. Sensitisation is normally irreversible and may be caused by both natural and synthetic products.

Having selected the least hazardous UV-curable product possible, the following factors should be taken into account to reduce the risk of injury from handling inks and coatings and from cleaning presses:

Handling inks and coatings

- Automatic ink dispensers reduce the need to handle ink, and where the quantity handled is large, consider pump application from a drum or storage area. Where this is not possible and inks are applied to ducts by hand, appropriate gloves should be worn.

- Powered mixing and stirring etc which gives rise to airborne emissions should take place in designated areas with suitable and effective exhaust ventilation.

- Keep containers for uncured materials closed when not in use.

- Identify procedures to deal with web breaks or random failure of a UV source which can produce large quantities of web coated with uncured material, along with suitable disposal arrangements (see under 'Cleaning and spillages').

- Personal protective equipment should be cleaned or disposed of as special waste after any obvious contamination as it may otherwise be a method of transferring uncured material. Send contaminated clothing for specialist laundering in labelled bags. Such clothing should never be taken home by employees for laundering.

- If uncured material enters the eye, rinse with plenty of clean water and seek medical assistance. Deal with skin contact by washing with soap and water. Adequate facilities are best located close to the point of use.

Cleaning and spillages

- Cleaning of machinery and associated equipment, ink ducts, rollers etc will be needed regularly, for example at change of colour, end of shift or the working day, or change to other inks.

- Provide impervious aprons (including a bib), long gauntlet gloves and eye protection such as a clear plastic face shield. See Acrylate Preference Criteria for advice on glove type.

- Make sure all the local exhaust ventilation and personal protective equipment provided is used. Remember that maintenance personnel are also at risk from contact with uncured materials that can inadvertently accumulate in normally inaccessible parts of plant and machinery.

- Provide suitable lidded containers labelled to indicate that skin contact should be avoided for the safe disposal of contaminated cloths etc. These should be removed from the workroom at the end of the shift.

- If cleaning solvents are intended to be used several times before eventual disposal, keep them only for cleaning machines using UV-curable materials, and store in closed containers that are clearly identified and labelled.

- Cloths dampened with solvent for cleaning will become contaminated with uncured material. Skin contact with these cloths is likely to be a serious cause of skin irritation owing to the 'defatting' action of the solvent and the deposition of uncured material on the unprotected skin. Dispose of cleaning cloths immediately and do not put them in overall pockets or leave on benches where others may handle them.

- Remove permeable clothing that becomes accidentally splashed with cleaning solvents and/or uncured materials at once. Clean or dispose of such clothing as special waste. Send contaminated clothing for specialist laundering in labelled bags.

Ink mist

Ink mist or fly can be significant as press speeds increase, particularly in offset and letterpress processes, and the mist formed can irritate the skin and respiratory tract, with the potential for respiratory sensitisation.

- Where ink mist generation is identified, and roller/plate/blanket pressures are correct and properly maintained, try to reduce exposure by ink reformulation. Cooling of rollers and cylinders will help to reduce fly by maintaining the correct ink viscosity. Other factors, apart from press speed, that may have a bearing include the amount of material on the rollers, the size of the roller, air temperature and the relative humidity. Ask for advice from your suppliers.

- If ink fly persists, consider fitting shrouds at relevant rollers on the press and the provision of local exhaust ventilation. In all cases workrooms should be well ventilated, for example by mechanical ventilation systems.

Ozone

UV curing lamps give off considerable heat and convert some of the oxygen present in the air into ozone. Mechanical extraction cools the air, but also leads to continuous generation of ozone by the conversion of oxygen present in the freshly supplied air around the UV lamp. Ozone gas is harmful even at relatively low concentrations. Levels about the occupational exposure standard (currently 0.2 ppm, 15 minute time-weighted average (TWA)) can lead to eye, nose and throat irritation. Higher levels of exposure sometimes cause headache and nausea. At levels about 15 times the occupational exposure standard, chest pain and coughing may occur.

- Provide extraction to control ozone and duct this outside the building to a safe place where it cannot return to the workroom. Monitor to ensure that the system is working satisfactorily and make arrangements for 14-monthly examination by a competent person.

- Units using water cooling, fed through specially designed quartz tubes, allow curing and, as well as removing heat, block or filter some of the higher energy (UV-C) light responsible for ozone generation. These water-cooled or 'cold-cure' UV lamps do not require air-cooling and therefore there is no bulk air movement around the UV lamp and ozone is not likely to be continuously generated in significant amounts. This should be confirmed during installation.

Further information is given in Guidance Note EH38 *Ozone: Health hazards and precautionary measures*.

UV light

Exposure to UV light from curing units can cause particularly acute effects as they are much more powerful than those used in platemaking. See 'Radiation' later in this chapter.

Provide fixed or interlocking screens to prevent direct or reflected UV light being emitted into the workroom. The reflective substrates common in label and screen printing create a greater hazard if the UV lamp cowling is not kept properly adjusted to minimise escape of light. In some cases, a tunnel extension may be required. No attempt should be made to inspect printed sheets under the lamp because of the high levels of reflected light; sheets should be removed from the press for inspection.

Screens should be regularly checked, and broken or damaged screens or filter glasses should be replaced.

A summary of the potential health hazards and the precautions to be taken in the use of UV-curable materials is given in Table 4.

Table 4 UV-curable materials - health hazards and precautions

Type of exposure	Health hazard	Precautionary measures
Contact with UV-curable materials	Skin irritation Skin sensitisation	Consider possibilities for less irritant substitutes, and enclosed handling systems or automatic dispensers. Use impervious aprons, gloves and eye protection
Inhalation of UV ink mist or ink fly	Upper and lower respiratory tract irritation Potential for sensitisation	Reformulation of inks, cylinder cooling etc Shrouding of rollers, and local exhaust ventilation
Contact with wash-up solvents	Skin irritation Upper and lower respiratory tract irritation	Consider use of local exhaust ventilation. Devise and use safe systems of work including use of PPE where necessary (eg spillage and leakage)
Inhalation of ozone	Eye, nose and throat irritation Headaches and nausea	Local exhaust ventilation
UV light	Occular irritation to varying degrees which may temporarily cause difficulty with vision Skin burns (ie erythema)	Fixed or interlocking screening Suitable goggles and skin protection during certain maintenance work

Health surveillance

Health surveillance of those using UV-curable material is required and should include inspection of all exposed areas of skin by a responsible person who has been instructed to recognise the skin disorders described. Any person can be nominated and trained as the responsible person but often a first-aider or supervisor is best. There should be inspections at least once a month and employees should be encouraged to check themselves for signs of skin disease. Cases of suspected dermatitis should be referred to a doctor or nurse for further investigation.

Where the main risk is from ink fly, promote awareness of possible respiratory problems using pre-employment enquiries and information about symptoms, and encourage employees to report symptoms to the responsible person. Where pre-employment enquiries and information about existing respiratory conditions and symptoms of tightness and pains in the chest, breathlessness etc are used, remember that they are simply a baseline against which any future health problems can be assessed. Such enquiries are not a substitute for proper control of exposure.

Health records for each employee subject to health surveillance should be kept. The first signs of harmful effect - reddening of the skin and a rash - may not appear until 24 hours after exposure, and may get worse over two or three days. A system of skin inspection will identify any printers who develop problems.

Wash-up solvents with traces of UV-curable materials are a particular danger. Organic solvents de-fat and damage the skin, making it easier for all organic materials to penetrate the surface of the skin and reach the vulnerable layers beneath. Keep such solvents off skin and clothing.

If contact does occur, wash off immediately with plenty of soap and water. Remove contaminated clothing immediately. Send it for laundering, but make sure it is properly packaged to prevent inadvertent contact and labelled, indicating the hazard, to protect other people who may handle it. If eyes are affected, clean with plenty of water and get medical help.

Screen printing and cleaning

Screen printing is a process using inks and auxiliary products (including surface coatings) that are solvent- or water-based, or cured by ultra-violet light (UV). Printing may be done manually or by using machinery with varying degrees of automation.

Screen printing inks and solvents may contain glycol ethers and their esters. Like many other solvents, glycol ethers can cause dizziness, headaches, loss of co-ordination and nausea. Some are more hazardous than others, as they can also affect the bone marrow and cause aplastic anaemia and ought not to be used. Particular care and a very high standard of control are required where inks containing N-vinyl pyrrolidone (NVP) and Michler's Ketone are used. Check with your supplier if in doubt and substitute safer alternatives.

Screen preparation

Adhesives used to attach the mesh to the screen frame often contain isocyanates (see the section on the use of isocyanates later in this chapter). Use impervious protective gloves and a face visor when degreasing or preparing the mesh before applying the stencil, especially when using corrosive degreasants.

UV lamps used to prepare the stencils can give rise to a number of risks (see the section on UV-curable materials earlier in this chapter). Impervious gloves should be worn during the preparation of direct and indirect stencils, and for the use of fillers to blank out the remainder of a screen not covered by an indirect stencil. The preparation should be carried out in a well-ventilated area.

Printing and drying

Screen printing areas need local exhaust ventilation or extraction that prevents or adequately controls the risk of inhalation. As a minimum the ventilation system should comply with the occupational exposure levels for the substances used. Position mechanical ventilation so that it draws fumes away from the printers. Arrange the workflow so that drying racks are positioned in an area of forced ventilation, so the airflow across them draws the fume away from the working area. Vent drying tunnels and ovens to a safe place outside.

Screen cleaning and reclamation

After printing always remove as much wet ink as possible from the screen, wearing suitable impervious gloves to prevent skin contact (seek advice from your glove supplier if in doubt). Clean screens in a mechanically ventilated area such as a booth. Do not use high-pressure water jets to clean screens doused with solvents, as this will result in unnecessarily high levels of airborne solvent. Jet them when they are free from ink and solvent.

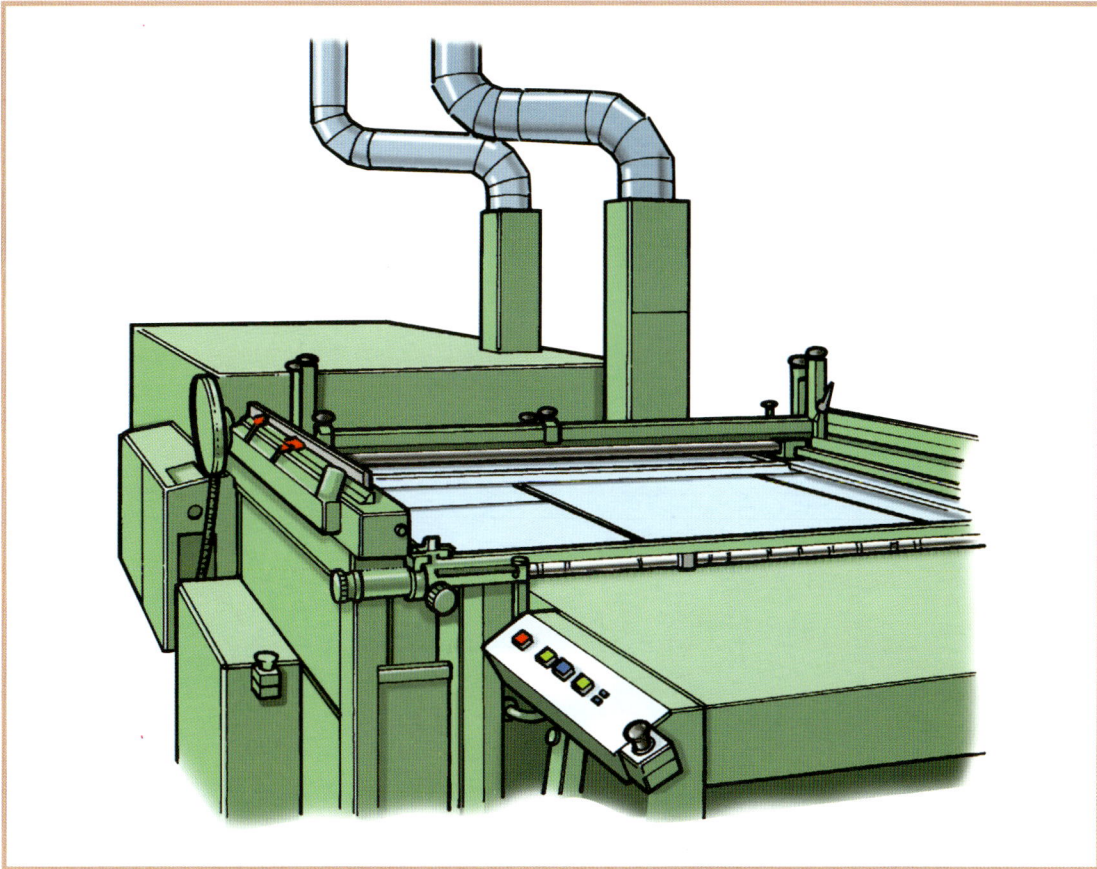

Figure 9 Screen printing areas need very good ventilation to keep the air clear of fumes

If the quantity of work allows, enclosed automatic systems provide the best method of screen cleaning and reclamation.

Operators should wear eye protection (goggles or visors), aprons, gloves or gauntlets and waterproof boots when using high-pressure water/steam cleaners. Ventilation, electrical safety, hearing protection and drainage need to be planned when the wet cleaning area is set out. Further information is available in Guidance Note PM29 *Electrical risks from steam/water pressure cleaners.*

Use of isocyanates

Isocyanates may be found in adhesives used in laminating, polyurethane lacquers, primers and certain specialised inks. They are respiratory sensitisers and have the potential to cause asthmatic attacks, which may occur immediately on exposure or after a delay of several hours. Health surveillance will be necessary in most circumstances - seek specialist advice from an occupational health professional about this.

Try to choose products that do not contain isocyanates if possible, but if they are unavoidable, choose those that have the minimum isocyanate content necessary and are the least volatile to fulfil production requirements. Remember there is always a risk of respiratory sensitisation when isocyanates are used, even if they are present in products at very low levels and appropriate controls should be provided.

Care is needed to ensure that control measures are selected and implemented to prevent inhalation of isocyanates. Local exhaust ventilation that prevents the risk of inhalation will be appropriate in many situations. As a minimum the ventilation system should ensure

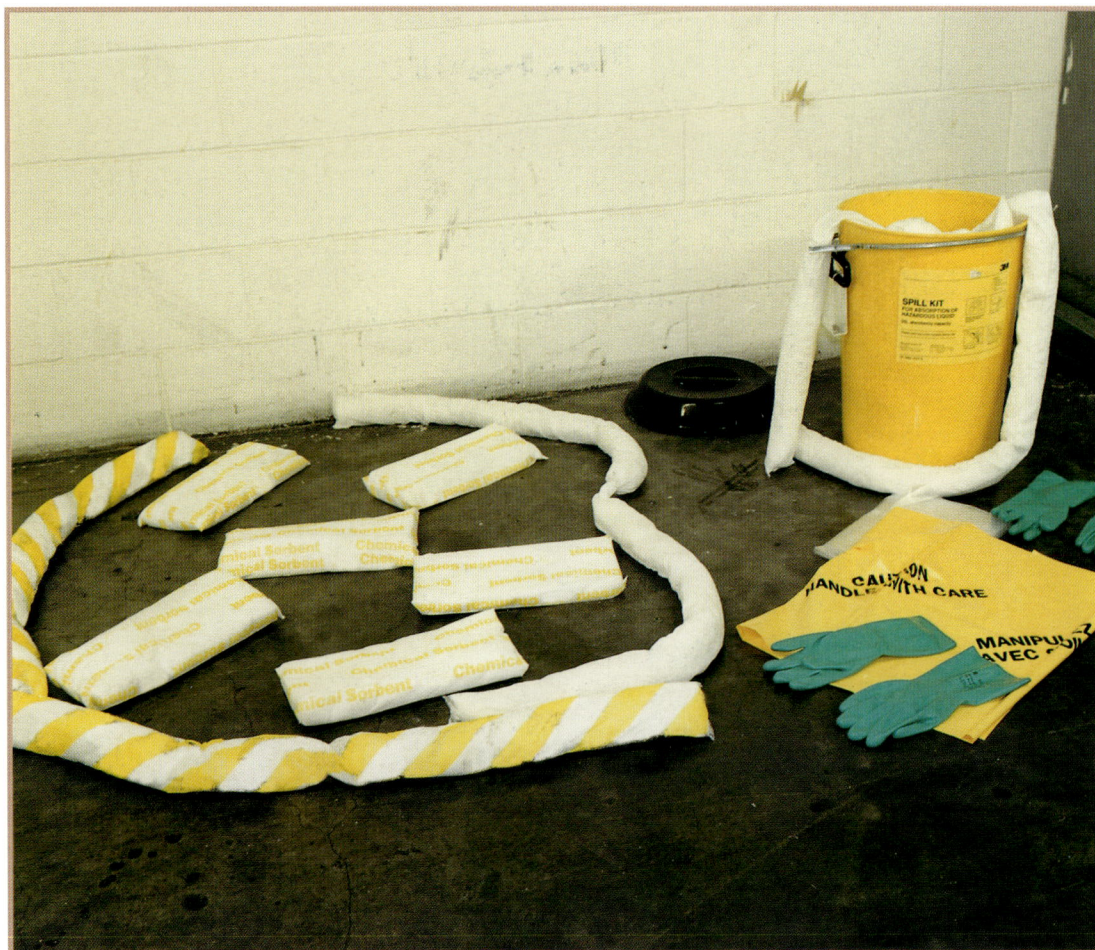

Figure 10 *Provide facilities for dealing with spillages such as a spill kit*

compliance with the relevant occupational exposure level for the substance being used. Risk is likely to be greater in situations in which the substance is heated, or when misting or aerosol formation may occur (the operating speed of the machine will affect this).

Air monitoring should be carried out. There can be serious risks to health if the local exhaust ventilation or other control measures fail, deteriorate or do not work properly. You should keep a record of any exposure monitoring you carry out for at least five years. You can find more information on monitoring in the guidance booklet *Monitoring strategies for toxic substances* (HSG173) and *Methods for the determination of hazardous substances: Organic isocyanates in air* (MDHS25/3).

General protective clothing, including gloves and eye protection, will be necessary and in certain situations respiratory protective equipment will be needed - this will be determined by the COSHH assessment.

Provide facilities for first aid and for dealing with spillages, skin and eye contamination and other emergencies. See the booklet *Safe use of isocyanates in printing and laminating* for further guidance.

Disposal of waste

Remember that the disposal of waste materials and nominally empty containers are subject to environmental regulations. Take advice from your waste management contractor and the waste regulatory authority (Environment Agency etc).

Noise

Loud noise at work can cause irreversible hearing damage. It accelerates the normal hearing loss that occurs as we grow older. It can cause other problems such as tinnitus (troublesome noises in the ear), interference with communication, and stress.

Civil claims against employers are common, and many are successful because not enough has been done in the past to protect the hearing of people at work.

Do you have a noise problem?

As a rule of thumb, if you cannot hear a normal conversation in your workplace clearly when you are 2 m away from the speaker, the noise level is likely to be around 85 dB(A) or higher. If you cannot hear someone clearly when you are about 1 m away, the level is likely to be around 90 dB(A) or higher.

If you think you may have a problem, find out what the noise levels are in your workplace by taking measurements.

Measuring noise levels

Noise is measured in decibels - you will usually see it written as dB(A). The noise level (sound pressure) is measured logarithmically so that every 3 dB(A) increase means a doubling of the noise energy, for example 93 dB(A) is twice as hazardous as 90 dB(A).

In most jobs, the risk depends not just on the noise levels, but also how long people

are exposed, including any overtime. For more information see the booklet *Reducing noise at work* (L108).

Noise and the law

The Noise at Work Regulations 1989 are intended to reduce hearing damage caused by loud noise and they lay down three action levels. The Regulations require employers to assess the risks and take action when workers' daily exposure to noise reaches the 85 dB(A) ($L_{EP,d}$)* 'first action level' and further action if it reaches the 90 dB(A) ($L_{EP,d}$) second or 140 dB(A) 'peak' action levels. When measuring noise exposure no account is taken of the effect of any personal ear protectors worn.

Figure 11 Do you have a noise problem? Loud noise at work can cause irreversible hearing damage

If you find that the noise level is at the first action level or above you must:

- have the risk assessed by a competent person;
- tell your workers about the risks and precautions;
- make hearing protection freely available to those who want it where levels exceed 85 dB(A).

* *Daily personal noise exposure: the worker's noise exposure averaged over an eight-hour working period*

If you find that the noise levels are at the second action level or above, in addition to the above actions, you must also:

- do all that is reasonably practicable to reduce exposure without relying on hearing protection, eg use engineering controls;

- use recognised safety signs to identify and restrict entry to zones where noise reaches (or exceeds) the second or peak action levels. Employees, including managers and supervisors, must not enter these zones unless wearing suitable and effective hearing protection.

Noise reduction

Consider:

- choosing quiet machines or processes for new work. Makers must reduce noise by good design and construction and also provide noise data with their equipment if levels are likely to reach or exceed the first action level. If you are buying machinery, insist on this information. Once the machinery is installed, check the noise levels and take any steps necessary to reduce noise. Noise emission levels can be limited as part of the contract with suppliers and checked after installation;

- changing the machine and process to produce less noise. Don't forget that other changes you make might affect noise levels;

- enclosing noisy machines by providing acoustic enclosures. These have to be made of appropriate noise-reducing materials and be correctly installed. If they are not properly designed, noise escaping from holes, feed openings or poorly fitting panels may significantly reduce performance. Specialist advice will probably be necessary;

- putting noisy machines and processes in separate rooms, away from employees' work areas;

- fitting silencers to all exhausts and making sure they are kept in place and maintained.

Reducing exposure

Think about reducing the length of exposure by rotating jobs or providing a noise refuge, eg at machine control points.

Remember - hearing damage is cumulative. Make sure that young people in particular get into the habit of avoiding noise exposure, before their hearing is permanently damaged.

Providing hearing protection

Ensure that workers wear hearing protection where daily personal noise levels exceed 90 dB(A). Remember this is not a substitute for noise reduction at source.

Do not rely too heavily on hearing protectors. In practice they reduce noise exposure less than is claimed because they:

- have not been correctly selected;

- are not fitted and worn correctly;

- are not properly maintained;

- are uncomfortable or inconvenient to wear.

Plastic foam or mineral fibre/waxed plugs, if properly chosen and correctly worn, can be as good as ear muffs. To work, hearing protectors need to be worn all the time that people are in noisy areas. If they are left off for even short periods, even the best protectors cannot greatly reduce noise exposure. Supervisors should check this.

Protectors should:

- be suitable for the conditions in which they are to be used;

- provide enough attenuation to reduce the noise exposure level to below 90 dB(A) and preferably to below 85 dB(A);

- only be issued on a personal basis;

- never be removed in a noisy environment;

- be compatible with other forms of necessary PPE;

- preferably be marked to indicate conformity with BS EN 352: 1993 *Hearing protectors - safety requirements and testing* Part 1: *Ear-muffs.* Part 2: *Ear-plugs.* Part 3: 1997 *Ear-muffs attached to an industrial safety helmet.*

It will be beneficial for employees to have a choice of hearing protection from a range of types identified as suitable. See the free leaflets *Noise at work: A guide for employees* (INDG99), *Ear protection: Employers' duties explained* (INDG298), and *Protect your hearing!* (INDG299) pocket card.

Workers need to be adequately trained in the proper fitting, use and care of hearing protection. This will help to ensure that protectors maintain their efficiency and are correctly worn.

Common problems and solutions for printers

Experience has shown that there are certain areas that can usefully be targeted to reduce noise in a printing workplace.

- Sheet-fed buckle-folding machines in the finishing department create high noise levels. These machines should be fitted with acoustic hoods at all buckle plates to reduce the noise. Guidance is given in the publication *Noise reduction at buckle-folding machines*.

- Web-fed presses have several noise sources (in particular the folder), and various noise control measures may be appropriate. Guidance is given in the booklet *Noise reduction at web-fed presses*.

- Vacuum pumps and compressors, such as those associated with sheet-fed printing machines, gatherer-stitcher-trimmers and buckle-folding machines, can produce high noise levels and it is important to site such equipment away from the workroom or shield it in a suitable enclosure, as these can make a large contribution to the overall noise level.

- Sheet-fed printing machines (in general) do not create excessive levels of noise if they are properly spaced and housed, as long as noise from vacuum pumps and compressors is controlled.

- Regular preventive maintenance of machines can be important in avoiding the generation of excessive levels of noise. Worn bearings in buckle-folding machines are frequently found to be a significant source of noise.

- It is good practice to carry out regular hearing checks on all employees whose daily personal noise exposures equal or exceed 90 dB(A), and such checks should be carried out when noise levels reach or exceed 95 dB(A). Refer to the leaflet *Health surveillance in noisy industries* (INDG193) and the paragraphs under 'Hearing protection' in the 'Personal protective equipment (PPE)' section at the end of this chapter.

Hearing loss

Under the Management of Health and Safety at Work Regulations 1999, employees exposed to certain types of risk, such as high noise levels, should be provided with appropriate health surveillance. Such conditions are likely, for example, at large web-fed presses and associated folders. Health surveillance for hearing loss usually involves hearing checks called audiometry.

There is no simple formula to show when audiometry is necessary. The starting point is to assess the risk of employees becoming deaf because they are being exposed to loud noise.

This risk depends on the noise level and the length of exposure. Employers should arrange for a competent person to carry out an assessment of their employees' noise exposures, as required by the Noise at Work Regulations 1989.

Programmes for hearing checks need to be under the control of someone who can make sense of audiometric data and advise individuals on the state of their hearing and on follow-up action. This might be an occupational physician, a nurse with appropriate training and experience, an audiological scientist or a trained audiometrician able to refer employees to a more qualified person when they need more advice.

Health surveillance for employees in noisy jobs normally means:

- regular hearing checks in controlled conditions to measure the sensitivity of hearing over a range of sound frequencies;

- informing them about the results of their hearing checks;

- keeping records; and

- encouraging them to seek further advice from a doctor where hearing damage is suspected.

For more information, see Guidance Note MS26 *A guide to audiometric testing programmes*.

Manual handling

The law and manual handling

The Manual Handling Operations Regulations 1992 require all employers to:

- avoid the need for hazardous manual lifting and handling if it is reasonably practicable to do so, eg by redesigning the task and/or workplace layout, eliminating the need to move loads manually, using mechanical handling equipment etc;

- assess the risk of injury from any hazardous manual lifting and handling which cannot be avoided;

- take steps to reduce the risk of injury from manual handling, eg by providing mechanical assistance, improvements to the task, load or working environment;

- provide employees with information on the weight of the load and an indication of the heaviest side where a load has a centre of gravity that is not centrally positioned.

Risk assessment filter

A detailed assessment of every risk could be a major undertaking and involve wasted effort, so HSE has developed a filter to screen out straightforward cases. The filter is based on a set of numerical guidelines developed from published scientific literature, and its application will provide a reasonable level of protection to around 95% of working men and women although it should not be seen as providing safe weight limits for lifting.

The guidelines assume that the load is easy to grasp with both hands with the handler in a stable body position, and take into account the vertical and horizontal position of the hands as they move the load during the handling operation, as well as the height and reach of the handler.

Figure 12 gives a boundary mapped out by the guidelines. If the handler's hands enter more than one of the box zones during the operation, the smallest weight figures apply. If the task requires lifting or lowering of the hands outside the box zones, a more detailed assessment should be made.

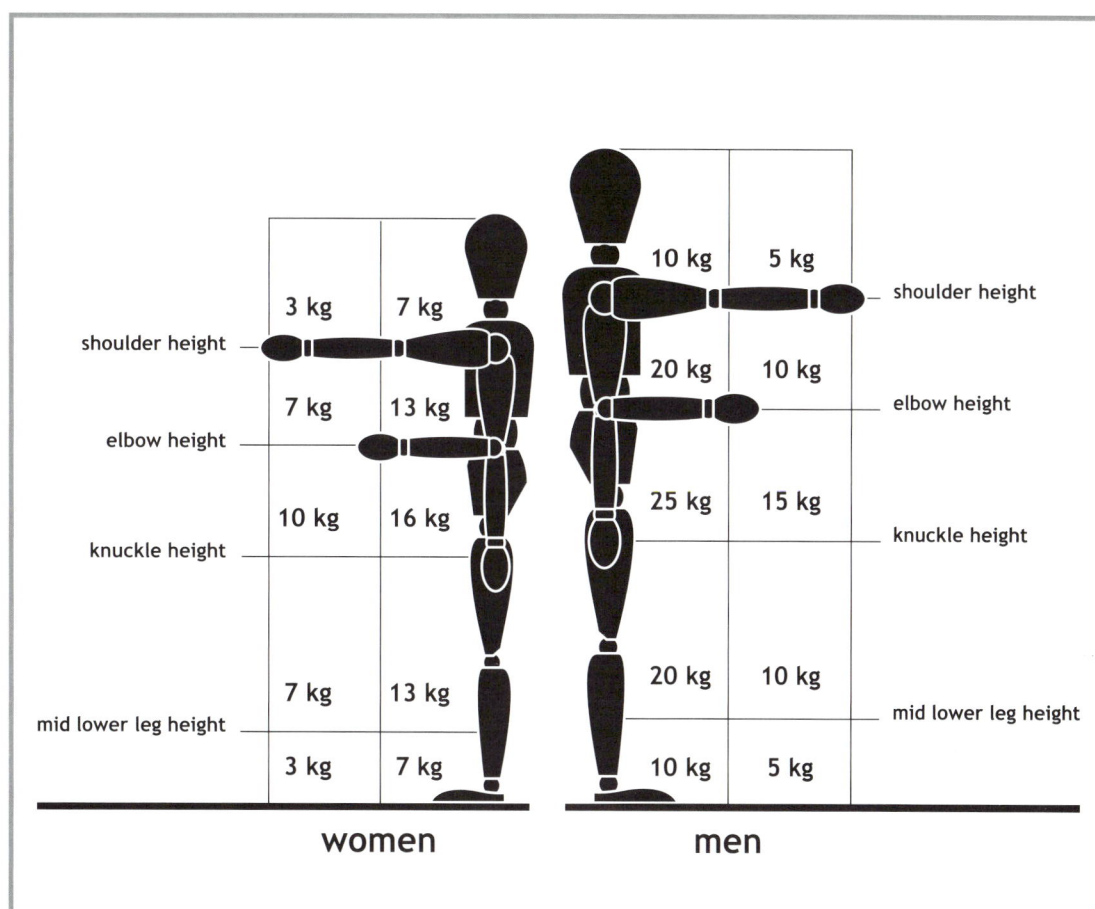

Figure 12 *Lifting and lowering*

What are the risks?

Although some people are more at risk, everyone can suffer injuries as a result of manual handling - this is why hazardous manual handling activities should be avoided if possible. If it is impossible to avoid such activity then it should be assessed and risk reduction measures considered. When making an assessment, you may have to give particular attention to the following groups of people:

- younger, more inexperienced employees;

- older and/or less physically fit employees;

- those with existing injuries or conditions such as asthma;

- pregnant employees.

Manual/materials handling can lead to injuries and musculoskeletal disorders in various parts of the body including the back, abdomen, neck, upper limbs and even lower limbs.

The cumulative effects of even minor injuries can become more pronounced over a period of time. Serious and lasting damage to the spine and other parts of the body can result. Careful job design can avoid the problems of restricting particular tasks to particular workers or the disruption that can follow if people are injured.

Poor lifting and carrying, pushing and pulling causes more than 25% of the work-related injuries reported in the printing industry each year.

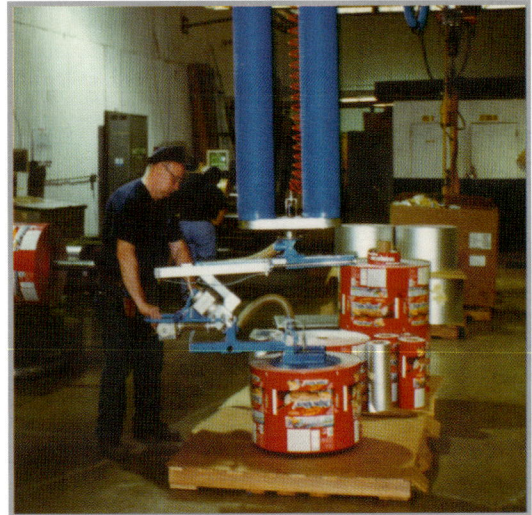

Figure 13 Reel and cylinder trolleys reduce the amount of manual lifting and carrying

Reducing the risks

When manual handling is unavoidable, look at the job and think about reducing the risk by providing mechanical help, for example:

- scissor lifts and elevating tables at folders and guillotines;

- pile turners and joggers to reduce the need for hand turning and 'knocking up';

- mechanical or free-running conveyors to reduce lifting and carrying;

- hoists and slings at reelstands to reduce manual lifting of paper reels, especially those mounted on swing arms;

- reel conveyor trolleys for localised movement of paper reels into and out of reelstands;

- cylinder and roller trolleys;

- reel shaft trolley;

- sack trucks.

Other ways of reducing the risk include:

- making the load smaller/lighter or easier to grasp, eg by buying in smaller paper bundles or chemical containers;

- reorganising or redesigning the tasks to reduce the effort required;

- altering workstation heights to suit the worker;

- improving the layout of the workplace to make the work more efficient;

- ensuring reasonable working temperatures;

- ensuring adequate manoeuvring space has been provided.

Handling newspaper and magazine bundles

Specific guidance is available on the control of risk from handling bundles, comprising two free leaflets (IACL105 *Handling the news: Advice for employers on manual handling of bundles* and IACL106 *Handling the news: Advice for newsagents and employees on safe handling of bundles*) and a training video *What the papers weigh*. The industry has agreed a maximum bundle weight of 18 kg, with a target to reduce this further to 17 kg to help reduce the risks to all those involved in the distribution chain - including delivery boys and girls, and newsagents.

Training

Consider providing every employee with basic training in manual handling techniques appropriate to the type of work they do. You will also have to consider other more direct ways to reduce risk.

Training should cover:

- how manual handling can cause injury;

ACCIDENTS

A printer lifting a magazine bundle weighing 12 kg onto a pallet injured his lower back. He had not been given any handling aids or training in correct lifting techniques.

An employee attempting to clear a jammed newspaper bundle on a conveyor injured her back. She had not been given any training or information on manual handling techniques or bundle clearing techniques.

A maintenance fitter suffered back pain after lifting press inking rollers weighing 23 kg. He had received no training or information on manual handling. Use of mechanical lifting equipment or assistance from a second person would have reduced the risk of injury.

- the essentials of the Manual Handling Operations Regulations 1992;

- how to recognise potentially harmful manual handling tasks/operations;

- appropriate systems of work;

- correct use of mechanical aids;

- appropriate handling techniques.

Further information on manual handling can be found in the booklet *Manual handling. Manual Handling Operations Regulations 1992. Guidance on Regulations* (L23) and the leaflet *Back in work: Managing back pain in the workplace* (INDG333).

Assessing and reducing risks

Job

Does the job require:

- lifting or lowering too far?
- rushing?
- carrying over long distances?
- lots of repetitions?
- twisting and turning?

Work area

Is the work area:

- too dark?
- too slippery?
- too congested/ obstructed?

Load

Is the load:

- too heavy?
- too large?
- too unstable?
- too sharp?
- too difficult to grasp?

Individuals

Are individuals:

- fit?
- in need of special consideration?
- trained?

Example tasks	Short-term action	Long-term solution
Loading and unloading deliveries by hand	Provide help for heavy loads. Reduce the load size.	Palletise loads. Use lift trucks, pallet trucks, boom conveyors, vehicles with tail lifts etc.
Moving materials to and from machines	Break down the loads into easily handled units. Fold or wrap over large sheets of paper.	Use conveyors/ hoists/lift trucks/ pallet trucks etc. Use air tables, eg at guillotines.
Loading and unloading machines	Raise pallets etc to the right height and position.	Automate loading/unloading operations. Use mechanical aids, eg scissor lifts and pile hoists.

Assessing and reducing risks

Example tasks	Short-term action	Long-term solution
Assembling and packing	Use appropriate, fit, trained personnel. Rotate the work to reduce repetition.	Provide a well-lit working environment with suitable seating where appropriate. Automate. Provide mechanical aids.
Preparing, maintaining, moving and repairing presses and other equipment	Use appropriate, fit, trained personnel. Ensure adequate working space.	Provide mechanical aids, eg hoists for removing cylinders etc.

Repetitive handling

Repetitive handling can present particular problems and give rise to conditions called work-related upper limb disorders (WRULDs) or upper limb disorders (ULDs). Sometimes the condition is called repetitive strain injury (RSI).

The musculoskeletal system (ie the muscles, bones, ligaments, tendons) in our hands, arms, shoulders and neck can be harmed by static or awkward postures, excessive force levels and repeated exertions. This is especially so when these are combined with little opportunity for variety or other means of recovery.

Work-related upper limb disorders (WRULD) can cause all of the following:

- pain;

- soft tissue swelling;

- restriction of joint movement;

- reduced sense of touch and manual dexterity;

- permanent disability if other symptoms go untreated.

Failure to take prompt action can result in:

- serious ill health. Well-motivated and productive people have had to give up work because of pain and disablement from WRULDs; others have been so badly affected that simple household tasks become difficult;

- lost production due to employees taking sick leave;

- compensation claims from employees that have had to stop working because of WRULDs;

- employees complaining of, or seeking medical attention for, persistent pain or actual injury;

- hidden costs, eg training new staff or providing extra staff where sickness absence is high. Substantial cost savings can occur when a preventive strategy is adopted.

Additional information about upper limb disorders is given in *Work-related upper limb disorders in the printing industry* (IACL91).

To protect your employees from upper limb disorders you need to be able to identify the operations that give rise to the risk and take steps to reduce that risk.

How to assess and tackle ULDs

Identify the hazards

The following are examples of operations which can give rise to upper limb disorders (ULDs):

- Using powered hand tools.

- Using pliers or scissors.

- Sealing boxes with tape.

- Hand feeding/unloading of machines.

- Assembly work.

- Counting, sorting, checking.

- Stripping, breaking, knocking-out, knocking-up.

- Flat pack wrapping.

- Manual handling of bundles.

- Hand insertion work.

- Jacketing of cased books.

Hazards may also exist if the work involves frequent, forceful or awkward gripping, squeezing, twisting, and repitition, pulling, pushing or lifting.

Warning signs of upper limb disorders can include complaints by workers and improvised changes to workstations or tools.

If any of the above are characteristic of your workplace you should do a full ergonomic risk assessment. Don't forget to consider the risks arising from the use of display screen equipment (see Chapter 3 for further advice). A systematic and ergonomic approach will help to assess risks and provide solutions.

Reduce the risk

Apply ergonomic principles to machines, workstations and work methods so that the job fits the person. For example:

- reduce high force levels (maintain equipment properly, spread force levels, use tools with appropriately designed handles);

- reduce highly repetitive movements (balance frequent repetition with non-repetitive work, carry out tasks with the other hand, introduce handling aids, use automation, provide more varied tasks);

- provide rest/recovery time by breaks or activity changes before fatigue starts;

- change postures (modify operation, redesign work so the wrist can be straight);

- change the operator's position in relation to work;

- where people remain in the same position, provide a mix of work requiring movement.

Other steps include:

- making sure operators receive adequate information, instruction and training;

- being aware of the main causes/symptoms and preventive measures;

- reporting problems early before they become serious;

- ensuring new employees start at slower work rates before gradual upgrading;

- rotating jobs (variation of tasks);

- ensuring that any incentive schemes do not adversely affect how the work is done (eg ensure sufficient breaks are taken).

Future control measures

- Examine risks from upper limb disorders when planning changes to work methods or purchasing new machinery. Check that ergonomic principles have been incorporated in the design.

- Consider health surveillance, eg record keeping and prompt medical assessment when problems are reported.

- Think about ways to encourage early reporting of symptoms.

- Look at sickness records and staff turnover.

- Consider the possibility of alternative work if a person cannot continue in a particular job or where it will assist a return to work.

- Introduce a system to monitor the effectiveness of current control measures.

- Be alert to any increase in ULDs in the workplace, eg after a change in process, and take appropriate action.

- Ensure that there are arrangements for effective rehabilitation (see 'Occupational health and rehabilitation' earlier in this chapter).

Radiation

Lasers

Laser use in the printing industry is increasing. Applications include laser printers and copiers, scanners, platemakers, engravers (in printing cylinder manufacture), package date marking, die cutting and typesetting.

Radiation hazards

A laser is a source of intense light. Laser emissions can be dangerous when viewed either directly or when reflected from a smooth surface. The greatest hazard is to the eye, because it focuses visible laser emissions to form a very small image on the retina. Power intensities can be increased by a factor of 100 000 so that even a few milliwatts of laser emission can cause serious and permanent damage to the retina, and therefore vision in the affected eye.

It is important to get an eye examination immediately following hazardous personal exposure, but routine eye examination as part of health surveillance is not recommended. Some types of laser produce invisible beams that may still be focused by the eye to produce a harmful image on the retina. Skin burns may also be a risk that needs assessment.

Fume hazards

Laser copiers and computer printers may give off ozone, dust and fume - this is seldom excessive and not normally a problem if the equipment is both well maintained and sited in a place that is effectively ventilated. Other types of equipment may need local exhaust ventilation (LEV) - your COSHH assessment will help you to decide the need for this, and your supplier should be able to advise.

Mechanical and electrical hazards

As with any machinery, dangers from moving parts and from electrical installations exist - these hazards should be evaluated as part of your risk assessment.

Safeguarding standards

Laser products are classified in accordance with their level of hazard. BS EN 60825-1: 1994 *Safety of laser products* Part 1: *Equipment classification, requirements and user's guide* gives information on class definitions. Laser products used in the printing industry will generally be Class 1 (safe by engineering design). This means the laser and workpiece will be fully enclosed during normal use.

Lasers are generally classified according to their output power, but remember that a Class 1 laser product may contain a high-powered Class 4 laser inside its casing. Tampering with or removal of shielding or enclosure from a Class 1 product may result in exposure to a high-powered laser emission. Also remember that harmful exposure can result from reflected laser beams as well as those that are viewed directly. Avoid use of mirrors or reflective glass near laser sources.

When you acquire laser equipment the supplier has a duty to provide adequate information to you (see 'Acquiring machinery and other work equipment' in Chapter 5). The information provided by the supplier will help you develop suitable systems of work for the safe operation of your equipment.

Only a competent person (usually a service engineer) should carry out any servicing or other work on your laser equipment. A competent person is someone who is properly trained in laser safety and who is able to follow a safe system of work which in many cases will include wearing suitable eye protection. It is your responsibility to assess eye protection needs and to ensure your workers wear it (see 'Personal protective equipment (PPE)' later in this chapter).

For further information on lasers see the booklet *Laser safety in printing*.

Ultraviolet (UV) light

UV light is used in photoengraving and lithographic platemaking and to cure certain inks, vanishes and lacquers, eg in lithographic, flexographic and label printing (see 'Hazardous substances' earlier in this chapter for hazards of UV-curable inks etc).

ACCIDENTS

An employee was dealing with a film misfeed on an imagesetter. He turned off the computer but forgot about the raster image processor (RIP). He opened the cover to the film and laser, and used an override key to run the film through manually so that he could find the misfeed. But stored information in the RIP caused the laser to start up unexpectedly, and the employee suffered eye damage from the reflected laser emission.

UV light is typically generated by a carbon arc, xenon discharge tube or mercury vapour discharge tube. Nowadays, carbon arcs are seldom used because of the fume they generate (primarily carbon monoxide and toxic oxides of nitrogen).

Radiation hazards

Excessive UV exposure can cause acute effects such as redness and burning of the skin and damage to the eyes (possibly causing painful conjunctivitis). The onset of symptoms may be delayed for several hours after exposure. People who have had the lens of the eye removed (aphakes) may suffer retinal damage from exposure to UV light.

Some people may have an abnormally increased sensitivity to the effects of UV light which may be a consequence of one of a number of uncommon medical conditions or may result from exposure to a sensitising chemical such as a prescribed drug, for example some antibiotics including tetracyclines and sulphonamides, thiazide diuretics, tricyclic antidepressants, phenothiazines and some other categories of drugs. Such sensitisation may result in an exaggerated sunburn response or in more varied and less well localised skin changes. Anyone who develops an abnormal condition affecting mainly the light-exposed areas of the body may have become photosensitised. Further occupational exposure to UV light should stop and the individual should be referred to a doctor.

UV exposure also increases the risk of developing various types of skin cancer and is associated with accelerated skin ageing and cataracts. Skin cancer risk increases with exposure level and with exposure time and is not thought to have an exposure threshold below which there is no risk.

When considering acute effects, as a general rule, UVB sources (those emitting at wavelengths between 280 and 320 nm (nanometres)) are more hazardous than UVA sources (those emitting at wavelengths between 320 and 400 nm). UVC sources emit below 280 nm and are potentially the most harmful. UVC radiation is, however, easy to remove as even glass is a heavy absorber. This is a technically complex area, and users may need to take advice from their suppliers about the adequacy of their precautions.

Fume hazards

UV light sources used for curing are usually much more powerful than those used in platemaking. It is important to ensure that where these lamps are aircooled they are well ventilated so that fume and ozone is removed.

Safeguarding standards

Fixed or interlocked screening at UV light units prevents direct or reflected UV emission from being emitted to the workroom where it would present a risk to

the skin and eyes. It is important that the screens, shutters and sealing brushes on print-down frames are well maintained, so that emission leakage is prevented. It is particularly important to check that lamp cowlings are adjusted so that UV escape, especially where reflective substrates are in use, is minimised. A common failure is the splitting of infill canvas screens. These should be regularly inspected and replaced as necessary.

Figure 14 Screen all UV light sources adequately, preferably with automatic curtains or blinds

Printed sheets should not be visually inspected under a UV lamp because levels of reflected radiation may be high: remove sheets from the press before inspection.

For some unusual maintenance work it may be necessary to run a UV lamp without screening. In such cases, suitable eye protection against UV emission will be necessary, together with clothing to cover exposed areas of skin.

For further information see 'Screen printing' and 'Basic rules of machinery safety' in Chapter 5.

Infrared sources

Infrared units are used typically for drying printed material at offset litho presses, as an alternative to the use of anti-set-off powder and for accelerated drying. The equipment may be fitted retrospectively to existing machines.

Radiation hazards

Infrared light may cause eye injury (especially to the lens of the eye). In the printing industry, however, it is unlikely that sources will be of sufficient output for this risk to be a serious problem. Exposure may also cause reddening and burns to the skin.

Fume hazards

The inks used on litho presses have a low solvent content. There are generally no fire, explosion or fume hazards arising from their evaporation, however you will need to assess the fume hazards and introduce control measures if necessary.

Safeguarding standards

Interlocking of lamp units with presses prevents the risk of fire when machines are stopped during a print run, or when there is a misfeed.

Dryers should be electrically isolated during wash-up at machines and using flammable solvents should be avoided on the infrared unit itself. Lamp enclosure may be necessary to shield operators from excessive exposure and to reduce levels of glare that might otherwise interfere with work.

Static eliminators

Static electricity may be a problem in some plants. As well as the possibility of operators experiencing painful static shocks, there is also the risk of static ignition of flammable vapours, for example where volatile, flammable solvents are used in processes such as web-fed gravure and flexographic printing. Polythene, PVC and other insulating substrates are particularly likely to generate static.

Static eliminators are used to prevent the build-up of unwanted electrostatic charges and so avoid the potential for static ignition of flammable vapours. Static eliminators need to be designed so that they cannot produce incendiary sparks, and where relevant need to be constructed to a suitable explosion protection standard. Static eliminators may be used in conjunction with 'static assist' devices, or may be used to control static generated by the movement of the web.

Some static eliminators contain small amounts of sealed radioactive material, which ionises the air. It is also possible to use static eliminators such as carbon fibre brushes, and high voltage types, which do not contain radioactive material.

It is important that static eliminators are kept clean and properly maintained.

The correct fitting of any static eliminators is a skilled task and it is recommended that advice be taken from the suppliers. Static eliminators containing radioactive material should not be tampered with or dismantled. If you suspect they are not working correctly, call the supplier.

Skin disease (dermatitis)

A detailed study in the printing industry has identified that about 40% of printing workers are likely to have suffered from a skin complaint at some stage and over 10% are likely to have a current problem. This highlights the fact that skin problems are an important problem in the printing industry, which were previously underestimated. People working in the printing area and involved in cleaning printing machinery showed the greatest tendency towards skin problems, but the evidence suggests that some problems can exist in all areas of printing.

What is dermatitis?

Dermatitis is a common skin condition, which is reported to affect between 15 to 20% of the UK population. The causes are varied. It is often quite simply an inflammation of the skin, and can arise as a result of:

- an inherited sensitivity to eczema (atopy);

- contact with irritants such as soaps, solvents and wet work;

- an allergy caused by contact with certain substances such as nickel or rubber.

In the workplace all these factors may be involved. The printing industry uses developers, etching solutions, solvents, inks, glues, gums, oils and greases that can all cause skin irritation.

Printing processes with a high occurrence of skin problems are:

- platemaking;

- correction of litho plates;

- solvent use;

- UV-cured ink use;

- materials containing isocyanates;

- cleaning of litho rollers and cylinders;

- guillotining;

- handling press room consumables.

Fifty per cent of workers involved in the correction of litho plates or cleaning of litho rollers and cylinders are likely to have had a skin complaint at some time.

Affected areas

The most commonly affected parts of the body are the fingers and the webs between the fingers, closely followed by the back of the hands, particularly those of printing press workers. These workers generally also have more problems on the wrist, forearm and elbows than other workers. Something like three-quarters of those who have ever had a skin complaint find the problem clears up away from work. A majority of skin problems first occur after the age of 16.

Symptoms

The most frequently reported symptoms by printworkers, and which are consistent with irritant contact dermatitis are:

- itching;

- rough skin;

- dry skin;

- redness.

Work-related substances

The most common work-related substances which generally aggravate skin conditions are:

- wash-up solutions;

- inks and cleaning solvents;

- UV varnishes;

- UV inks;

- developers;

- thinners;

- hand cleansers.

Washing powders, cleaning agents and personal soaps both at work and in the home can also cause problems. Handling of paper, constant washing and contact with water can all lead to dryness, and itchy and sore skin conditions.

The disappearance of symptoms away from work, found in about three-quarters of all printers with a skin complaint, reinforces the need for better skin care provision in the industry and more awareness.

Why employers should take action

The Management of Health and Safety at Work Regulations 1999 and the Control of Substances Hazardous to Health (COSHH) Regulations 1999 require employers to assess risks to health as well as safety, such as dermatitis, and take action to prevent it. Also, dermatitis costs money - from sickness absence, loss of production, staff turnover, retraining etc.

As part of their overall COSHH assessments employers need to assess the risks of dermatitis from the materials and processes they use. **Health surveillance should be carried out and employees properly informed, trained and supervised** (see earlier in this chapter under 'Health surveillance').

Where there is exposure to substances that may cause dermatitis and the hands and forearms are likely to be affected (for example where UV-curable inks, lacquers and varnishes are used) the following measures will help protect employees.

- Arrange for a responsible person such as a supervisor or first aider to be given training by an occupational health professional on the symptoms and signs of dermatitis, and set up a system of periodic skin inspections. The frequency of the inspections will depend on the individual circumstances, eg the likely severity of the dermatitis that might develop, but would normally be at least monthly.

- Arrange for new employees to have their hands and forearms inspected before they start work with the substance that might cause a skin reaction.

- Refer any employee found to have relevant symptoms or signs to a suitable medical practitioner (normally an occupational health physician) who is familiar with the risks of the process and the principles of health surveillance.

- Train employees so they can recognise and report relevant symptoms and signs of illness to the responsible person.

Further guidance is given in the booklet *Assessing and managing risks at work from skin exposure to chemical agents* (HSG205) and *Skin problems in the printing industry* (IACL101rev1).

Other health issues

Workplace stress

Stress is the second biggest occupational health problem in the UK, after back pain. About 5 million workers suffer from high levels of stress at work. How employers design and manage jobs affects the mental and physical health of their employees.

What are the effects of stress?

Stress is people's natural reaction to excessive pressure - it isn't a disease. But if the stress is intense or goes on for some time, it can lead to mental and physical ill health, such as depression, nervous breakdown or heart disease. The symptoms of stress can also include indecision, anxiety, altered appetite, changes in weight, headaches, backache, skin rashes and difficulty in sleeping.

What must employers do?

It is the duty of all employers to make sure that their employees are not made ill by their work. Where stress caused or made worse by work could be, or is, leading to ill health, employers must assess the risk.

A risk assessment for stress involves:

- looking for pressures at work which could cause high and long-lasting levels of stress;

- deciding who might be harmed by these; and

- deciding whether the employer is doing enough to prevent that harm.

If necessary, employers must then take reasonable steps to deal with those pressures. Simply relying on employees to manage their own stress, for example by training them in relaxation techniques, or just providing counselling when they experience high or sustained levels of stress is not enough. Refer also to the section on occupational health services at the beginning of this chapter.

Managing stress

Most of the 'things to do' on stress boil down to good management, including good management of health and safety. They are ongoing processes that need to be built into the way a company is run.

- Taking stress seriously, and being understanding towards people who admit to being under too much pressure.

- Encouraging managers to have an open and understanding attitude to what people say to them about the pressures of their work, and looking for signs of stress in their staff.

- Ensuring that staff have the skills, training and resources they need, so that they know what to do, are confident that they can do it and receive credit for it.

- If possible, providing some scope for varying working conditions and flexibility, and for people to influence the way their jobs are done. This will increase their interest and sense of ownership.

- Ensuring that people are treated fairly and with consistency and that bullying and harassment are not tolerated.

- Ensuring good two-way communication, especially at times of change, and not being afraid to listen.

Workplace stress and mental health

Workplace pressure can keep staff motivated and be the key to a sense of job satisfaction, but people's ability to deal with pressure is not limitless. Excessive workplace pressure and resulting stress can be harmful and damaging to both your employees' health and to your business performance.

Employers have a responsibility under the HSW Act to take reasonable care to ensure that health is not put at risk through sustained levels of stress arising from the way the work is organised, the way people deal with each other or from day-to-day demands.

It is known that too little personal control over the work, not being allowed to use skills fully, being overworked or underworked, and boring work can all contribute to stress.

Learn to recognise signs of stress and encourage employees to discuss problems openly - are people distracted, tense or worried?

Give help, be sympathetic and, if appropriate, advise employees to see their doctor. Delay can make matters much worse.

Further information on stress at work can be found in the employer's guide *Tackling work-related stress: A manager's guide to improving and maintaining employee health and well-being* (HSG218) and the leaflet *Work-related stress: A short guide* (INDG281).

New and expectant mothers at work

Employers are required to take particular account of risks to new and expectant mothers when carrying out risk assessments. Particular attention should be given to lifting and carrying, hours of work including night work, work requiring long periods of standing and work involving exposure to chemicals, eg exposure to lead. Employers need to ensure that exposure to carcinogenic, mutagenic or teratogenic substances is prevented, as such exposure may create a risk to the unborn child.

If a risk is identified then suitable alternative work should be offered. If this is not possible the worker should be given paid leave for as long as possible to protect her health and safety and that of her child.

Further information can be found in the booklet *New and expectant mothers at work. A guide for employers* (HSG122).

Drugs and alcohol

The misuse of alcohol and drugs can affect work performance and potentially pose a threat to health and safety. Employers can benefit by developing an alcohol and drugs policy. This policy should form part of the overall health and safety policy. It should help employers identify problems at an early stage, encourage affected people to come forward for help and treatment and ensure appropriate controls.

Work such as operating machinery or driving demands clear thinking and sound judgement. Where performance is impaired, people should not be allowed to undertake such duties. All activities of employees who are in a place of work while under the influence of drugs or alcohol should be strictly controlled.

HSE's Employment Medical Advisory Service can advise on all aspects of occupational ill health including drug abuse. Further information for employers is available in the leaflet *Drug misuse at work* (INDG91).

Passive smoking

Passive smoking is the breathing in of other people's tobacco smoke. It can cause damage to health, make asthma worse and cause lung cancer.

Think about agreeing rules with the workforce to protect non-smokers and encouraging and helping smokers to give up. Advice is given in the booklet *Passive smoking at work* (INDG63).

The Workplace (Health, Safety and Welfare) Regulations 1992 require that rest rooms and rest areas include suitable arrangements to protect non-smokers from discomfort caused by tobacco smoke. This can be achieved by providing separate rest areas or rooms for smokers and non-smokers or by prohibiting smoking in rest areas and rest rooms.

Humidifier fever

Humidifier fever is a flu-like illness caused by inhalation of fine droplets of water from humidifiers that have become contaminated by micro-organisms. It should not be confused with Legionnaires' disease (see 'Legionellosis').

The symptoms of humidifier fever vary from mild fever with headache, malaise and muscle weakness, to acute illness with high fever, cough, chest tightness and breathlessness on exertion. The onset of symptoms is delayed, beginning four to eight hours after the start of the working shift. The symptoms usually occur on the first day back at work after a weekend or other break and tend to resolve over 12 to 16 hours.

Humidifiers are sometimes used in print companies to stabilise paper size and condition. They are also present in building air-conditioning systems.

Contamination of humidifier systems is most likely to occur in internal reservoirs within the humidifiers and in holding tanks, especially if the water is recirculated. Paper dust or anti-set-off powders may act as a nutrient for the growth of micro-organisms if allowed to accumulate. Exposure then results from spray emitted from the contaminated system.

So far, cases of humidifier fever in the printing industry have been associated with spinning disc and spray-type humidifiers incorporating holding reservoirs.

Prevention and control

Choose the humidification equipment that is least likely to become contaminated, eg steam humidifiers, compressed air atomisers that take water directly from the mains, or evaporative type humidifiers that do not create water spray.

Maintain cleanliness - weekly cleaning may be necessary in process environments, every two to three months may be acceptable for offices. Ensure that humidifiers are drained and kept dry during periods when they are not in use, and are thoroughly cleaned and disinfected before they are used again.

If humidifier fever is suspected, turn off the humidifiers and seek advice from both a medical practitioner and a competent ventilation engineer with the necessary specialised knowledge of humidifiers.

Legionellosis

Legionnaires' disease is a pneumonia that principally affects those who are susceptible due to age, illness, immunosuppression, smoking etc and may be fatal. Legionellae can also cause less serious illnesses that are not fatal or permanently debilitating but which can affect all types of people.

Infection is attributed to inhaling legionellae. These bacteria are widespread in natural water sources but may multiply under certain conditions if they enter man-made systems or water services. Most cases and outbreaks of legionellosis have been attributed to water services in buildings and cooling towers; other sources may include humidification systems and industrial coolants. Plant and systems containing water which is likely to have a temperature in the range 20-45°C, and which may release a spray or aerosol during operation or when being maintained, may also present a risk.

The law

The Notification of Cooling Towers and Evaporative Condensers Regulations 1992 require the notification to local authorities of wet cooling towers and evaporative condensers. *Legionnaires' disease: Control of legionella in water systems. Approved Code of Practice* (L8) gives guidance on complying with the requirements of the Health and Safety at Work etc Act 1974 and the Control of Substances Hazardous to Health Regulations 1999 in respect of this risk.

Asbestos

As a rough guide, if your building was built before the 1980s and you carry out any type of maintenance, repair or refurbishment work, even installation of new cabling in an office, you could be exposing people to asbestos dust without realising it. Any individual exposure may be small - but these can build up and may result in an asbestos-related disease later on in life. This is particularly relevant to maintenance personnel and contractors who could unknowingly disturb asbestos in premises built before 1985 if there are no records of what material is in the building.

See the section in Chapter 1 dealing with the control of contractors and Chapter 3 about the management of asbestos in workplace buildings.

Local exhaust ventilation (LEV)

Maintenance, examination, testing and the law

Under regulation 9 of the Control of Substances Hazardous to Health Regulations 1999, control measures must be maintained in an efficient state, in efficient working order and in good repair. Regular maintenance will ensure this is achieved. Employers must also ensure that thorough examinations and tests of LEV are carried out every 14 months, and appropriate records must be kept for at least five years.

Someone who has the necessary training, knowledge, skills and experience should carry out maintenance, examination and testing of LEV. Your insurance company may have the competence required.

Selection and use

LEV is frequently used and can be an effective way of controlling exposure to hazardous substances. It works by drawing hazardous emissions away from the breathing zones of workers into a hood or booth and ductwork connected to an extractor fan. LEV may also be used on machines for controlling hazardous substances at the point at which they are generated.

Examples of situations where LEV might be necessary include:

- screen printing and screen cleaning work;

- gravure printing using volatile solvents;

- UV units where ozone or ink fly is generated;

- hot melt glue stations and paper milling at adhesive binders.

In many circumstances LEV may be cheaper and more effective than general ventilation. (General dilution ventilation works by introducing fresh air into the workplace to lower the general level of hazardous substances in the air.)

Heat losses from LEV may be minimised by heat recovery systems or recirculation of filtered air. Recirculation should only be employed after specialist advice to prevent the recirculation of hazardous materials in harmful quantities.

Making the most of LEV

Get an expert to design and install the most appropriate system, with the right hoods/enclosures, ductwork, air velocities and cleaning and filtration systems. It is sensible to involve employees in discussions about the design of the systems, as they have to use the plant and will have views about what is workable. In general:

- Keep the extraction as close to the source of contamination as possible.

- Make sure the fan draws air away from the operator.

- Extract at the same level or below the source of contaminant unless there is need to control fume rising from a heated source. Extraction positioned above the operator's head will draw harmful substances into their breathing zone.

Check, clean out and maintain the system regularly, particularly flexible ductwork. If necessary, provide enough heating and lighting (suitably protected) within the enclosure to encourage work to be done inside the extracted area.

Common causes of LEV failure

The following are common causes of LEV failure and are easily checked by you. It helps to keep a record of these checks:

- physical damage to and poor positioning of hoods and booths;

- damaged and/or blocked ductwork;

- blocked, damaged, unsuitable or incorrectly installed filters;

- too high/low water levels in wet collectors;

- wear, corrosion or build-up of contaminant on fan blades;

- slipping or broken drive belts to fans;

- poor lubrication of fan bearings;

- poor fitment of the ductwork.

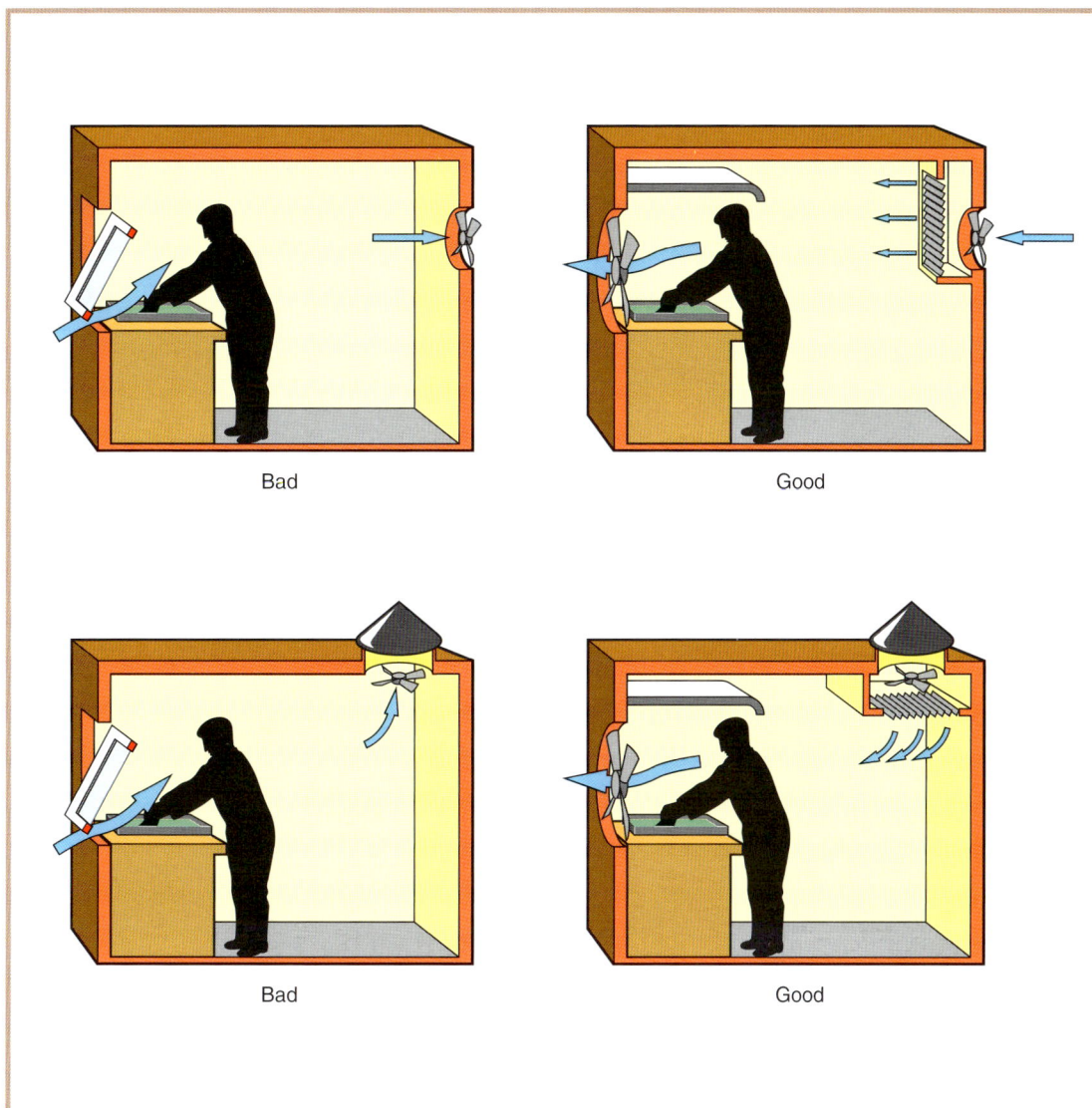

Bad　　　　　　　　　　　Good

Bad　　　　　　　　　　　Good

Figure 15 *Make sure fans draw air away from the operator*

Personal protective equipment (PPE)

If you are thinking of using personal protective equipment (PPE) to control employees' exposure to substances hazardous to health, remember that COSHH limits its use to situations where it is not reasonably practicable to use other control measures such as local exhaust ventilation.

PPE and the law

The Personal Protective Equipment at Work Regulations 1992 require employers to:

- assess risks to health and safety which have

not been avoided before providing PPE;

- provide suitable PPE free of charge to protect employees against risks which have not been controlled by other means;

- take all reasonable steps to ensure it is properly used;

- maintain PPE provided in clean and efficient working order with appropriate storage accommodation for it when it is not in use;

- give information, instruction and training in its use.

Employees must use the PPE provided and report any loss or obvious defect to the employer.

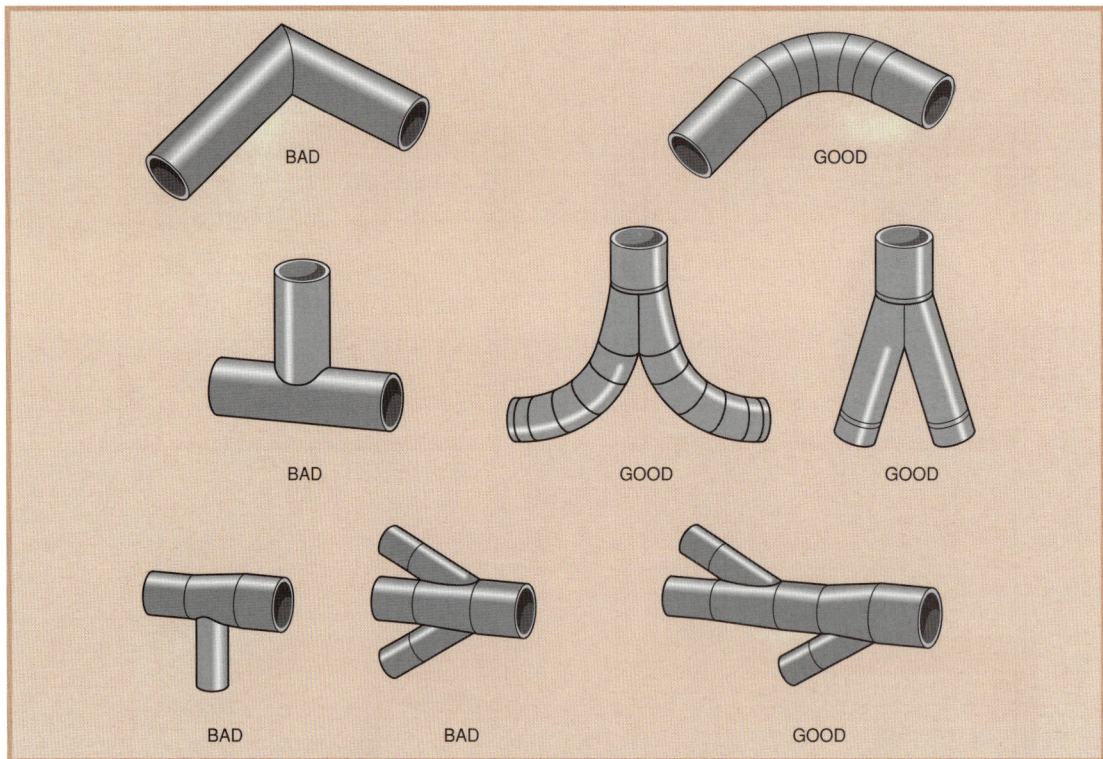

Figure 16 *Some principles of good ducting design*

Respiratory protective equipment (RPE)

Choosing

When choosing respiratory protection consider the job to be done in detail. Identify the contaminant and the likely level of exposure against which protection is required and take into account the working environment in which it will be worn.

Different types of RPE offer different levels of protection and the correct type has to be matched against the job, including the potential levels of exposure, and the wearer. Assess the work carefully and consult the suppliers of the substance in use and the protective equipment. British (BS) and European (EN) Standards set out the specifications for respiratory protective devices and filters. Check that equipment is marked to indicate conformity with a standard. Unless it is a good fit and properly worn, RPE will not offer effective protection and will not perform as designed.

Maintaining

Thoroughly examine and, where appropriate, test RPE at least once a month and more frequently where conditions are severe. (This does not apply to one-shift disposable respirators.) Half-mask respirators used only occasionally against dust or fumes of relatively low toxicity may be examined at longer intervals, but not less than once every three months. Make sure employees have facilities to clean respirators and know how to do this without damaging them.

Ensure that breathing air supplied to air-fed equipment is satisfactory; proprietary equipment to do this is widely available.

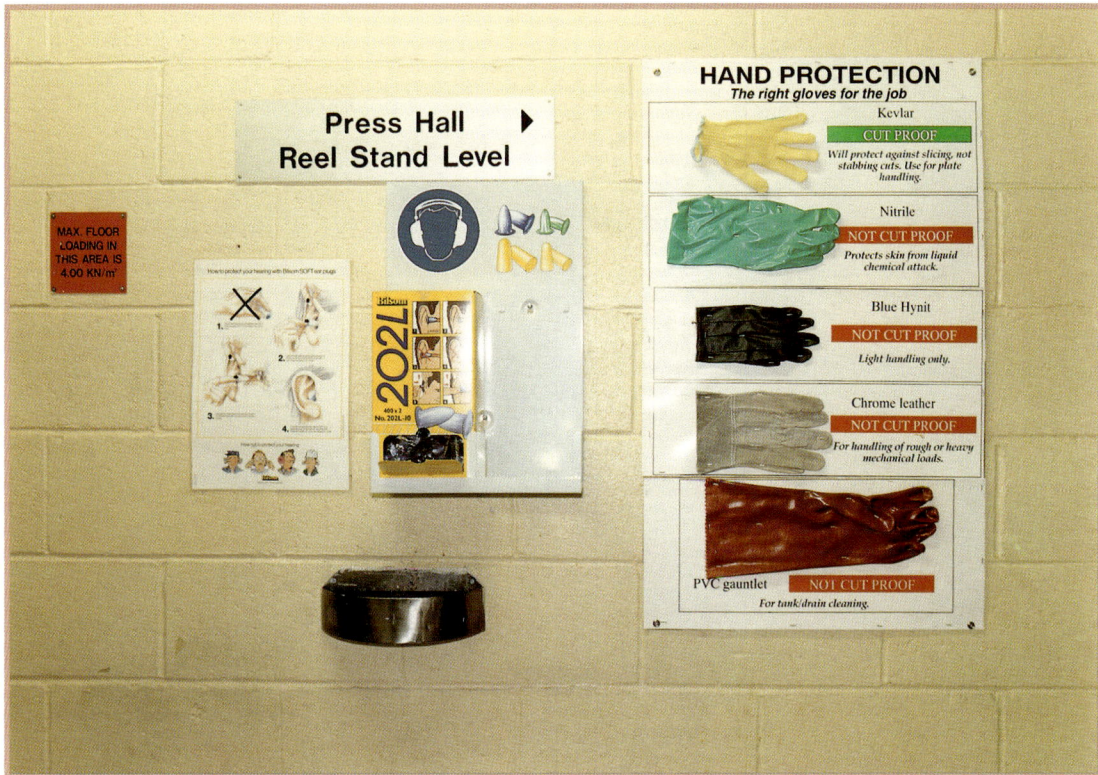

Figure 17 *Employers need to provide suitable PPE and information*

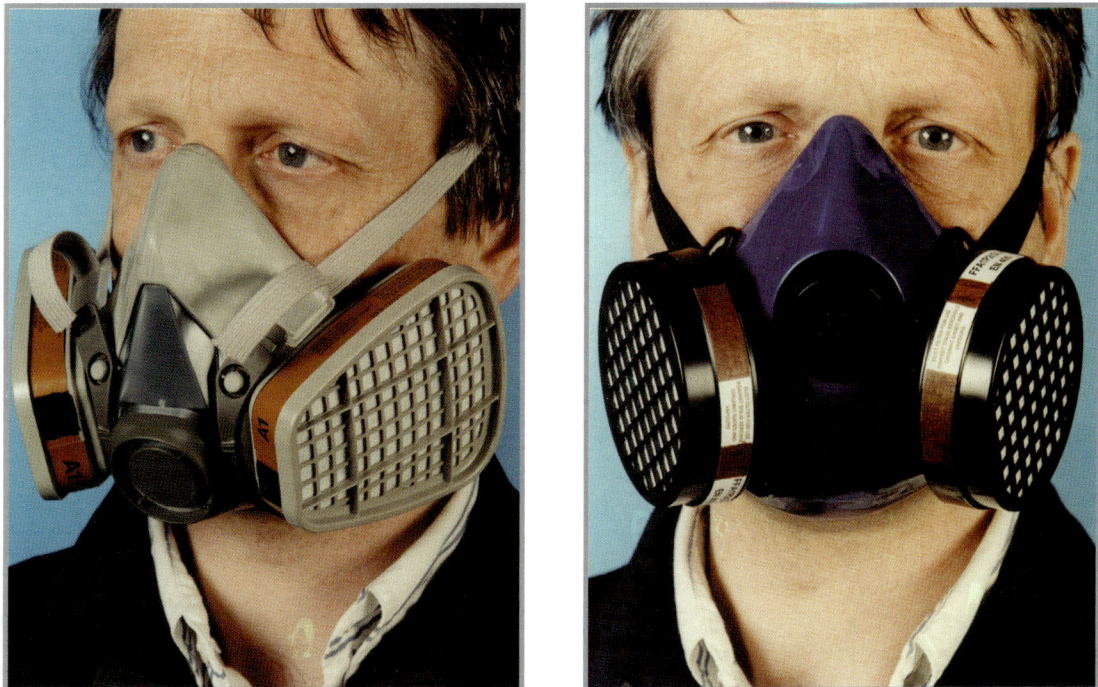

Figure 18 *Examples of respiratory protective equipment*

Eye protection

Eye protection will have to be provided and used (sometimes throughout the whole workshop) where work that puts eyes at risk is carried out, eg:

- the use of pressure-cleaning appliances which leads to the projection of spray and particles;

- the use of hazardous substances, such as solvents which may splash into the eye;

- in maintenance departments, grinding and other machining processes, which lead to the uncontrolled ejection of metallic particles.

BS EN 166: 1996 *Personal eye-protection. Specifications* sets out the standard for eye protection for industrial and non-industrial uses. Special arrangements are appropriate for people who normally wear glasses such as the use of goggles or safety glasses.

Skin protection

The selection of suitable protective gloves can be a complicated procedure. Seek expert help from manufacturers or distributors. For the glove to be suitable it must:

- be appropriate for the risk(s) and the conditions where it is used;

- take into account the ergonomic requirements and state of health of the person wearing it;

- fit the wearer correctly, if necessary, after adjustments;

- either prevent or control the risk involved without increasing the overall risk.

Further information, including a table with a simple guide to selection, is given in the leaflet *Selecting protective gloves for work with chemicals* (INDG330), the booklet *Cost and effectiveness of chemical protective gloves for the workplace* (HSG206) and the leaflet *Skin problems in the printing industry* (IACL101rev1).

For other protective clothing requirements see 'Work with UV-curable materials' earlier in the chapter.

Storage of PPE

Suitable accommodation should be provided for PPE when it is not in use. The storage should be adequate to protect the PPE from contamination, loss, or damage by, for example, harmful substances, damp or sunlight. Where PPE becomes contaminated during use, the accommodation should be separate from any provided for ordinary clothing, and where necessary be suitably labelled. Special arrangements may have to be made to clean PPE. Make sure you inform your cleaners about any hazards.

Chapter 5
PROCESS SAFETY

See the 'References' section at the back of the book for details of publications which relate to PROCESS SAFETY and also see Appendix 1 'Safeguarding terms'

Relevant legislation

The Health and Safety at Work etc Act 1974 (HSW Act) requires employers to ensure, so far as is reasonably practicable, the health, safety and welfare at work of their employees. This duty extends to the provision and maintenance of plant and machinery that is safe and without risks to health.

The Provision and Use of Work Equipment Regulations 1998 (PUWER 98) place general duties on employers to ensure that the work equipment they provide is suitable and safe for use.

Manufacturers and suppliers have duties under the Supply of Machinery (Safety) Regulations 1992 (amended 1994) to provide new equipment that meets certain essential health and safety requirements and is safe. Employers, however, should still assess all equipment to ensure it is safe and free from patent defects before bringing it into use. The fact that a machine is CE marked does not necessarily mean that it is safe for use in your printworks - you may have procedures and ancillary processes that were not considered by the manufacturer so you will still need to do your own risk assessment.

Provision and Use of Work Equipment Regulations 1998 (PUWER 98)

The main requirements of the Regulations which will need to be met by employers in the printing industry are to ensure that:

- equipment is suitable for the use that will be made of it and is not used for unsuitable applications (eg unprotected electrical equipment in potentially explosive atmospheres);

- equipment is adequately maintained;

- guards and protective devices are kept in good working order, eg by performing daily/weekly checks on the satisfactory operation of photoelectric or interlocked guards;

- equipment whose safe operation is critically dependent on its condition in use and where deterioration would lead to significant risk, such as power-operated guillotines and hand-fed platen presses, are inspected at suitable intervals by a competent person;

- adequate information, instruction and training is given to operators, eg lift truck operators;

- new equipment (including second-hand equipment from outside the European Economic Area) conforms with product safety legislation, eg the Supply of Machinery (Safety) Regulations 1992 and amendments;

- hazardous parts of machinery are guarded, eg in-running nips at cylinders and rollers;

- there is protection against specific hazards, eg disintegration and ejection of slitting discs;

- control devices are clearly visible, properly marked, unambiguous, reliable and perform all the tasks necessary for safe operation, eg provision of emergency stop and other controls where appropriate;

- equipment can be isolated from the electrical supply and other sources of energy, eg using a properly earthed electrical supply isolator adjacent to the machine, or isolating gas valves at heat-set ovens;

- adequate lighting is provided, eg at the test sheet removal area of a sheet-fed press;

- maintenance can be carried out safely, eg provision of ladderways and working platforms on large web presses for maintenance of free running rollers;

- equipment is stable, eg bolted to the floor.

Basic rules of machinery safety

Every year serious accidents occur in the printing industry as a direct result of unguarded or inadequately maintained machinery. Just because you haven't had an accident at a particular machine, don't assume that the machine is safe. Machinery may need upgrading to meet the right safety standards. Do a risk assessment to check whether your guarding is suitable, then take any necessary action to reduce risks. (See 'Planning and risk assessment' in Chapter 1.)

The following are examples of basic steps you can take to reduce the risk of machinery accidents at work:

1   Choose the right machine for the job.

2   Check that it is adequately guarded, eg is there protection from in-running nip hazards at inking rollers and printing cylinders, is transmission machinery enclosed, are all interlocks working correctly, are gap covers provided and used where necessary?

3   Ensure operators and supervisors are adequately informed, instructed and trained so they know how to work safely and how to use the guards and safety devices provided. Some machines, including guillotines and platen printing machines, are extremely hazardous. Young people in particular are likely to need additional training and a high level of supervision.

4   Check adequate lighting has been provided for work at all machines.

5   Provide clear working space around machinery.

6   Test and check machinery regularly to ensure safeguards are working.

7   Carry out maintenance work on a proactive rather than reactive basis.

Machinery guarding

All machinery must be guarded so that access is not possible to hazardous parts. Wherever possible, fixed guards should be used. However, if regular access is needed to hazardous parts, eg printing cylinders, then interlocking guards, trip nip bars, fixed nip bars, an electrosensitive safety system or a combination of the above will be more appropriate.

European Norm (EN) Standards give specifications for new machines. However, some of these standards may also be relevant to existing machines.

Guards should be carefully designed, constructed and fitted to ensure that they are:

- in accordance with the safety reach distances laid out in BS EN 294: 1992 *Safety of machinery. Safety distances to prevent danger zones being reached by the upper limbs* so that openings in or around guards do not allow access to the hazardous parts;

- sufficiently robust, eg nip bars do not become deflected;

- not heavy or awkward to use (eg some gap covers and lift-off interlocked guards provided for flexo presses);

- designed to allow operators to see certain machine functions (eg gluing unit on an adhesive binder);

- designed to be compatible with machinery operation (eg fitting of wash-up trays);

- of adequate electrical/electronic integrity (eg suitable for use within flammable atmospheres at gravure presses), and reliable enough for a safety application;

- are located close enough to rollers if they are nip bars (ie no more than 6 mm from the cylinder surface);

- designed so that they do not cause a hazard themselves.

The following are examples of machinery hazards - some or all of these may be relevant to your workplace.

Parts of the body, clothing and cleaning cloths can become entangled in rotating and in-running parts such as inking and damping rollers, printing cylinders, nipping rollers or transmission machinery.

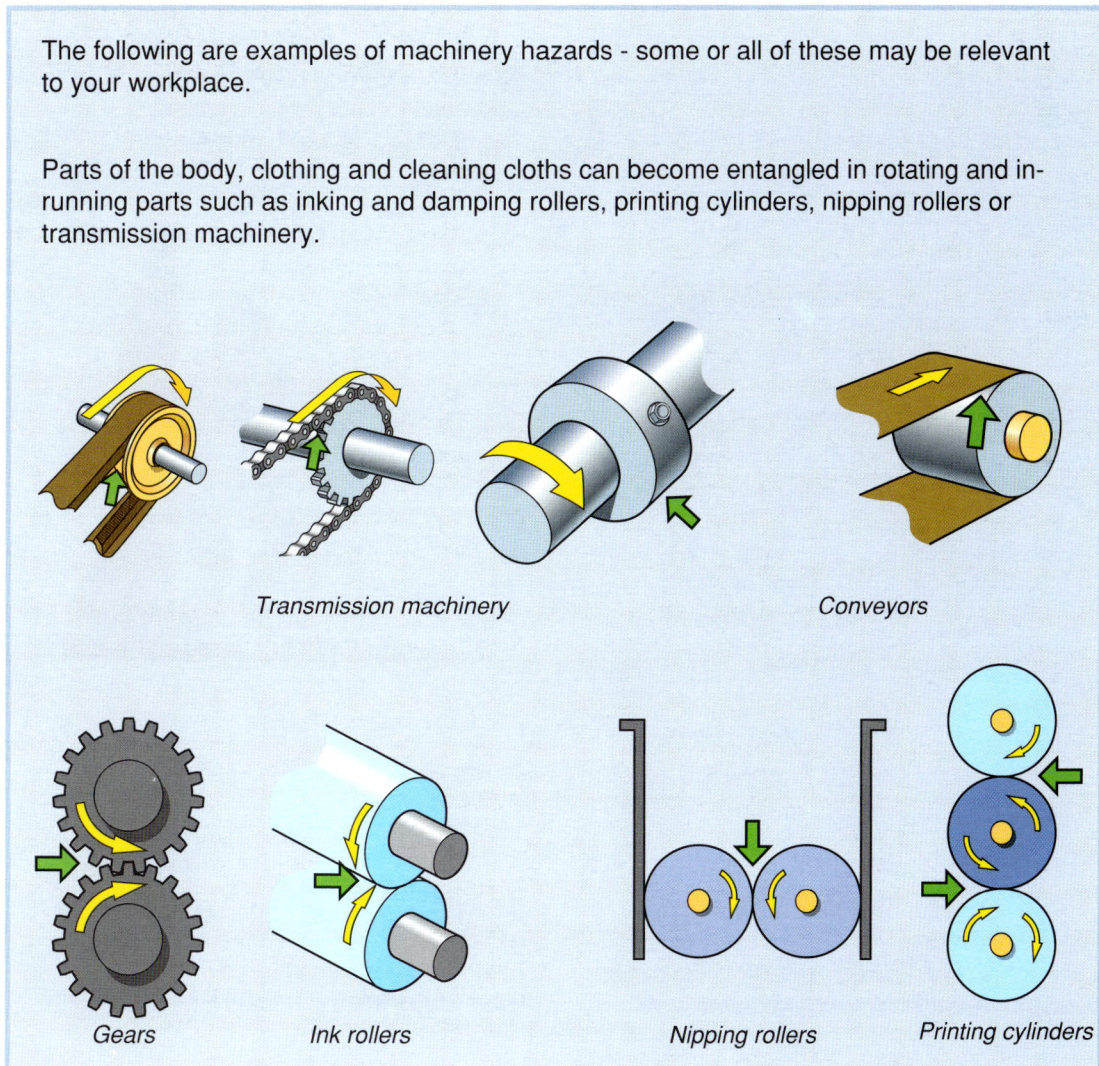

Transmission machinery

Conveyors

Gears

Ink rollers

Nipping rollers

Printing cylinders

Figure 19(a) *Identifying basic machinery hazards*

Shearing can occur between parts moving past one another.

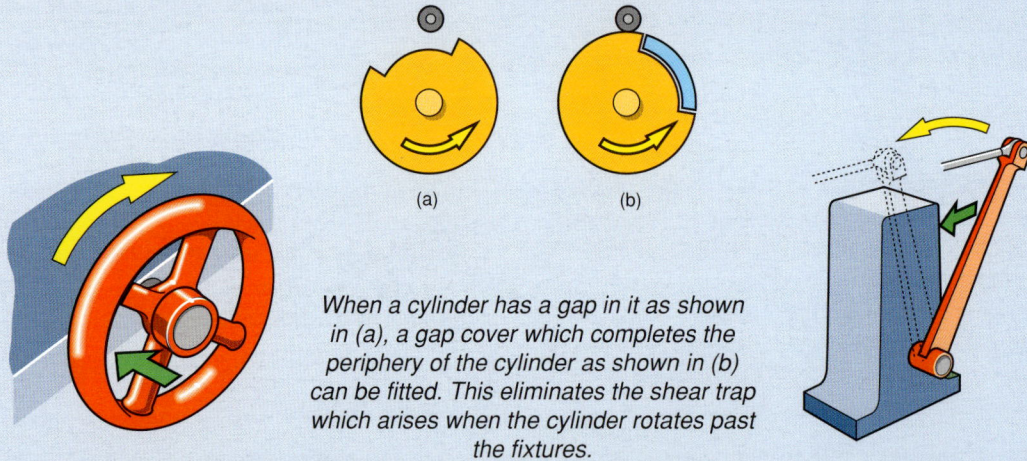

(a)

(b)

When a cylinder has a gap in it as shown in (a), a gap cover which completes the periphery of the cylinder as shown in (b) can be fitted. This eliminates the shear trap which arises when the cylinder rotates past the fixtures.

Crushing can occur between parts moving towards each other or between fixed and moving parts, eg the traps between gripper bars and machine body on certain litho presses, traps created by closing scissor lifts or traps created between moving parts of machines and fixed structures, eg litho proofing presses.

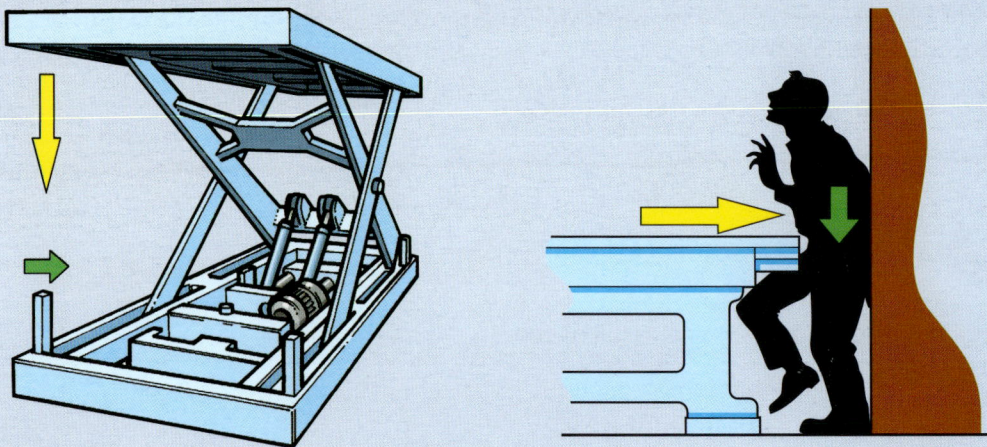

Figure 19(b) *Identifying basic machinery hazards*

Interlocking guards

Opening an interlocked guard should stop movement of hazardous parts before they can be reached. Alternatively, guard locking can be used to prevent the opening of guards until hazardous movement has stopped (this is particularly appropriate for machines with long rundown times). Interlocked guards should be used where there is a need for frequent access.

Cutting and severing can occur at sharp edges or surfaces, eg web-severers, slitters and guillotine blades.

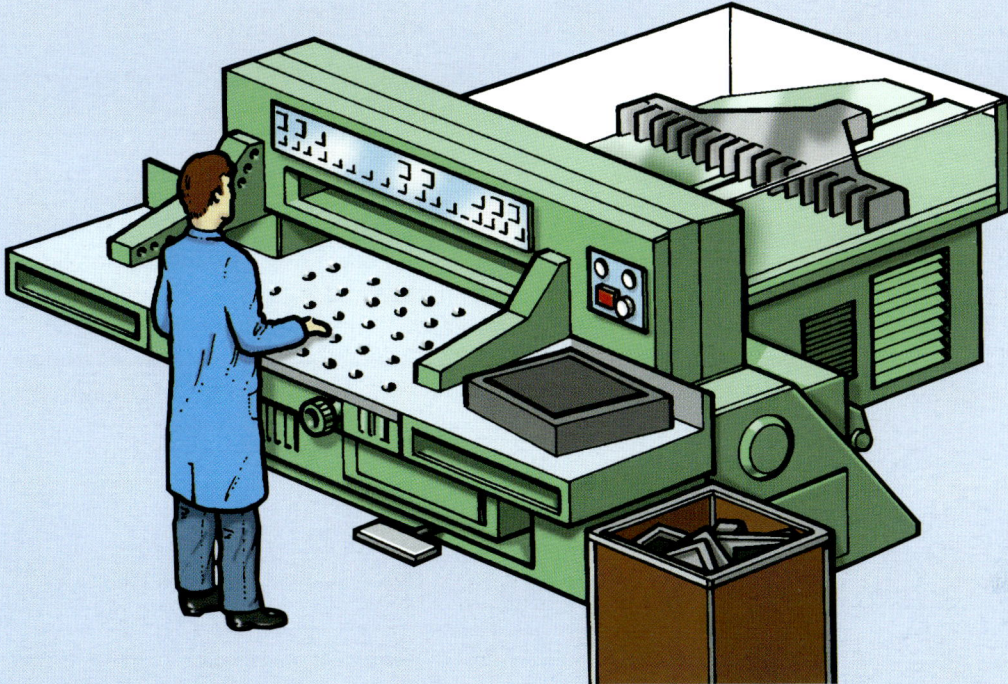

Materials can be ejected from machinery, eg reels from reelstands and hot glues from adhesive binding machines.

Electricity can also cause accidents at machines (see Chapter 6).

Figure 19(c) *Identifying basic machinery hazards*

Guard interlocks can fail as a result of age or rough treatment. They should be designed to work in the positive mode so that under normal circumstances a failure of the interlock switch prevents machine operation.

Switch A is installed in the positive mode, ie the contacts have been opened by the positive mechanical action of the cam. Switch B is installed in the negative mode, ie the contacts are opened by spring pressure when the cam is rotated. When switches are used singly, the positive mode should be used. Failure should prevent operation of the machine. Positive switches are also more difficult to defeat. The use of two cam-operated switches positioned next to each other but operating in opposite modes provides an even better standard.

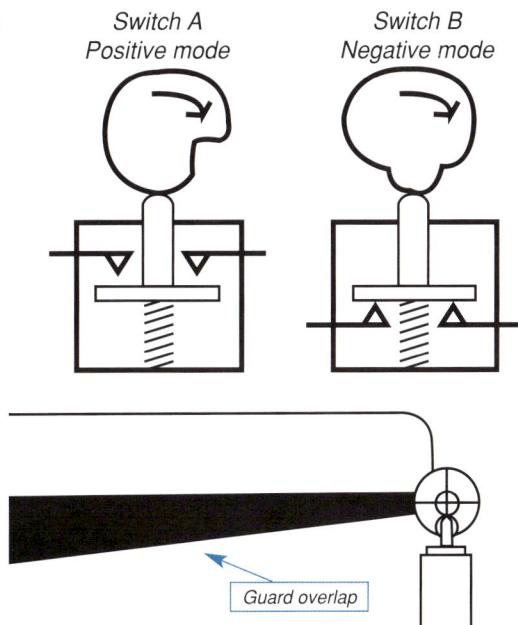

Switch A
Positive mode

Switch B
Negative mode

Guard overlap

Figure 20 *Integrity of guard interlocks*

Machine controls

Control switches should be clearly marked to show what they do. Emergency stop controls should be provided where necessary, eg red mushroom-headed buttons on a yellow background, within easy reach of operator positions that stop all hazardous motion and require positive resetting.

Operational controls should be designed and placed to avoid accidental operation, eg by the use of shrouds on start buttons and pedals. Presses with reverse facilities should have the reverse controls distinguishable by touch. This is usually done by the use of deep shrouds. Hinged flaps can also be used.

Multi-operator equipment

Multi-operator presses should have pre-start warning devices which automatically give an audible warning when an inch, crawl or run button is depressed. An acoustic signal of one to three seconds duration should be given. From the moment the signal is activated, at least three seconds should elapse (waiting time) before the machine can be started by repeated activation of the same or different control element.

After the waiting time or after a preceding operation in the inch mode (not continuous run mode) the machine can be started within 0 to 12 seconds (release time) without another audible warning.

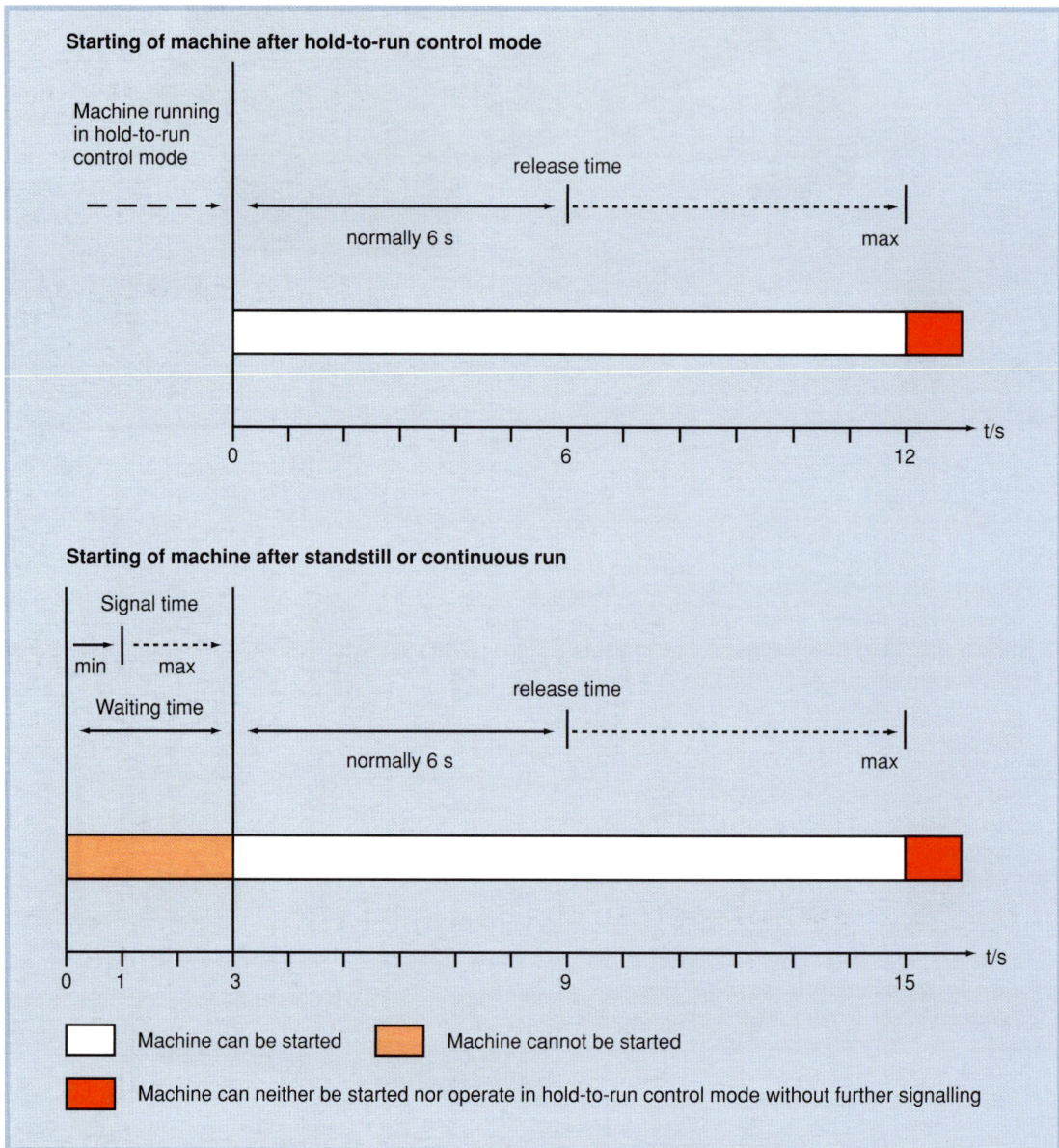

Figure 21 *Audible pre-start warning signal sequences*
....

After the release time or activation of a stop control, or the emergency stop, it should only be possible to operate the machine after repeating the whole of the above sequence (see Figure 21).

Zoning of controls should be used on multi-operator presses or other equipment where the vision of a second operator may be obscured. A zoned control will only allow limited movement (slow crawl or inch) of a specific press area with a guard open, such as one side of a print unit, or a single section of a gatherer-stitcher-trimmer, when all other guards are in the closed position.

Where hazardous parts have long rundown times, interlocking methods incorporating braking and/or guard locking should be used. Systems should be designed to incorporate a device to either cause the hazard to be eliminated as the guard is opened (by applying a brake), or prevent the guard from being opened until the risk of injury from the hazard has passed (guard locking). The Standard prEN 1010 *Safety of machinery. Safety requirements for the design and construction of printing and paper converting machinery* requires guard locking to be provided on new presses with rundown times in excess of ten seconds.

Control definitions for press movement

True inch - a single depression of the control button causing a movement of 25 mm measured circumferentially. It should not be possible to cause uninterrupted movement of the cylinders by repeated depression of the inch button.

Limited inch - a single depression of the control button causing a movement greater than 25 mm but less than 75 mm circumferentially. It should not be possible to cause uninterrupted movement of the cylinders by repeated depression of the inch button.

Hold-to-run slow crawl - uninterrupted movement of the cylinders at 1 m/min (5 m/min for web-fed machines) caused by continued depression of the control button. Crawl speed may be increased to a maximum of 5 m/min (10 m/min for web-fed machines) **only** if there is no substantial increase in hazard.

Continuous slow crawl - uninterrupted movement of the cylinders at 1 m/min (5 m/min for web-fed machines) which does not require continued depression of the control button. Crawl speed may be increased to a maximum of 5 m/min (10 m/min for web-fed machines) **only** if there is no substantial increase in hazard.

Note: Certain other types of machines, eg gatherer-stitcher-trimmers, folders, have increased slow crawl speeds necessary for setting purposes. These are referred to where relevant later in this chapter.

To measure crawl speed - count the number of revolutions per minute and multiply by the cylinder circumference.

Trip nip bar performance standard - after tripping the stop function, the length of movement of the trip bar should be greater than the stopping distance of the cylinder, ie cylinder movement should cease within the deflection travel distance of the trip bar. (See box insert below Table 6 for testing procedure.)

Safe systems of work

A safe system of work is an agreed, documented, safe job method based on risk assessment that is designed to reduce the risk of accidents or ill health. Examples are the 'inch-stop-clean' or 'inch-stop-lock-clean' safe systems of work which minimise the risk of fingers being drawn into in-running nips. It is essential that the correct system of work is used for the task - for press cleaning, see the tables under the sections dealing with each press type.

Safe systems of work for press cleaning

There are three main safe systems:

- *Inch-stop-lock-clean.* In this system, the press is subject to limited movement

using the inch button, stopped and the power isolated using the emergency stop button before applying the solvent-soaked cloth. In multi-operator operation, each person must retain control over the re-setting of their own emergency stop button so that it is not possible for another person to cause the press to move unexpectedly.

- *Inch-stop-clean.* In this system the cylinders are rotated enough to expose the next section of cylinder surface to be cleaned. The hand with the cleaning cloth is held clear of the cylinder while it is rotating. The cylinder should be stationary before the solvent-soaked cloth is applied. For machines with a true or limited inch control, several depressions of the button may be required to expose enough of the

Figure 22 *Emergency stop controls should be provided within reach of all operating positions*

cylinder surface to clean. Multi-operator cleaning is acceptable using this system only where zoned print unit controls are provided, ie cylinder movement at each print unit can occur and be controlled independently of the rest.

A variation of this system can be used on sheet-fed presses with semi-automatic plate change. By making use of the plate change cycle, and pre-cocking the cylinder position, there is almost a complete revolution at slow speed which is sufficient to allow cleaning of the whole cylinder surface without allowing exposure to the cylinder gap.

- *Slow crawl cleaning*. In this method, the cleaning cloth is applied to the cylinder as it rotates at very slow speed. Movement is controlled using hold-to-run slow crawl controls or non-hold-to-run controls (continuous slow crawl). **Note:** *This method is* **only** *acceptable where the defined trip nip performance is met and rigorous guard checking is done. See box insert below Table 6 for the definition of trip nip performance.*

ACCIDENT

An operator was cleaning the blanket cylinder of a press on continuous slow crawl. The rag he was using was drawn into the nip between the plate and blanket cylinder. The press was fitted with a trip-nip bar which stopped the machine but only after the printer's hand had been taken in up to the wrist. The accident could have been prevented by using the appropriate safe system of work and checking the performance of the trip bar.

Other essential safeguards

- Operators should know how to stop a machine before they start it.

- All guards should be in position and all protective devices working.

- Cylinder gap covers should be used where provided by the manufacturer.

- Hickeys (fluff) should only be removed from moving cylinders using a proper

hickey picker (such as a rubber blade mounted on a wooden handle).

- Rags should never be applied to moving rollers or other parts such as duct rollers or oily transmission machinery.

Machinery maintenance

- All guards and other safety devices should be kept in good working order and checked regularly, eg daily checks on guillotines and hand-fed platens, and weekly checks on presses.

- Machinery should be isolated from all power sources before maintenance work, including lubrication, is carried out, especially if the work involves the removal of guards.

- Safeguards should be checked after any modifications to machinery.

- Maintenance needs should be considered before installing new machines.

- Preventive, rather than breakdown, maintenance procedures should be implemented.

Safety hazards by process

Pre-press

Manual design and art work

Although this is generally a low-risk area, take care with scalpels which should be sheathed when not in use. Provide inclined lay-up boards with a high lip at the base to prevent scalpels falling from them. Dispose of used scalpel blades safely - don't just put them into waste bins.

Electronic/digital image preparation

Typesetting and electronic pre-press involve large amounts of work at visual display units (VDUs). The use of VDUs by the employed and self-employed is covered by the Health and Safety (Display Screen Equipment) Regulations 1992. Employers have a duty to make sure that the display screen equipment is safe and does not affect the user's health.

Experience has shown that repeated use of input devices like a mouse can lead to upper limb disorders so it is important to consider all the risks.

Workers using VDUs need well-designed work areas with suitable lighting and comfortable, adjustable seating. This helps to prevent undue tiredness, reduce eye strain, and prevent pains in the hands, arms, neck, shoulders and back. Place VDUs in a position where lighting will not cause reflections or glare on the screen. No special precautions are necessary against radiation - the levels emitted from VDU equipment are well below the recommended safe levels.

Employers must:

- analyse the workstations of employees covered by the Regulations and assess and reduce the risks;

- ensure the workstations meet minimum requirements;

- plan so there are breaks or changes of activity;

- train and inform display screen users about the health and safety aspects of their work;

- provide eye examinations and tests for users on request and special spectacles where required - for a definition of users and further advice see *VDUs: An easy guide to the Regulations* (HSG90).

Trailing electrical and digital data cables can cause accidents. Run cables in ducts, under the floor, around the walls or in a pendant dropped from the ceiling.

Computer and digital data handling equipment often generates large amounts of heat. Good general ventilation and/or air conditioning should cope with this. Automatic gas-flooding fire-protection systems may be used to protect major systems. Set up procedures to ensure that when personnel enter the protected space the automatic fire protection system is switched to manual and illuminated indicators are provided to show the system's operating mode.

Graphic reproduction and platemaking

Screen all UV light sources adequately. Screening on printdown frames can take the form of curtains (preferably automatic or interlocked), automatic shutters or automatic roller blinds. Blinds should be maintained in good condition. Brushes should be used to reduce leakage of UV light around the periphery of the frame on printdown boxes.

On large format printdown frames, as found in screen printing, the UV sources should be positioned so that light is directed away from doors, windows and passageways, and screened from other work areas, eg by using curtains. Timer switches (or other on/off controls) should be located outside the screened area.

Provide laser containing equipment such as scanners and image setters with interlocked covers as part of the laser beam screening to ensure that Class 1 conditions are met (ie the output of the laser light is inherently safe) and to prevent access to rotating parts of machinery.

See the 'Radiation' section in Chapter 4 for more information.

Rollers on automatic film and litho plate developers need periodic cleaning. The best method is to remove the rollers before cleaning. In-running nips need to be guarded (this is usually achieved by using interlocked guards) except where the rollers are held in position by their own weight and the maximum force that could result is 50 newtons. Rollers should not be cleaned while the machines are running as fingers may be drawn into in-running nips.

Make sure drip trays have been provided beneath auto film and plate processors. Hot surfaces on plate developer pre-heat and baking ovens should be shielded to prevent contact.

Assess the ergonomic risks arising from handling and loading of plates and film into computer-to-plate units (see 'Manual handling' in Chapter 4).

Plate bending machines need to either be adequately safeguarded or provided with a simultaneous two-hand control. On plate punching devices the movement of the punching tool should be safeguarded either by design or by providing guards.

During flexographic platemaking, moulding presses are frequently used to impose heat and/or pressure to rubber or synthetic compounds. The closing movement of these presses should be safeguarded. Local exhaust ventilation should be provided for the heat and fume generated. Also consider extraction for solvent wash-off from photopolymer plates and personal protective equipment such as suitable gloves where there is a possibility of skin contact with uncured photopolymers. (See 'Personal protective equipment' in Chapter 4.)

Conventional litho proofing presses

The danger of hands being trapped in the shear traps created by the moving carriage of litho proofing presses should be eliminated. Trip devices should be provided at each end of the carriage which actuate a fail-safe stop device to arrest movement of the carriage.

Where hazardous in-running nips exist at the stationary damping and inking roller units, they should be guarded, eg by fixed nip bars. Many litho proofing presses avoid this hazard by having 'lift out' rollers or stopping these rollers when the carriage moves away.

The inking and damping rollers on the moveable carriage should be safeguarded either by interlocking guards, fixed nip bars or other effective means. The action of 'sheeting off' is a hazardous operation which should be prohibited.

Regularly maintain and check safety features on all proofing presses.

Digital printing and copying

Many of the health and safety considerations required for traditional printing are also relevant to digital printing and copying. The main risks include:

- Manual handling - paper is heavy and it is important to keep the area around machines clear to allow easy access to clear paper jams etc (see Chapter 4).

- Electrical - maintain electrical equipment and ensure cables and connectors do not become damaged (see Chapter 6).

- Fire - maintain a clear airflow to allow proper cooling of the machine and remove rubbish regularly (see Chapter 7).

- UV light - take precautions to ensure that strong light sources in photocopiers and large reprographics installations are adequately shrouded (see Chapter 4).

- Hazardous moving parts - feeder trays, staplers and other attachments have the potential to trap fingers. Remember to isolate the machine before clearing blockages and to replace guards and covers before operating. Associated finishing machinery, such as guillotines, should be properly guarded and those guards maintained.

- Chemicals and ozone - always handle and change toner or cleaning agents in accordance with the manufacturer's instructions. Provide adequate ventilation to prevent build-up of heat and ozone (see Chapter 4).

- Broken glass - the top glass of copiers can break if abused.

Printing

Litho sheet-fed

Where access to moving parts is needed, eg for cleaning and make-ready operations on printing machines, the guard control circuits should be interlocked so that with guards open the machine can be operated by hold-to-run controls (or on slow crawl only where a trip nip device meeting the performance standard detailed later in this chapter is achieved). The hold-to-run control devices should be designed to allow:

- machine movement limited to 25 mm (true inch) on each depression of the control or a maximum operating speed of 1 m/min; or

- where the measures defined above would reduce the ability of the machine to perform its function and where there would be no substantial increase in risk, machine movement limited to a maximum

of 75 mm (limited inch) or a maximum operating speed of 5 m/min.

Where interlocked guards allow hold-to-run slow crawl or inching, cylinder trip nip bars within 6 mm of the cylinder surface which stop printing cylinder movement within the deflection travel distance of the bar should be provided to prevent the risk of entanglement in contra-rotating rollers or cylinders, especially where gap covers are not provided. Fixed nip bars are only acceptable in conjunction with cylinder gap covers where there is a slow crawl function. The print unit guarding options for sheet-fed presses are summarised in Table 5.

Figure 23 *Two-colour press fitted with slotted, interlocked, all-enclosing guards*

Figure 24 On multi-operator presses an audible pre-start warning device should be fitted

Table 5 Safeguarding sheet-fed offset presses

Hazard	Safeguard
Sheet-fed offset	
In-running nips between inking and damping roller assemblies	All-enclosing interlocked guards with either no powered movement or true inch only when the guard is raised.
In-running nips between the plate, blanket and impression cylinders	An enclosing interlocked guard which allows limited powered movement when raised by means of true or limited inch, or hold-to-run or continuous slow crawl; **and** a trip nip bar adjusted to within 6 mm of the cylinder surface which either meets the performance standard detailed in the box insert under Table 6, or is supplemented by cylinder gap covers for both plate and blanket cylinders, or there is no facility for continuous slow crawl; **or** an enclosing interlocked guard as above supplemented by fixed nip bars adjusted to within 6 mm of the cylinder surface and gap covers for both plate and blanket cylinders. Fixed nip bars are not adequate in the absence of cylinder gap covers unless there is no facility for continuous slow crawl; **or** on certain old machines, trip nip bars which do not meet the performance standard (see the box insert under Table 6) or fixed nip bars, in either case adjusted to within 6 mm of the cylinder surface and close-fitting gap covers for both plate and blanket cylinders. There should be no facility for continuous slow crawl. Users should plan to upgrade such presses by the addition of enclosing interlocked guards.

Table 5 Safeguarding sheet-fed offset presses (continued)

Hazard	Safeguard
Sheet-fed offset (continued)	
In-running nips between impression/ transfer cylinders	An enclosing interlocked guard which allows limited powered movement when raised by means of true or limited inch. An emergency stop (or 'stop-lock') control should be provided at each print unit.
Unexpected start-up during multi-operator cleaning	Pre-start audible warning device.

Safeguarding other parts of litho presses

Guarding is required for the hazardous parts of feed tables, including:

- in-running nips associated with chains and sprockets;

- rotating shafts;

- swing arm grippers.

Transfer cylinders and delivery mechanisms need high standards of guarding due to the severity of injury they cause. Interlocked and/or fixed guards are essential. The interlock arrangement should only allow the press to be 'inched' (true or limited) due to the severity of the hazard and usual lack of nip bars. The delivery mechanism guarding should permit the safe removal of test sheets.

Clearly mark all press controls. Emergency stop controls should normally be provided at all operating consoles and within easy reach of all other operating positions and print stations, and should stop all hazardous movement. On certain smaller existing presses without powered inching/crawling, additional emergency stop controls will not be necessary as they will not enhance the overall safety of the machine. Control stations on units should preferably be laid out so that hold-to-run controls are above, or immediately adjacent to, the emergency stop controls.

On multi-operator presses, or those on which it is not possible to clearly see all over the press from any control station, an audible pre-start warning device should be fitted (see under 'Machine controls' in the 'Basic rules of

machinery safety' section earlier in this chapter). Guards and other protective devices need to be regularly maintained and checked (see Chapter 8). A weekly check of the guards, their operation, the hold-to-run controls and the emergency stop control should ensure that presses remain properly guarded.

Hickeys (fluff) should never be removed from a moving cylinder except with a proper hickey picker. Rags should never be applied to moving inking or damping rollers including duct rollers, even if adjacent rollers are well guarded, because of the risk of entanglement.

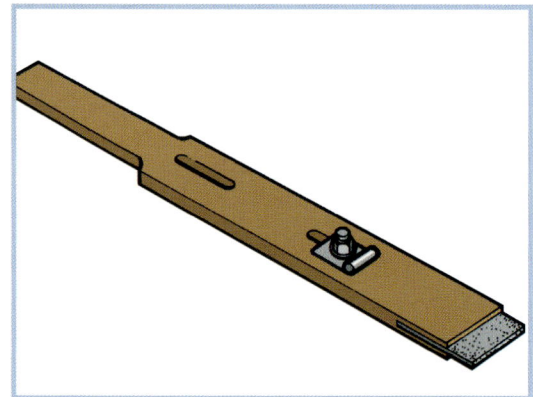

Figure 25 *Hickeys should not be removed from moving cylinders except with a proper hickey picking stick*

Safe systems of work for sheet-fed press cleaning

A very high proportion of the accidents to printers result from cleaning tasks (see Chapter 1). Use Table 6 to select the appropriate safe system of work.

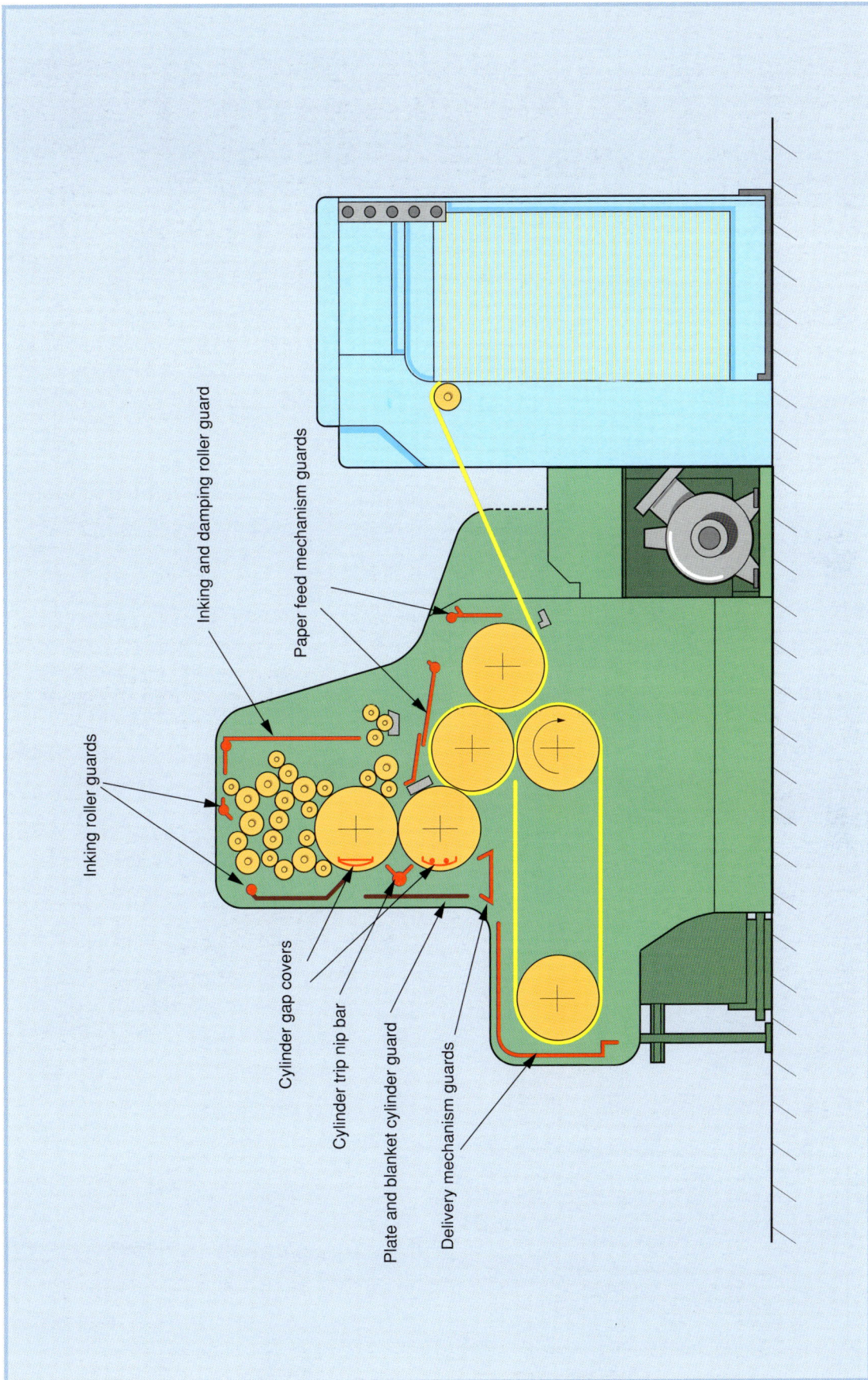

Figure 26 *Basic guards for a single-colour press*

Inking and damping roller guard

Paper feed mechanism guards

Inking roller guards

Cylinder gap covers

Cylinder trip nip bar

Plate and blanket cylinder guard

Delivery mechanism guards

Table 6 Safe systems of work for press cleaning

Warning: failure to ensure the safeguarding conditions for the appropriate system of work could result in contravention of the requirements of PUWER 98.

Task	Risk factors	System of work
Sheet-fed offset		
Cleaning inking rollers, multi- or single-operator cleaning	It should not be possible to access rollers when in motion	• Use of demountable wash-up tray.
Cleaning plate and blanket cylinders, single-operator cleaning	Frequent lack of gap covers with resultant accessibility behind trip nip/nip bars	• Auto wash-up. • Inch-stop-clean, forward motion. • Forward slow crawl cleaning only if there is safeguard checking and a trip nip to the defined performance standard.
Cleaning plate and blanket cylinders, multi-operator cleaning	Frequent lack of gap covers with resultant accessibility behind trip nip/nip bars Unexpected start-up	• Inch stop-lock-clean. • If press has zoned controls allowing independent movement of print unit cylinders, inch-stop-clean, forward motion. • Forward slow crawl cleaning only if there is safeguard checking and trip nips to the defined performance standard.
Cleaning impression and transfer cylinders, multi- or single-operator cleaning	Relative inaccessibility; absence of nip bars and hazard from grippers	• Inch-stop-lock-clean. • For presses with dedicated, zoned true inch controls beneath the foot board **only**, inch-stop-clean.

Trip nip performance standard - on tripping, the length of movement of the trip bar should be greater than the stopping distance of the cylinder, ie cylinder movement ceases within the deflection travel distance of the bar. To test:

• With the press stationary, measure the total deflection of the trip nip bar (t).

• Mark the cylinder and machine frame.

• Operate the crawl control.

• Push the trip nip with a cardboard tube when the two reference points are in line.

• Measure the distance moved by the cylinder (c) and compare measurements (t) and (c); (t) should be greater.

Web offset presses

Webbing-up

One of the main additional hazards associated with web-fed presses arises from the need to web-up following a web break and/or a format change. It is extremely important to ensure that a safe system of work is devised and a written procedure laid down and adopted. On new presses this will be supplied by the manufacturer. On older presses management may need to develop a safe system of work in conjunction with press crews and safety representatives.

The safe system of work should take account of the different web path configurations (including paths through colour satellite units in newspaper printing) and through the folder, involving cross-association if appropriate. It should also deal with the use of part-width webs where web lead-in devices may not be usable. The written procedures will need to include a clear diagram of the press showing all possible web paths.

Manual webbing-up should be carried out with the press stationary and off impression so that the web can be passed between/around the cylinders. Web lead-in devices can significantly reduce the hazard associated with webbing-up and should take the web from the reelstands, through the print units and dryers to the top of the folder, but not including turned or bay window web paths where the tapes may be terminated.

On older presses, or machines not fitted with web lead-in devices, the practice of tucking in or attaching the web to the cylinder with adhesive tape should be used so that all operators can withdraw completely and stand away from the press when the crawl controls are depressed.

Traps associated with driven web lead-in tapes or chains should be guarded where there is a risk of injury, eg by providing disc guards.

Safeguarding of print units

Inking and damping rollers must be guarded (see Table 7). On certain old installations the inking and damping rollers may be guarded by non-interlocked enclosing guards. These should be upgraded by providing nip bars or by interlocking the enclosing guards. Where alcohol damping systems have a separate drive which continues after the interlocked guard is opened, the in-running nips should be guarded by nip bars.

Plate, blanket and impression cylinders must be guarded. Guarding can take the form of robust fixed nip bars if the printing and blanket cylinder gutters are less than 4 mm deep and 8 mm wide (or exceptionally 19 mm wide on newspaper presses) and the press's throw-off (cylinder movement going on impression and off impression) still keeps the nip bars within 6 mm of the cylinders during make-ready and wash-up.

Following web breaks, nip bars should be checked by operators to ensure they have not been deflected away from the cylinders leaving gaps in excess of 6 mm.

In some situations, such as the blanket-to-blanket nip, the web path precludes the use of a single fixed nip bar. In these circumstances, a dual fixed nip bar or 'letterbox' guard may be used. There needs to be a large enough gap to allow for web flutter, but the guards should be positioned far enough away from the nip to prevent risk of injury.

Certain types of presses require some nip bars to be removed for make-ready. A hinged nip bar secured when the press is in the run mode is acceptable as long as measures are taken to ensure it must be in position when the press is run, eg by interlocking.

On unit arch type presses, access must be prevented to roller/cylinder intakes within the arch. This guarding can take the form of internal guarding, eg nip bars or fixed guards or interlocked unit gates. With interlocked gates open, movement of rollers/cylinders within the arch should be via local hold-to-run controls only allowing crawl speeds of no more than 5 m/min (10 m/min may be acceptable in exceptional circumstances, eg on some older presses).

The print unit guarding options for web-fed presses are summarised in Table 7.

Table 7 Safeguarding web-offset presses

Hazard	Safeguard
Web-fed offset In-running nips between adjacent inking (and damping) rollers	All-enclosing interlocked guards with either no powered movement or true inch only when the guard is raised; **or** fixed nip bars adjusted to within 6 mm of the roller surface.
In-running nips between plate, blanket (or impression) cylinders	Interlocked guards allowing true or limited inch or hold-to-run slow crawl only where nip bars are not fitted. All danger points should be within view of a single operator, or of several operators each of whom needs to operate a hold-to-run control. Nips out of view should be safeguarded; **and/or** fixed nip bars adjusted to within 6 mm of the cylinder surface; **and/or** fixed or interlocked 'letterbox' distance guards; **and/or** sweep-on nip bars interlocked with reverse crawl or no facility for reverse crawl. Where nip bars are provided and continuous slow crawl is available, this should always be supplemented by an emergency stop (or 'stop-lock' control) at each print unit.
Unexpected start-up during multi-operator cleaning	Pre-start audible warning device.

Safeguarding other parts of web presses

Draw rollers

Draw rollers may be incorporated into the reelstand, between the reelstand and the first print unit, or within the frame of the printing units. Where the intake between draw rollers is accessible, it should be guarded using a nip bar, a split bar with a bell-shaped mouth to assist hand webbing-up, or an enclosing guard.

Web severers

Web severers within unit arches and elsewhere on the press need to be guarded or be safe by design. Tunnel guards are frequently used. Precautions need to be taken to ensure that the web severers do not automatically fire when operators or others are in the vicinity. Interlocked access gates to units can be used.

Guide rollers

Due to the high speeds of many of these machines and the inertia of web-driven guide rollers, these rollers should be safeguarded. Guarding such as nip bars can be provided or the rollers can be separated from other contra-rotating rollers and the machine's frame by a gap of at least 120 mm.

Drying unit

Ovens at heat-set offset presses may have opening hinged tops. Ensure that these will not close inadvertently, trapping the operators. The controls to close the oven should be of the hold-to-run type and be located so that the closing movement of the oven can be seen along its entire length. See Chapter 7 'Explosion risks in blanket wash systems' for guidance on avoiding fire and explosion risk.

Chill rollers

A gap of at least 120 mm should be allowed between accessible in-running chill rollers, or a guard should be fitted. Guards should be fitted over any accessible balance weights at the ends of the rollers.

Propeller rollers

Propeller and slitter roller intakes should be guarded. This guarding is often associated

Figure 27 *Propeller and slitter rollers should be guarded*

with dust collection hoods and should also eliminate the laceration hazard posed by slitters. The guarding should cover at least 300° of the roller.

Controls

Clutches used to disengage the drive to press units on older presses should be provided with interlocks which ensure that the controls on a disengaged unit remain ineffective with the exception of the emergency stops.

Misinterpretation of indication lights on presses has resulted in a number of accidents. It is therefore extremely important that the indicator lights are clear and unambiguous.

Folding units

Guard all in-running nips and other mechanical hazards on folders. In-running nips should be protected with nip bars and/or enclosing guards, eg nipping and cross-association rollers. Guidance on folders is given under 'In-line folders, sheeters and die cutters' later in this chapter.

Incorporate noise control measures in enclosing guards and, where possible, extend controls, locking nuts and adjusting devices through the guard.

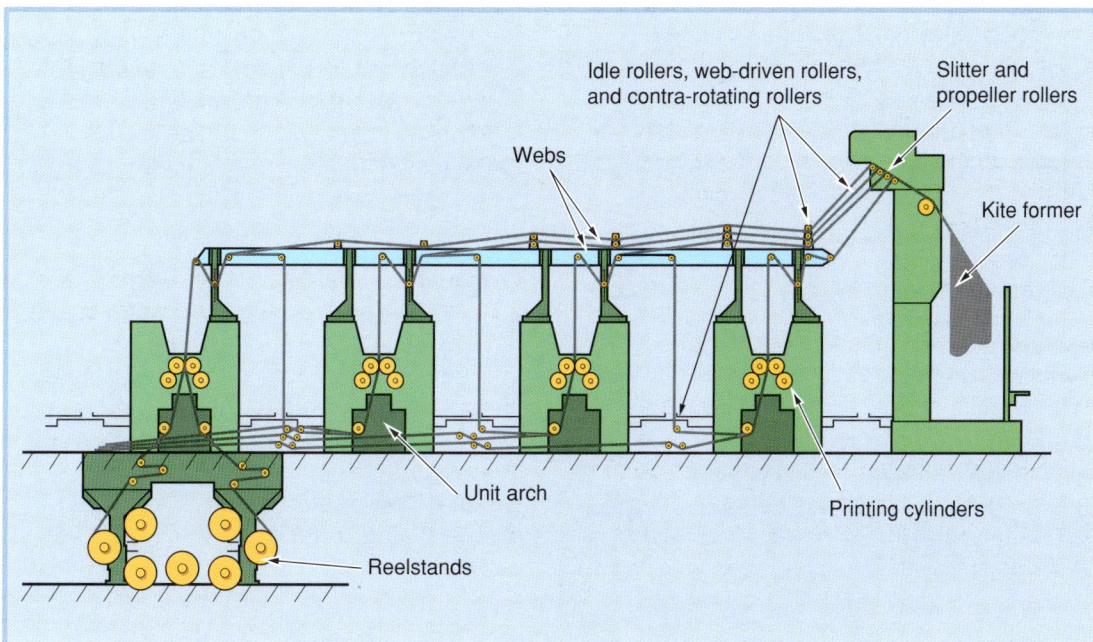

Figure 28 *Examples of areas that need safeguarding at web-offset printing presses*

Table 8 Safe systems of work for web-fed offset press cleaning

Task	Risk factors	System of work
Web-fed offset		
Cleaning inking rollers, multi- or single-operator	It should not be possible to access rollers when in motion	● Auto tray wash-up.
Cleaning plate, blanket (and impression) cylinders, multi- or single-operator	'Smooth' cylinders only (gutter not exceeding 4 mm radially by 8 mm circumferentially (exceptionally, 4 mm x 19 mm on newspaper presses))	● Inch-stop-lock-clean, forward motion. ● Forward slow crawl cleaning **only** if nip bars and an emergency stop are provided and a suitable guard checklist is completed.
Cleaning transfer/path rollers, multi- or single-operator	Relative inaccessibility; absence of nip bars	● Inch-stop-lock-clean where rollers are powered, or by hand turning where free running.

Cleaning and make-ready

To facilitate make-ready, cleaning operations etc, hold-to-run controls should be provided which may allow movement of the press with the interlocked guards open. On new and existing installations hold-to-run slow crawl speeds should be less than 10 m/min. Certain older installations may not be able to achieve this speed and the slow crawl speed at these should be as low as practicable.

Safe systems of work for web-fed offset press cleaning

A very high proportion of the accidents to printers result from cleaning tasks. Use Table 8 to select the appropriate safe system of work (see Chapter 1).

Reel unwinds and rewinds

For the purposes of this book, the term 'reel unwinding and rewinding devices' applies to simple single-reel, non-automatic equipment for the provision and collection of paper, polythene, foil or other types of web. The term 'reelstands' applies to larger installations capable of holding two or more paper reels and installations associated with automatic operations such as splicing.

The following safeguards are appropriate for reel unwinding and rewinding devices:

● Unwind units are usually of two types, shafted or shaftless. On unwinds the in-running nips between the reel and pressure roller should be protected either by a trip device or guards.

● Devices for bringing the reels up to speed should be guarded if danger points are accessible, eg at running tension belts.

● In-running nips associated with the pressure/rider rollers should be guarded over the entire reel diameter. This may be achieved by the provision of trip devices, self-adjusting nip bars or area interlocked guards. At reel-up, the latter are best designed on castors with tongue-operated interlock switches to allow hold-to-run movement only when removed for access during reel change.

● Tickets to mark defects etc should be self-adhesive and attached to the web at an accessible location away from the guarded nip between the forming reel and lay-on roller. Consider also providing devices which will allow remote placing of marker tickets.

● Any shear hazards created by movement of the reel lifting arms or other reel lifting devices should either be guarded or reel lifting/lowering should only be possible using hold-to-run controls restricted to a speed of no more than 5 m/min.

- Where shaftless unwinding or rewinding is used, the chucking cones should be designed so they can only be inserted using a hold-to-run control. The hold-to-run speed should not exceed 5 m/min for new machines. The control system of the machine should prevent start-up until the chucking cones have been fully inserted.

- Ejection of a reel due to a 'core chew out' or inadvertent opening of the chucking cones must be prevented. The controls should not allow separation of the chucking cones while the press is in motion.

Safeguarding reelstands

- Existing reelstands should have a minimum 500 mm clearance between the surface of the largest reel that the stand is designed to accept and any obstruction such as a full reel, mounted on an adjacent stand, or a wall, unless fixed or interlocked barriers prevent whole-body access.

- Since any reel being loaded will encroach on the 500 mm gap mentioned above, reels should not be left standing within the reelstands on the sub-trucks.

- Perimeter fence guarding should also be provided where hand/arm access is possible to in-running traps/nips created between rotating and stationary reels on the same reelstand, unless a minimum separation distance of 120 mm can be maintained between the reels.

- Additional dangers created by an adjacent stand indexing during automatic splicing will need to be addressed, eg unexpected start-up of the reel, splicing unit movement and spider arm movement. A safe system of work should be implemented to address such hazards in conjunction with safeguarding. Safeguarding may be provided by electrosensitive devices and trip bars.

- Where turrets or spider arms rotate automatically, pressure-sensitive mats or similar should be provided to prevent rotation when a person is in the pit. Where rotation is manually controlled, movement should be by means of a hold-to-run control.

- Where reels are driven by belts on the reel circumference, the danger point between the reel and the belt should be safeguarded by interlocked or other effective guards. Guards should also be provided to protect operators from in-running nips created at drive-belt guide rollers.

- Where flying splicing devices are fitted, they must either be safeguarded by fixed and interlocked guards or be 'safe by position' (ie out of reach of any work platform).

- On presses fitted with reelshafts, guards or loose sleeves need to be provided for any exposed ends of the shafts. Any brake discs should also be guarded.

- Safeguarding for draw and festoon/dancer rollers is necessary to protect operators from in-running nips and roller movement. This may be achieved by a combination of fixed nip bars, interlocking guards, tunnel-type guards or by ensuring a spacing of at least 120 mm between the rollers.

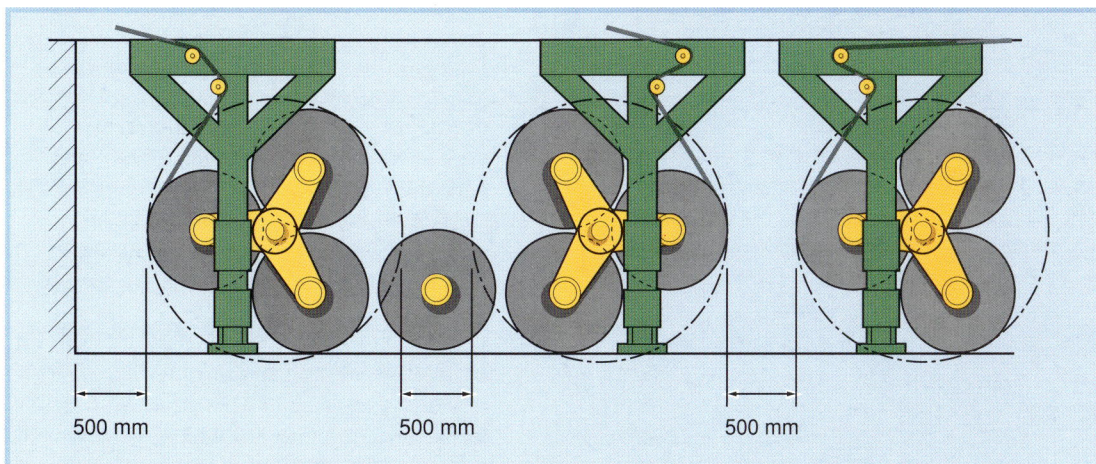

500 mm   500 mm   500 mm

Figure 29 *Reelstands should have a minimum 500 mm clearance between reels or fixed parts*

Reeler/winder slitters used in paper conversion and flexible packaging

These machines vary in size from less than 1 m to several metres wide and are used widely for converting paper and printed paper and flexible packaging materials. The diameter of the reels being rewound can vary from less than 100 mm to 1 m and above. The machine speeds also vary. All machines have in common a significant accident history.

Common issues to all types of machine

- Prevent reel ejection by ensuring that there is gradual start-up and speed control and provide interlocked restraints where the reel shaft rests on open-topped bearings.

- Prevent the risk of trapping between the reel loading arms and the reel shaft by ensuring the loading arms are operated under hold-to-run control.

- Prevent the risk of trapping between the chucking cones and reel by insertion of cones under hold-to-run control and within the view of the operator.

- Where there are web-driven contra-rotating rolls, nip guards should be provided if the size and weight of the rolls could cause injury. Webbing-up should only be undertaken when the machine is stationary. Power-driven rolls should be provided with post-box type guards, or, where the web angle makes webbing-up difficult because of the distance between the slot and the nip, a combination of fixed guards below the web path and a hinged interlocked guard above.

- Make sure there is a gap of at least 120 mm to prevent nips between driven rolls and fixed parts or provide fixed guarding.

- Make sure guarding is provided where there are running nips between the web and web-driven rolls for flexible packaging material and paper with a high breaking strength.

- Guard the whole of the surface of slitting knives (except that in immediate contact with the substrate) by individual fixed plates or interlocked hinged guards along the length of the knife shaft. Adjustments should not be made on the run unless this can be done remotely.

Two-drum reelers

- Prevent access to the in-running nip between rewinding reels and the drive drum by one or more of: perimeter fencing with interlocked doors; localised fixed/interlocked guarding; photoelectric devices; pressure-sensitive mats.

- Where the rider (lay-on) roll is held under hydraulic or pneumatic pressure, or has a self weight at a pressure greater than 300 newtons, interlocked guarding or a self-adjusting nip bar will be required.

- Where a trap under the descending rider roll occurs under power, a two-section guard with a trip function which descends in advance of the roll should be provided. Machines without ratchet-operated rider rolls should have a scotch to prevent gravity fall.

- When repairing a paper break, a single operator should control the machine using hold-to-run slow crawl at no more than 5 m/min.

Centre winders

- The nip present between the centre and the surface drive roll until the forming reel has reached a diameter of 120 mm should be safeguarded by localised fixed/interlocked guarding, photoelectric devices or pressure-sensitive mats.

- Automatically adjusting nip guards are necessary to safeguard the nip between forming reels and the surface drive roll, as the position of the nip will change with the increasing diameter of the forming reel.

- The operation of cross-cut knives should be operated by a hold-to-run control positioned out of reach of the knife where the operator can see the knife movement.

- Intervention by the operator to insert tickets, 'smooth' the web, check for binding between slit reels, feel the sides of the forming reel to identify telescoping and to correct problems with trim must not be done with the machine running at production speed.

ACCIDENTS

An operator of a small slitting machine converting a polyester web was injured when his fingers were drawn into the nip between the patent roller and an unpowered rubber coated roller. He had attempted to remove a piece of adhesive tape used to label the patent roll from an unpowered tension roller.

The operator of a winder suffered a fractured finger when it was taken into the nip between the polyester foil web and the take-up roller. He had been smoothing creases in the foil.

Friction burns were sustained by the operator of a winding machine when he was feeding a tail of paper to web-up. The interlocked guard was open and the machine was being operated on crawl using a foot pedal control. An air feed was subsequently fitted.

Flexographic press safeguarding

Safeguarding of unwind and rewinding units is explained under 'Reel unwinds and rewinds' earlier in this section.

Safe webbing-up procedures need to be implemented. Much of the advice under 'Web offset' earlier in this chapter is applicable, though many older presses will not have web lead-in devices.

Flexographic printing units on all size presses, eg label presses to flexible packaging presses, are a frequent source of accidents. It is particularly important to ensure that they are properly guarded.

Removable enclosing interlocked guards or gate/barrier interlocked guards are generally considered acceptable. The former are usually more suitable for small- to medium-sized presses, and presses with web widths up to 1 m, and the latter for larger machines.

Adjustable nip bars have not proved satisfactory as they are frequently removed or incorrectly adjusted (due to the use of stereo cylinders of variable diameter). They are only likely to provide a satisfactory standard of protection on presses which carry out long-run work with few or no cylinder changes where strict controls are in place to ensure they are always correctly adjusted.

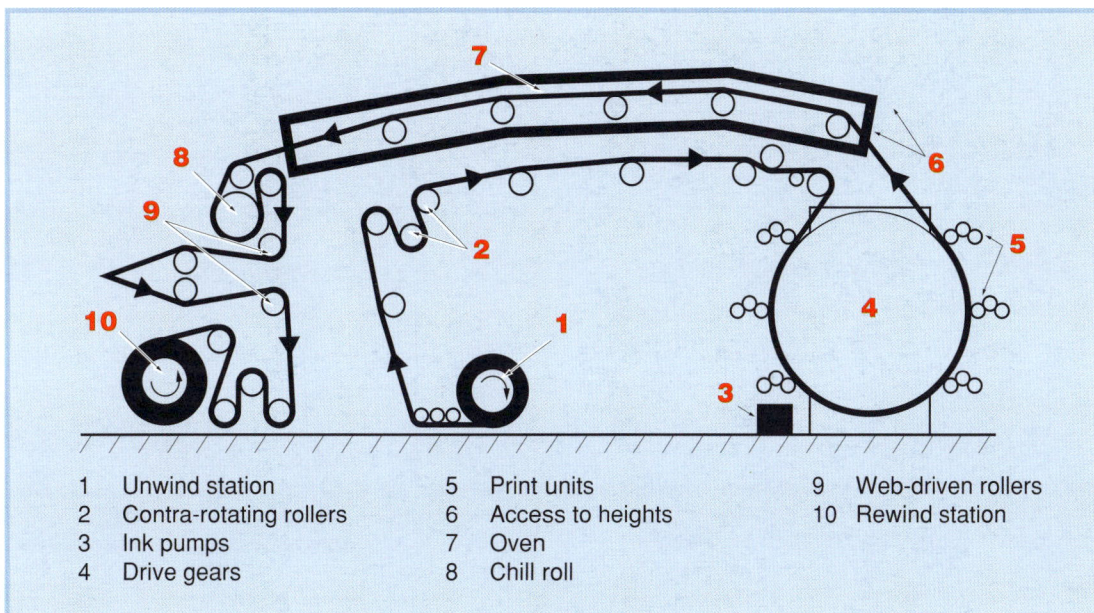

1	Unwind station	5	Print units	9	Web-driven rollers
2	Contra-rotating rollers	6	Access to heights	10	Rewind station
3	Ink pumps	7	Oven		
4	Drive gears	8	Chill roll		

Diagram of a flexographic printing press

Standards for flexographic presses with removable interlocked guards

The following standards should be met on flexographic print units guarded by removable enclosing interlocked guards:

- A removable enclosing guard should be provided which prevents access to intakes between impression/stereo and stereo/anilox cylinders as appropriate, for the entire range of stereo cylinder diameters. This guard should be electrically interlocked with the drive so that, with the guard removed, the press may only be run at slow crawl speed, ie no more than 5 m/min. The operation of the slow crawl should be via a hold-to-run button. On some small presses where cylinders may be turned by hand then interlocking should be to stop, ie not to slow crawl or inch.

- Electrical interlocking should be via proximity switches designed for safety applications, and in presses using highly flammable inks and lacquers should be suitable for potentially explosive atmospheres (see Chapter 7).

- In addition to the enclosing guard, a fixed nip bar should be provided at the intake between anilox and duct roller on the down-running web side, as these rollers often have an auxiliary drive to prevent the ink from drying when the press is stopped. The distance between this nip bar and the surface of the cylinder should be no more than 6 mm. On some presses a chamber doctor blade arrangement may be fitted. This device is mounted directly onto the anilox roller and the duct roller is removed. Consider using plastic doctor blades to minimise the risk of cuts during handling and cleaning.

- Gears driving the cylinders should be adequately guarded by either fixed sheet metal enclosing guards or interlocked guards (which often take the form of interlocked side-opening doors).

Standards for flexographic presses with gate/barrier interlocked guards

The following standards should be met on flexographic print units guarded by gate/barrier

ACCIDENT

An employee crushed his fingers between the central impression cylinder and stereo cylinder when cleaning the stereo during making-ready. Non-interlocked guards were fitted and the machine was able to run on continuous slow crawl. The safeguarding and the system of work used for cleaning were inadequate.

New and recently installed presses should already be guarded by one of the methods outlined in this booklet. Many older machines will not be adequately guarded, relying on non-interlocked lift-off covers or adjustable nip bars. You will need to upgrade these.

interlocked guards. These guards usually take the form of distancing hinged mesh barriers situated at the front of each print unit:

- Side-opening doors should be provided on the drive and operator's side of the press to guard the drive gears and intakes accessible from the side of the press. Any openings around and/or between the gate guard and doors should prevent access to hazardous parts (see also BS EN 294: 1992 *Safety of machinery. Safety distances to prevent danger zones being reached by the upper limbs*). On some older presses the side lay can only be adjusted when the press is running at a speed greater than 5 m/min so provision should be made for this, eg by extending the adjustment mechanism outside the guarded area.

- The guards should be interlocked so that with the guard open the press may only be run at slow crawl speed.

- The fixed nip bar for the intake between anilox and duct roller on the down running web side should be fitted as detailed for flexographic presses with removable interlocked guards.

Table 9 summarises the safeguarding options for flexographic and rotary letterpress machines.

Table 9 Safeguarding flexographic and rotary letterpress machines

Hazard	Safeguard
Flexographic and rotary letterpress - small- to medium-size, up to 1 m web	
In-running nips between inking rollers (rotary letterpress), duct, anilox, stereo and impression cylinders	Interlocked guards allowing limited inch and hold-to-run slow crawl only when removed or opened; **and** a fixed nip bar adjusted to within 6 mm of the anilox/duct rollers where these have a separate auxiliary drive which is not stopped by opening of the interlocked guard.
Unexpected start-up	Pre-start audible warning device.
Flexographic - larger format, eg flexible packaging	
In-running nips between duct, anilox, stereo and impression cylinders	Interlocked guards allowing limited inch and hold-to-run slow crawl only when removed or opened; **and** a fixed nip bar adjusted to within 6 mm of the anilox/duct rollers where these have an auxiliary drive.
Unexpected start-up	Pre-start audible warning device.

Safeguarding other parts of flexographic presses

As well as the guarding of the printing units on flexo presses there are often other hazardous intakes or other parts that will require guarding, eg between chill and pressure rollers, between other contra-rotating but non-contact rollers, and at unwind/rewind points. Gaps of less than 120 mm between contra-rotating powered rollers will require guarding and this can normally be achieved using nip bars or fixed guards.

Where fixed nip bars are used, they should be positioned to comply with the maximum permissible gap of no more than 6 mm from the cylinder or roller surface. Ideally, right-angled nip bars should be used.

There may also be in-running nips on non-powered riding or guide rollers driven by the movement of the web. Assess whether there is a need for safeguarding - this will depend on a number of factors, such as type of material, wrapping angle and web speed.

Enclosing guards are best made of weld mesh material on a rigid frame as this makes them reasonably lightweight and allows good visibility of the cylinders and printed web. It is likely that operators will want sheet metal sections at the duct roller to prevent ink splashing, and in some cases a means of replenishing ink by hand without removing the guard.

- It is very important that safe systems of work are implemented for cleaning and make-ready operations which cannot be carried out without removing guards. Table 10 lists the appropriate safe system of work for various tasks. Give particular attention to developing and implementing safe means of access and methods of work when accessing the upper section of a common impression cylinder on a large press.

Table 10 Safe systems of work for cleaning flexographic and rotary letterpress machines

Task	Risk factors	System of work
Flexographic/rotary letterpress		
Cleaning duct/anilox rollers, single-operator	Absence of nip bars	• Inch-stop-clean.
Cleaning duct/anilox rollers, multi-operator	Absence of nip bars	• Inch-stop-lock-clean. • If press has zoned controls allowing independent movement of print unit cylinders, inch-stop-clean.
Cleaning stereo mid-run, single-operator	Accessibility to in-running nip when interlocked guard raised	• Inch-stop-clean.
Cleaning stereo mid-run, multi-operator	Accessibility to in-running nip when interlocked guard raised	• Inch-stop-lock-clean. • If press has zoned controls allowing independent movement of print unit cylinders, inch-stop-clean.
Cleaning stereo at end of run	Stereo removed from press	• Off-machine manual or auto-washing.

Standards of safegarding at the rewind unit should meet those set out under 'Reel unwinds and rewinds' earlier in this chapter. See also 'Reeler/winder slitters used in paper conversion and flexible packaging'.

Where hold-to-run controls are being used to safeguard a danger point, starting the machine in the hold-to-run mode after opening an interlocking guard should only be possible when other interlocking guards outside the area viewable by the operator are closed. Controls should be zoned - this is particularly relevant to new machines.

Care should be taken when cleaning sharp doctor blades. Anti-cut gloves should be provided, or plastic blades can be used.

Safeguarding gravure web-fed presses

Reel unwind and rewind units on gravure printing presses must be adequately safeguarded. The requirements for the differing types of reelstands are set out under 'Reel unwinds and rewinds' earlier in this chapter. See also 'Reeler/winder slitters used in paper conversion and flexible packaging'.

Gravure printing cylinders need to be guarded. This can be difficult to achieve as the print cylinders and gears vary in diameter to determine the pattern repeat. Guarding should take account of access needs for safe cleaning of doctor blades.

Where presses are used for long-run work, adjustable nip bars can be used to guard the gravure/impression intake and impression/back impression (boule) rollers. These should be designed so that they can be adjusted to within a maximum of 6 mm from the surface of the cylinders and are often best mounted off the doctor blade carrier. Safe systems of work will need to be implemented to ensure the nip bars are always used correctly.

Where presses are used for short to medium runs, guarding should be provided in the form of interlocking guards. These can either be fitted along the side of the presses or over individual print units.

Give careful consideration to the need for doctor blade wiping. Slots can be cut in the guards which allow the doctor blade to be wiped with a long pencil but prevent finger access to the hazardous parts. Alternatively, you may be able to reduce the need for wiping doctor blades by introducing reformulated inks - contact your supplier.

Make sure all equipment is suitable for use in potentially explosive atmospheres (see 'Explosion risks in flexo and gravure' in Chapter 7).

Table 11 summarises the safeguarding requirements for the print units of gravure presses.

Table 11 Safeguarding gravure presses

Gravure - long-run presses	
In-running nips between gravure and impression cylinders	Nip bars adjusted to within 6 mm of the gravure/impression and impression/back impression (boule) cylinders which are designed to allow adjustment for the full range of gravure cylinder diameters. Continuous slow crawl should be supplemented by an emergency stop (or 'stop lock') control at each print unit. If wiping of the doctor blade is required during the print run, provision for safe access should be made. The safe system of work should consider other aspects including lighting and provision of a purpose-designed tool.
Unexpected start-up	Pre-start audible warning device.
Gravure - short-run presses	
In-running nips between gravure and impression cylinders	Interlocking guards fitted either at each print unit or along the length of the press which allow limited inch and hold-to-run slow crawl only when open. If wiping of the doctor blade is required during the print run, provision for safe access should be made either by means of a slot in the interlocked guard, or by means of an adjustable nip guard. The safe system of work should consider other aspects including lighting and provision of a purpose-designed tool.
Unexpected start-up during multi-operator cleaning	Pre-start audible warning device.

As these presses are usually multi-operator, audible pre-start warning devices must be fitted. Use hold-to-run controls for make-ready, cleaning etc and develop safe systems of work for make-ready, cleaning and webbing-up etc.

Remember that many of the accidents that occur in printing happen when it is necessary to intervene on a machine in these ways. Safe systems of work are listed in Table 12 for the various cleaning tasks likely to be required.

Table 12 Safe systems of work for cleaning gravure presses

Task	Risk factors	System of work
Gravure		
Wiping doctor blades	Approach close to in-running nips at production speed	• Use of purpose-made tool and properly adjusted nip bar or slot in interlocked guard.
Cleaning gravure/impression cylinders mid-run, single-operator cleaning	Accessibility to in-running nips when interlocked guard raised	• Inch-stop-clean. • Forward slow crawl cleaning **only** if nip bars and emergency stops are provided and a guard checklist completed.
Cleaning gravure/impression cylinders mid-run, multi-operator cleaning	Accessibility to in-running nips when interlocked guard raised	• Inch-stop-lock-clean. • Forward slow crawl cleaning **only** if nip bars and emergency stops are provided and a guard checklist completed.
Cleaning gravure/impression cylinders at end of run	Gravure cylinder removed from press	• Off-machine manual or auto-washing.

Safeguarding screen printing presses

The main risks from screen printers are from:

- crush risks from either the screen rise and fall mechanism or squeegee movement;

- in-running nips from feeder and delivery mechanisms;

- shear points from gaps on lower cylinders on cylinder-type presses;

- hazardous substances, such as inks or varnishes, either when in use, when curing or when cleaning screens.

Most screen print operators add ink or varnish while the press is moving. Although this is not inherently dangerous, it prevents perimeter guarding from being used to prevent screen crush injuries.

Screen crush risks

There are several situations which can create a risk of crushing the upper body or fingers:

- When the frame holding the screen is raised to allow access under the screen it must not be possible for the frame to

descend, crushing the upper body. On some machines, light beams are provided, but these can sometimes be ineffective as it is possible to reach over the beam without interrupting it. It is often not practicable to extend the beam over the whole area as machine components may interrupt it. Sensitive edges may be a practical solution, or light curtains in front of the machine to detect the operator's legs rather than the upper body. Safe systems of work must be used to isolate the machine before entering the area below the screen.

- The squeegee rise and fall mechanisms can provide crush points for fingers. Provide a fixed guard around them.

- The oscillating squeegee carriage can create a crush or shear point as it moves to the end of its travel. While this could quite easily have been designed out, it is generally not practicable to shield these.

Semi-automatic presses

On semi-automatic flat-bed machines, take precautions to minimise the likelihood of the reciprocating table striking the operator, by providing sensitive edges, presence-sensing devices or chain rails to prevent access. The traps between the vertically reciprocating frame-holder and the four main machine pillars will also need to be guarded.

Cylinder type machines

These machines can pose a risk when making ready, though this risk is removed in normal operation. The risks occur from:

- shear points between gaps in the cylinder (by the grippers) and the fixed structure. Safe systems of work must be in place to address this risk and it should never be necessary for the operator's fingers to be in this area;

- in-running nips between exposed drive gears and the fixed structure. These gears tend to have teeth large enough to trap a finger. It may be desirable to increase the gap between the gear and the structure so that a finger is not drawn in.

Hinged presses with power closure

Hinged or clam-type screen process printing machines with power closure should be fitted with efficient trip guards around the three edges of the screen (unless the closing force is less than 300 newtons and there are no sharp edges). These will stop the screen or make it retract if anyone becomes trapped. Regular testing of the safety devices should be carried out to ensure they continue to operate effectively.

Safeguard the crushing point between the squeegee and screen frame by adjusting the stop gauge to ensure a minimum 25 mm gap. If the descending squeegee creates a crushing risk, make sure that the lifting path is as short as possible.

Feed and delivery in-running nips

Belt drives on many machines have inadequate nip guards where they pass over rollers. Belt tensions tend to be low which reduces the potential severity of the injury, but nip guards should be provided.

Hazardous substances

Where UV-cured inks or varnishes are used, appropriate controls must be provided to limit skin contact. Emptying ink from screens at the end of the run involves moving a significant amount of ink and appropriate precautions should be taken to prevent contamination. Also, great care must be taken when washing screens using water jetting techniques to avoid sprays of UV-cured inks hitting the operator. Vertical strip curtains, similar to those provided in doorways for fork-lift trucks, can be used to both prevent the spray from hitting the operator and to make any local exhaust ventilation more effective.

For more information see 'Screen printing and cleaning' in the 'Hazardous substances' section in Chapter 4.

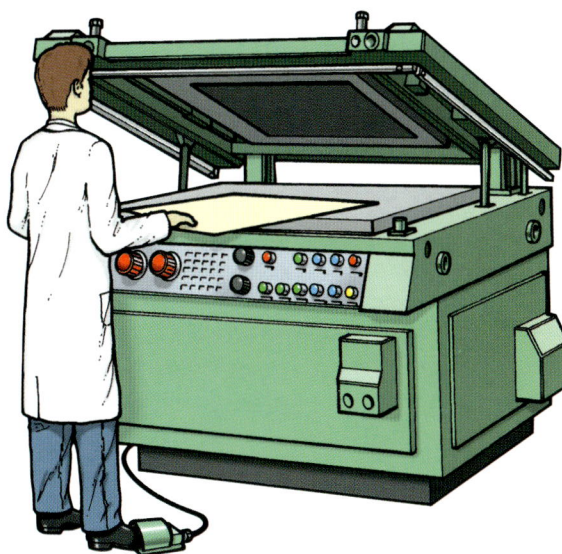

Figure 31 Hinged or clam-type screen printing presses with power closure should be fitted with safety trip bars

Label printing machines

Presses with twin side frames should meet the standards laid out under the headings 'Web offset' and/or 'Flexographic' earlier in this chapter. Label presses of the cantilever type should meet the following standards.

The gear wheels and in-running nips on cylinders and rollers of the print units on cantilever label printing machines should be safeguarded, for example with:

- hinged or rise and fall interlocked guards; or

- removable enclosing interlocked guards.

Hinged or rise and fall interlocked guards are often designed to cover all print units with one guard. This often prevents operators from being able to make adjustments or add ink on the 'run' so provision should be made for these adjustments by extending controls/ink troughs through the guard.

Removable enclosing interlocked guards can be used to safeguard each print unit individually and, if properly designed, allow adjustments and topping up of ink while the press is running. Detailed information on their design is given under 'Flexographic' earlier in this chapter.

Some older machines may be provided solely with adjustable nip bars as guarding. They are usually found to be removed or incorrectly adjusted and are therefore not adequate. Pacing/draw rollers should be provided with enclosing interlocked guards or suitable nip bars where access is possible to in-running nips created by contra-rotating rollers.

As well as the enclosing guard on flexographic print units, a fixed nip bar should be provided at any in-running intake between anilox and duct roller as these rollers often have an auxiliary drive to prevent the ink from drying when the press is stopped. The distance between this nip bar and the surface of the cylinder should be no more than 6 mm. Low powered drives may also be acceptable if they prevent injury. On some presses a chamber doctor blade arrangement may be fitted. Adequate procedures should be laid down for the safe handling of doctor blades.

Finishing section

The hazardous parts of the finishing section of label printing machines must be safeguarded. These sections will comprise some or all the following units: rotary die-cutting units, flat-bed die-cutting units, slitting knives, trim removal/rewind, punching units, perforating (cross and inline) etc. Combinations of fixed nip bars and interlocking guards need to be used to guard these finishing/processing stations. It is important to ensure that the

guarding arrangements are adequate for all web paths including the different trim/label stripping paths. These areas often produce a lot of dust and high noise levels so the guarding arrangements should take these hazards into account.

To facilitate make-ready and cleaning, label printing machines may be fitted with hold-to-run controls to allow operation of the press at slow crawl speeds with guards opened. Table 6 under 'Flexographic' earlier in this chapter details appropriate safe systems of work for cleaning.

In-line folders, sheeters, die-cutters etc

All in-running nips and other mechanical hazards on folders and other in-line processing equipment need to be guarded. Guard design may need to take account of other hazards such as noise and dust.

On new and recently installed folder installations, the folder should be totally enclosed with fixed and interlocked guards. Guard locking devices should be fitted where there is a high risk of severe injury (ie chopper folder) and the press has a rundown period of more than 10 seconds even after actuation of the emergency stop control.

Totally enclosed folders should be provided with arrangements for the remote control of folder settings either by electrical/electronic or direct mechanical means. The bending rollers and delivery area are likely to be outside the 'enclosed area'.

The bending rollers need to be provided with a 'nose' guard at the base of the former (kite) and adjustable guards for the portion of the bending rollers behind the former. The delivery area must be adequately guarded. However, a hold-to-run guard override control button may be provided for the delivery tunnel guard. Depression of this hold-to-run control will allow operators to open the guard at speeds up to 8 m/min to allow removal of the first incomplete product copies.

All-enclosing guards may not be practicable on older folders and localised guarding of the hazardous parts should be provided. In these circumstances the following areas need to be safeguarded: the nipping/pinching rollers, cross-association rollers, folding drum, cutting cylinders, cross-perforating cylinders, jaw cylinder, quarter folder etc. Hazardous nips between delivery belts and pulleys should also be guarded.

On sheeting units the main areas of danger are the draw rollers and the rotary knife. The draw rollers should be guarded by either fixed nip bars or enclosing interlocked guards. The rotary knife is a high-risk area and on a large installation should be guarded by a high-risk interlocking arrangement (ie dual-circuit interlocking) and with the provision of guard locking if the rundown time is long enough to make it necessary.

Make sure that precautions have been taken to control employee's exposure to noise and dust (see Chapter 4).

Business forms presses

The hazardous parts of finishing sections of business forms presses must be safeguarded. These sections and the means used to guard them are the same as those for label printing machines. If wander leads are provided, allowing access to parts with guards open, they should be of a simultaneous two-hand control type. These may allow speeds in excess of 10 m/min where specified by the manufacturer and where there is appropriate guard zoning.

Where, on business forms presses, the web is delivered by a spiral folder as in a zig-zag folded continuous stationery pack, the delivery guard may be fitted with an enable guard override control button. This operates as a hold-to-run control allowing the guard to be opened at slow run speeds to facilitate removal of the first incomplete copies.

A minimum gap of 25 mm should be maintained between the spirals by the provision of adjustment stops. Where the spirals need to be closed to less than 25 mm, a local guard preventing access into the nip must be provided. Fixed guards must be provided for the spiral drive gears.

Publishing rooms

Types of conveyors, counters, stackers, tyers and strappers vary considerably so the following guidance is general.

Conveyors

Effective means for stopping newspaper conveyors which enter the publishing room should be provided for use in emergencies. Where dump gates are provided at folders to divert copies, it should be possible to stop the insert conveyor leading to the publishing room without stopping the press. Where dump gates cannot be fitted, it may be necessary to provide stop buttons in the publishing room which stop the press as well as the conveyors where these are mechanically linked. Normal press stops should be carried out from the press room, and a signalling system provided so that publishing room staff can request that the press is slowed down or stopped.

Overhead conveying mechanisms out of reach, ie 'safe by position' will not normally require additional guarding. However, access may be possible to these mechanisms while they are running so some localised guarding may be required. Operators have been known to use ladders or moveable steps for copy or blockage removal etc.

Hazardous parts associated with conveyors such as belt and chain drives must be safeguarded including those situated below the conveyors. Lift-up conveyors on these units should be arranged so that access to hazardous parts is not possible when the conveyor section is raised, usually achieved by interlocking the conveyor section.

Where conveyors enter the publishing room from below, adequate barriers and toe-boards should be erected around the conveyor and floor opening.

Copy pick-up points should be designed to prevent access to hazardous parts by providing fixed or interlocked guards.

Figure 32 *Conveyors, counters, stackers, tyers and strappers in publishing rooms need to be safeguarded*

Counter stackers

Counter stackers should be provided with guards preventing access to hazardous parts, for example rotating collection hoppers. Safety reach distances to prevent hazardous parts being accessed will apply (see BS EN 294: 1992 *Safety of machinery. Safety distances to prevent danger zones being reached by the upper limbs*). Where guards have to be opened by operators, they should be interlocked to the counter stacker drive. Otherwise they should be fixed in position and require a tool for removal.

String-tyers and strappers

Conveyor-fed automatic string-tyers and strappers may be divided into two groups:

- those with a low-pressure clamp not capable of inflicting injury, eg less than 300 newtons and where an elastic bottom plate cover has been provided;

- those with high-pressure clamps.

Machines which fall into the second category should be provided with a combination of fixed and interlocked guards preventing access from the sides, in-feed and delivery ends. Safety reach distances in BS EN 294: 1992 apply. Lift-off guards and guards that need to be opened frequently for cleaning jams, replacing string etc will need to be interlocked, including any lift-up conveyor sections.

Some strapping machines may have force-limiting devices, eg slip clutches on the clamp as well as a resilient rubber facing, and may have no other associated hazardous parts. Gravity-fall crucifix-turn devices can become hazardous when laden, and screen-guarding should be fitted. This may require interlocking if access to other hazardous parts is possible. Where you rely on force-limiting devices, these should be regularly tested using a load-cell pressure gauge or other suitable instrument.

Insertion equipment

- The risks posed by insertion equipment are primarily those related to in-running nips or pinch points from moving equipment. On modern equipment, these are either housed behind fixed or interlocked guards or are above 2 m from the floor. Equipment must not be run with the guards removed or interlocks overridden. Regular checks must be run to test the continued correct operation of the interlocks.

- Where it is necessary to run the equipment with the guards open during make ready, then it must only be possible to run it using a hold-to-run button and at crawl speed. Systems of work must restrict such operations to appropriately trained personnel.

- Systems of work must be in place for elevated work, eg maintenance, near insertion equipment or their associated conveyors. Such work must only be carried out with this equipment isolated and locked off. Equipment is normally autonomous and so you need to isolate insertion equipment and conveyors separately.

Automatic insertion disc equipment

Control stations should not be located in the path of automatically moving discs of insertion material. Make sure there are no accessible shear traps between the moving discs and control/electrical panels and separate moving discs and personnel. Ensure trip wire/pressure-sensitive edge devices provided on the disc carriages give adequate protection to operators and that these are maintained in full working order. The integrity of the interface between the guarding devices and the programmable control systems for the disc carriages should be assessed. Disc carriages should stop safely, without trapping operators or ejecting their load.

Inserting and stitching drums

Front and end covers of inserting and stitching drums should be interlocked so that when they are open only movement by hold-to-run slow crawl is possible.

Adequate safeguarding should be provided at the rear of the drums to prevent injury when removing misfed copies.

Interlocked or fixed guards should be provided to prevent access to hazardous parts from steps, working platforms or other areas. Accidents have occurred when operators have attempted to clear blockages by reaching over interlocked guards by standing on pallets and short steps. Overhead chain drives should be safe by position or guarded. Full-length guarding may be more practical than multiple localised guards. Stitching heads should be fitted with interlocked hood guards where otherwise accessible, eg from work platforms.

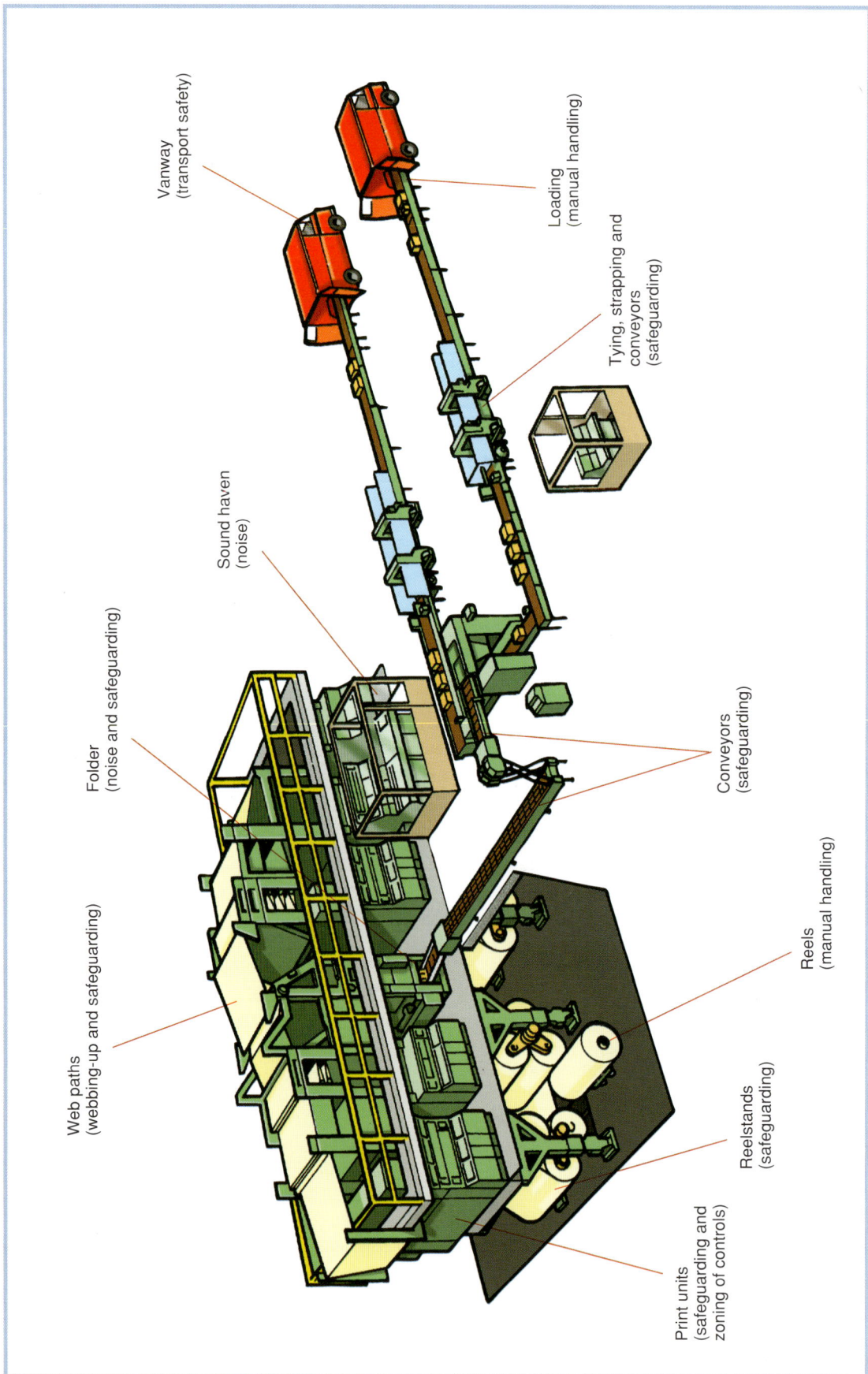

Vanway (transport safety)

Loading (manual handling)

Tying, strapping and conveyors (safeguarding)

Sound haven (noise)

Folder (noise and safeguarding)

Conveyors (safeguarding)

Web paths (webbing-up and safeguarding)

Reels (manual handling)

Reelstands (safeguarding)

Print units (safeguarding and zoning of controls)

Figure 33 *Newspaper production - printing and publishing operations*

Envelope-making machines

There are two broad categories of envelope-making machine, blank-fed or web-fed. Both types of machine usually consist of printing units, gumming station, window-patching station, folding and gluing station, a collator drum and a take-off section. Blank-fed machines have a feed plate or feed pillar. Web-fed machines will have a reelstand, profile cutting system and rotary or flying knife as well.

The hazardous parts of these machines include the in-running roller nips, gumming wheels, knives, reciprocating feed devices, gear wheels and drum-related shear traps - these must be safeguarded. Many of these hazardous parts can be guarded by fitting side guards to the machines. These should be interlocked to the machine's movement so that opening any one of these guards stops the machine. Localised interlocked or fixed guarding can also be used. In-running nips on folding rollers where safeguarded by tunnel-type guards may, in exceptional circumstances, have openings of 30 mm where the safety distance to the danger point is 200 mm.

Machines may be fitted with two-hand, hold-to-run controls for set up. The speed should be limited to 10 m/min and guard zoning provided. In exceptional circumstances, where the use of stroboscopes is needed at production speeds for fault-finding, the following should be provided:

● hold-to-run control;

● guard zoning;

● a selector switch;

● a safe system of work which includes using the slowest speed possible.

Additional local fixed, interlocked and adjustable guards are necessary on many of the machine's individual units. The feed plate or feed pillar will need local profiled guards for the draw, hook rollers and any score rollers. Any hinged gumming units should be interlocked to prevent them being left out of position, exposing hazardous parts when not in use.

Standards for reelstands on web-fed machines should meet those outlined under 'Web offset' earlier in this chapter. The print units on both types of machine should be guarded in accordance with the standards set out under 'Flexographic' earlier in this chapter.

Seal flap, window and bottom flap gumming units will all require guarding to prevent access to in-running nips or contact with hot glues. All-enclosing interlocked guarding may not be feasible as access may be needed to the glue bottles. A combination of fixed and interlocked guards is often most successful. Think about the handling of the glue bottles as this may pose a significant manual handling risk.

The intakes associated with the glassine tissue knife and tissue applicator in-running nips need to be guarded. Any shear trap between the delivery table and drying drum should be safeguarded. This may be achieved by providing fixed or interlocked guarding or a hinged table end of at least 25 mm. Any belt or pulley intakes should also be guarded. Delivery guarding can usually be achieved either by fixed tunnel guarding or by adjustable plates.

On web-fed machines, areas of high risk include the profile cutting system and separating knife. These must be adequately guarded by providing fixed or interlocked guards. Guarding should take account of the rundown times of the knives and the frequency of access.

Noise can cause serious problems on envelope machines so it is often a good idea to combine guarding and noise-reduction measures. New machines with high noise levels should be supplied with noise control measures incorporated as standard.

ACCIDENT

An employee was fatally injured when his head was trapped between the rotating spokes of a drying wheel and the fixed frame of the envelope-making machine. The access doors to the wheel were not secured. Fixed or interlocked guards should be provided at both sides of the drying wheel to prevent access to the shear hazard created between the rotating wheel and fixed machine frame.

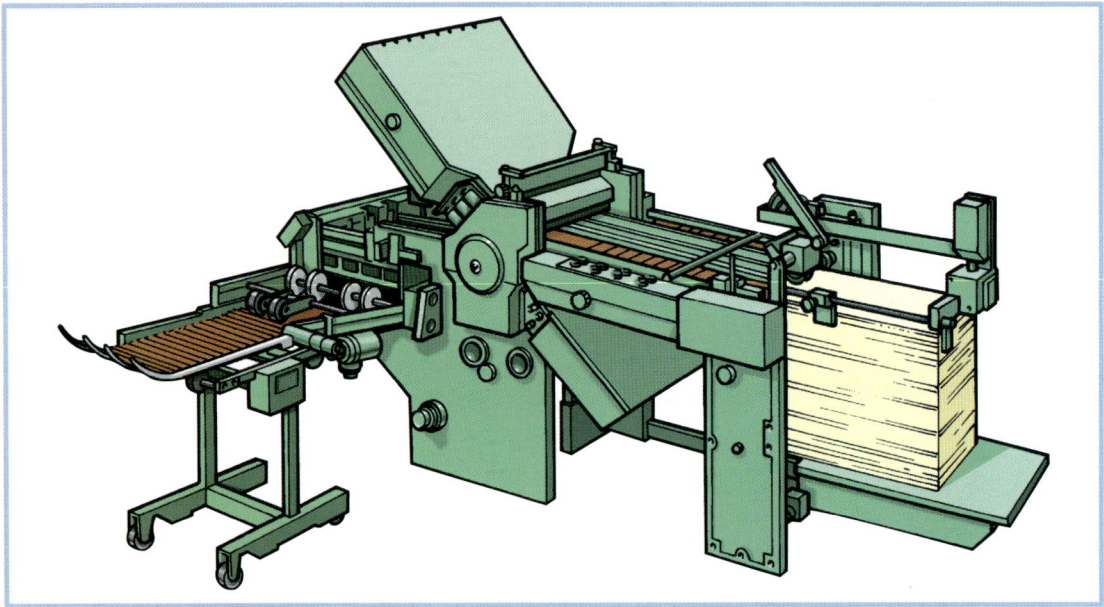

Figure 34 *Suitable noise-hoods should be provided for buckle plates*

Sheet-fed folding machines

The danger points on sheet-fed folding machines must be guarded. The two main types of machine, buckle and combination, give rise to similar risks. One of these is noise which can be addressed by providing suitable noise-hoods for the buckle plates. On new machines noise-reduction measures should be provided as part of their standard specification (see 'Noise' in Chapter 4).

The main in-feed rollers should be provided with fixed or interlocked guards with a narrow slot for sheet entry. Access to the folding rollers should be prevented by a combination of guards, the machine's frame and the buckle plates.

In-running nips associated with drive tapes should be guarded. This can be achieved by designing the transport/feed tables to 'fit' the pulleys, ie reach to a point no more than 6 mm from the in-running belt/pulley nip, or the provision of nip bars. Give particular attention to the nips associated with tensioning pulleys.

The hazardous parts involved with folding knives should be guarded. On new machines this may be in conjunction with the delivery area of the buckle-folding unit, ie an all-enclosing interlocked guard. On older machines a more localised fixed or interlocked guard should be provided.

Perforators, creasing units and slitters are often fitted to this type of machine. The intakes associated with these devices should be guarded, including any in-running nip created between them and fixed parts of the folding machine. Precautions also need to be taken to prevent access to the periphery of running slitters and perforators.

For setting purposes, interlocked guards may need to be opened. In these circumstances, the machine should only start under hold-to-run control with a maximum speed of 70 m/min measured at the folding rollers. Guards in areas outside the operator's view should be closed, a selector switch should be provided and the run speed should be as slow as possible.

Guillotines

Power-operated paper-cutting guillotines are potentially the most hazardous machines in the printing industry. They must be adequately safeguarded, regularly checked by both operators and competent guillotine engineers, and operators must be properly trained.

Further guidance on the guarding, maintenance and testing of guillotines is available in the Printing Industry Advisory Committee booklet *The guide to safe use of power-operated paper-cutting guillotines*. This publication also contains information on training and knife change procedures.

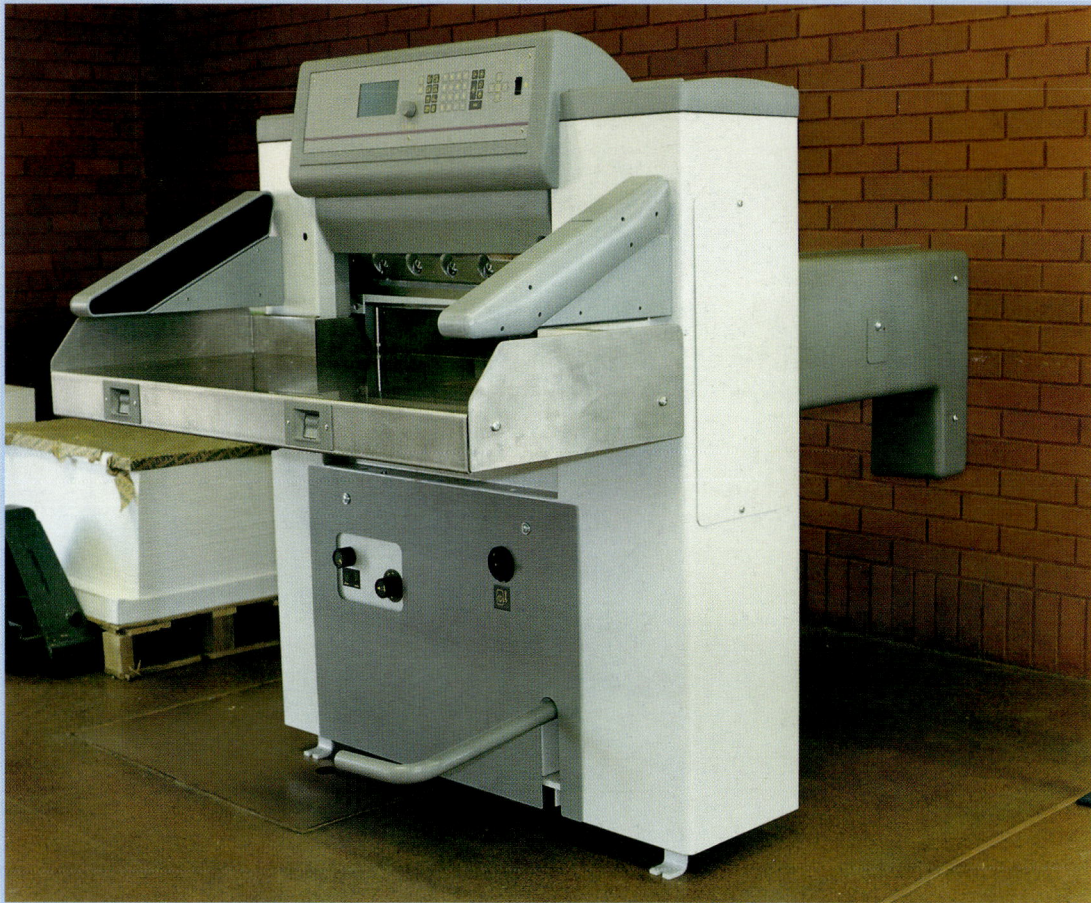

Figure 35 *Guillotine fitted with photoelectric curtain and simultaneous two-hand controls*

Common accidents

● Amputations following double stroking of the knife due to faulty brakes and poor maintenance (including top dead centre cams).

● Crush and amputation injuries by the clamp particularly when the dynamic gauging force exceeds 500 newtons.

● Amputation injuries caused by trapping fingers in the screw adjustment holes of the clamp when the clamp returns.

● Trapping accidents between the moving backgauge and clamp.

● Accidents due to incorrect guard positioning or guards being defeated.

● Accidents during knife changing.

Photoelectric (electrosensitive) safety systems

Photoelectric safety systems for guillotines should meet certain minimum standards with full function monitoring (FFM) as the lowest acceptable level for old machines. Newer machines will need to meet more stringent standards.

In general, guillotines supplied before 1974 with original photoelectric curtains will require upgrading to meet the standards in *The guide to safe use of power-operated paper-cutting guillotines.* Guillotines supplied between approximately 1974 and 1987 should have electrosensitive safety systems designed and operating to full function monitoring (FFM) standards. However, on some guillotines, certain modifications will need to be carried out such as the removal of the fully automatic facility. A competent guillotine engineer should be able to advise you.

Guillotines supplied after 1987 should comply with BS EN 61496-1: 1998, IEC 61496-1: 1997 *Safety of machinery. Electro-sensitive protective equipment. General requirements and tests*.

Guillotines supplied after 1 January 1995 should be 'CE' marked and comply with the Supply of Machinery (Safety) Regulations 1992 as amended.

It is extremely important that the photoelectric curtain (light curtain) is located correctly. Serious injuries have occurred when the curtain has been incorrectly mounted and operators have accidentally reached over or under the curtain without breaking the beams.

As a general rule, the outermost beam should be approximately 635 mm from the cutting stick and no more than 185 mm above the table.

Where new machines have a usable pile height of more than 185 mm, the outermost beam may be at a position 610 mm minimum and 700 mm maximum from the cutting stick and no more than 205 mm above the table. An electrosensitive protective device (additional beam) should also be provided at a distance of between 400 and 550 mm from the cutting stick and at a height of between 0 and 205 mm above the table. An additional beam should be fitted on all new machines fitted with fully automatic cutting operation. Where the machine design is such that the curtain extends down to the machine table, the outermost beam should be at least 400 mm from the cutting stick if the beam is less than 38 mm from the table.

The separation distance of the curtain from the cutting stick must be consistent with the overall stopping performance of the machine. Older machines will generally have a distance of at least 460 mm between cutting stick and curtain.

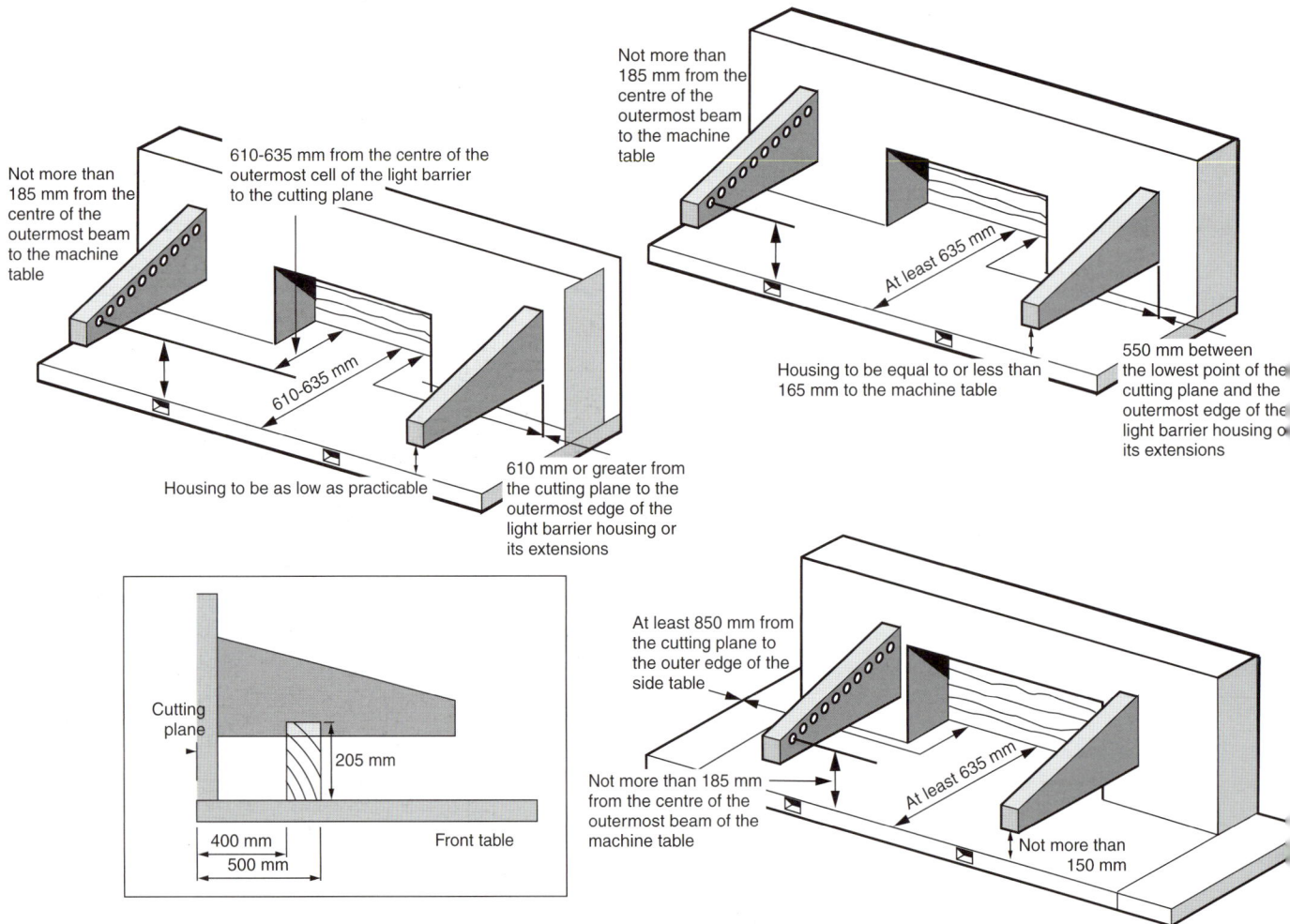

Figure 36 *Positioning of the electrosensitive protective devices (beams) and curtain housing*

Six key points to check on photoelectric safety systems:

- The system meets the required standards and is upgraded if necessary.

- The photoelectric curtain is located correctly.

- Two final switching devices are provided for fully automatic machines.

- Simultaneous two-hand controls are fitted.

- The dynamic gauging force of the clamp is less than 500 newtons.

- Suitable rear table guarding is fitted (see 'Interlocking guards' below).

Body push guards

Body push guards fitted to guillotines are no longer considered adequate safety devices. Guillotines fitted with body push guards should have been withdrawn from service.

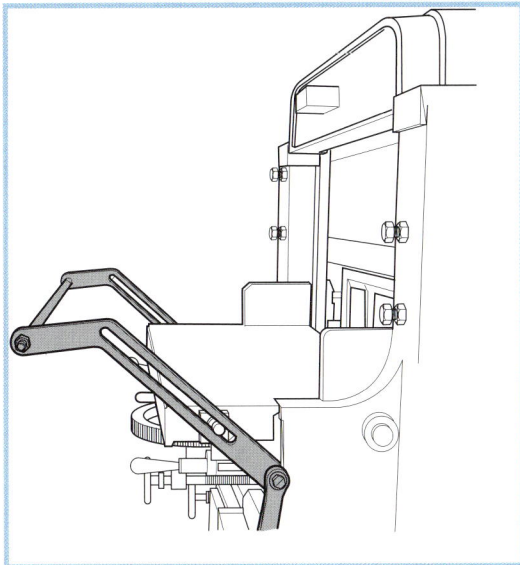

Figure 37 *Guillotines with body push guards should no longer be in use*

Interlocking guards

Four key points to cheek on interlocking guards:

- The guard prevents access to the danger zone (ie you shouldn't be able to reach over, around or beneath the guard when it is in the down position and lifting of the guard stops the machine before you can reach the blade or clamp).

- The interlocking arrangement is of the required standard (this will normally need to be a dual-channel control system - your supplier should be able to confirm this).

- Simultaneous two-hand controls are fitted.

- Suitable rear table guarding is provided which prevents access to dangers created by the moving clamp, blade or backgauge.

Automatic sweepaway guards

These are designed to push operators' hands away from the cutting area before they can be injured by the knife or clamp.

Five key points to check for guillotines fitted with sweepaway guards:

- The guard sweeps towards the operator to a point 500 mm from the face of the clamp before the clamp or knife have descended 50 mm. You may find it useful to put a mark at the 500 mm point on the table to help you check this.

- Additional guard bars/mesh are provided to prevent access over/through the guard.

- Side access to the danger zone at the front of the machine is prevented when the guard is extended, eg by providing large side tables or fixed guards.

- Simultaneous two-hand controls are provided.

- Suitable rear table guarding is provided.

Guillotines with sweepaway guards should not be supplied second-hand or sold on. Sweepaway guards should not be changed for electrosensitive systems if a non-fail-safe brake is fitted.

Sweepaway guard in extended position (side guards omitted for clarity)

An unacceptable sweepaway guillotine

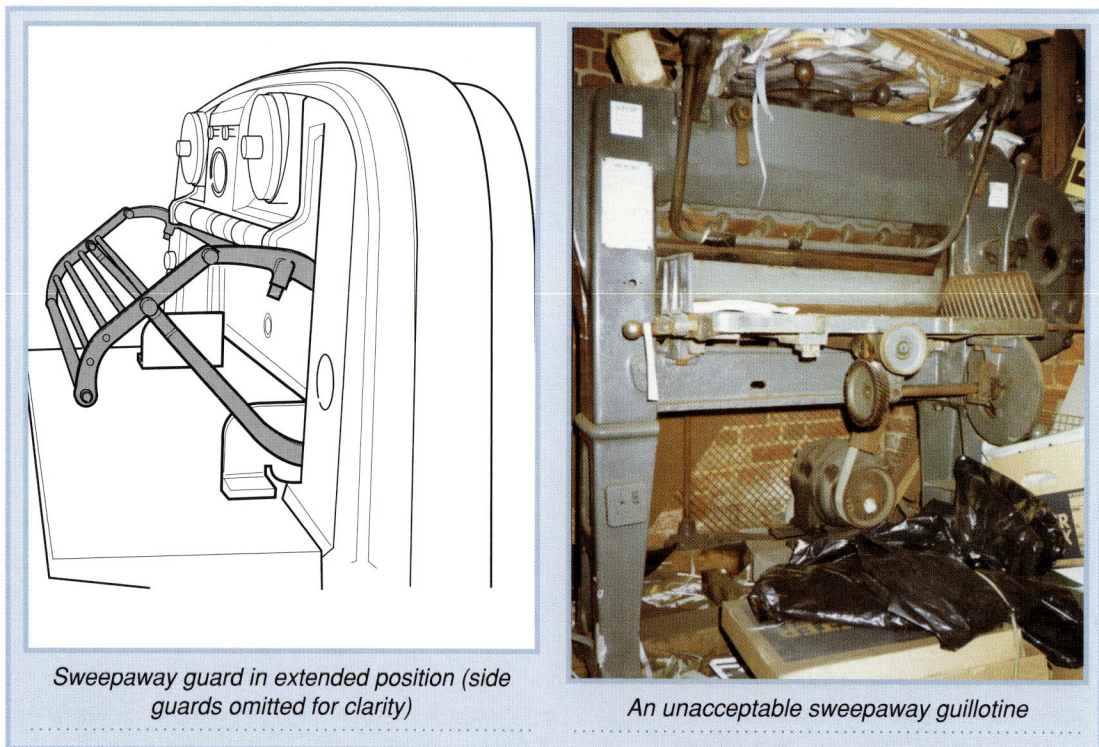

Figure 38 Automatic sweepaway guards

Common requirements for all power-operated paper-cutting guillotines

Modifications to guillotine safety systems should only be carried out by competent guillotine engineers, manufacturers or suppliers because of the complexity of the systems and the potential dangers resulting from inadequate modifications.

Simultaneous two-hand controls should be fitted to all machines other than those with high-integrity, all-enclosing interlocked guards. These would have cross-monitored dual-channel control using two guard position switches operating in opposite modes. Older machines may need their controls upgrading. The two-hand control should meet the following basic standards:

- both buttons should be operated within approximately 0.5 seconds of each other before the machine will operate;

- if one control is released, both buttons should have to be released and re-operated for re-initiation;

- the controls should not be capable of being spanned by one hand;

- if one or both controls are released, the machine should stop or return to top dead centre.

The above guidelines are very general and the detailed requirements of individual machine types and models should be checked with the manufacturer/supplier and against the guidelines in the Printing Industry Advisory Committee booklet *The guide to safe use of power-operated paper-cutting guillotines.*

Operators should carry out daily tests and checks of guillotines fitted with electrosensitive (photoelectric) safety systems or interlocking guards. These checks should also be carried out after knife changing.

Sweepaway guards on guillotines should be checked by operators on a monthly basis. All tests should be recorded. The checks should also be carried out after knife changing.

Six-monthly examinations and tests should be carried out on all guillotines by competent and trained engineers and cover safety components (eg brake and clutches, interlock switches and cams), stopping performance and gauging pressures to comply with regulation 6(2) of PUWER 98 (see Chapter 8).

Further information and example test forms can be found in the Printing Industry Advisory Committee booklet *The guide to safe use of power-operated paper-cutting guillotines*.

The integrity of guards and braking systems on guillotines can only be maintained by regular testing and examination - failure to maintain a guillotine could result in a serious and avoidable incident.

Knife changing

Special precautions are necessary to prevent injury when knives are changed. The guillotine manufacturer's instructions should be followed. These usually entail procedures involving devices such as knife handles or slides and supports for safe removal, mounting boards for safe transport and storage, and the use of an assistant when changing knives on larger machines. Precautions should also be taken to keep others away during knife changing, eg by using barriers and a table near the front of the guillotine.

Other cutting machines

Three-knife trimmers

These usually consists of three guillotine blades or knives (the head and tail knives and the forage knife). The knives reciprocate automatically throughout the run. Guarding for the blades and other hazardous parts is essential. Access to the blades with the guards open will be required for knife changing and adjustment. Three-knife trimmers must be adequately guarded. This is usually achieved by providing fixed or interlocked guards.

Manually fed machines

- Provide interlocked tunnel-type guards to prevent access to the knives from the rear of the machine.

- Feed-side guarding should incorporate trip devices, for example a tripped flap running the length of the feed opening or

tripped side guards or both. The trip devices should operate at minimal deflection and should instantly cut power and movement of hazardous parts if an operator's hands are carried into the feed opening.

- Provide adjustable feed-side guards where book sizes vary. These will need to be maintained in the correct position to allow feeding of the work but prevent operator access to the danger area. Front table dimensions may need extending to give operators extra protection by keeping them further away from the feed opening.

- Simultaneous two-hand hold-to-run controls should be provided on new manually fed machines. Similar standards should be provided on older existing equipment.

Automatically fed machines

Guarding usually takes the form of a sliding tunnel guard or a large hood split into two sections hinged at the middle. These should be interlocked.

Common provisions

Openings in the guards should comply with the safety reach distances in BS EN 294: 1992 *Safety of machinery. Safety distances to prevent danger zones being reached by the upper limbs.*

Photoelectric curtains can also be used to provide protection at the feed-side.

Emergency stop devices, including lift-up bar devices at certain older machines, are not a substitute for the trip devices referred to in the previous paragraphs.

You will need safe systems of work for knife changing and setting, incorporating the use of knife covers.

For setting purposes, two-hand-controls should be provided which do not allow running or jogging of the trimmer section with the guards open. Operating the two-hand control with the trimmer guards open should allow no more than a single stroke by the trimmer blades however long the controls are actuated, ie if the controls are operated and held in for several seconds the trimmer blade should do no more than one stroke and then come to a complete rest.

Where operation of the knives is not restricted to a single cut with the trimmer guards open, machines should be designed to allow necessary running adjustments with guards closed.

Loose knife punching machines

Manually operated loose knife punching/cutting machines have caused finger and hand injuries when operators have not withdrawn before the platen descends or have attempted to reposition a toppling knife. Access should be prevented during the stroke by a combination of a sliding front feed table, simultaneous two-hand controls and either interlocked/falling screen front guards or self-adjusting tunnel/screen front guards, together with either localised fixed guarding for the sides and rear, or perimeter-type fencing. Cutter balancing springs should be used to stop small cutters falling over.

Automatic machines need a higher standard of safeguarding as the two-hand controls only offer protection for the operator during the initial strike on. The feed-side should be safeguarded by either a hinged interlock guard or an electrosensitive safety system. You should ensure that the safeguarding arrangements at the feed-side comply with BS EN 294: 1992 *Safety of machinery. Safety distances to prevent danger zones being reached by the upper limbs.*

Locate the photoelectric curtain incorporated in this system correctly to prevent people reaching the danger points or being able to stand between the photoelectric curtain and machine. The sides and rear can be safeguarded by a combination of fixed and interlocked guards.

Shear and trapping points on the paper feed and take-off systems should be either designed out or safeguarded using trip devices or other methods.

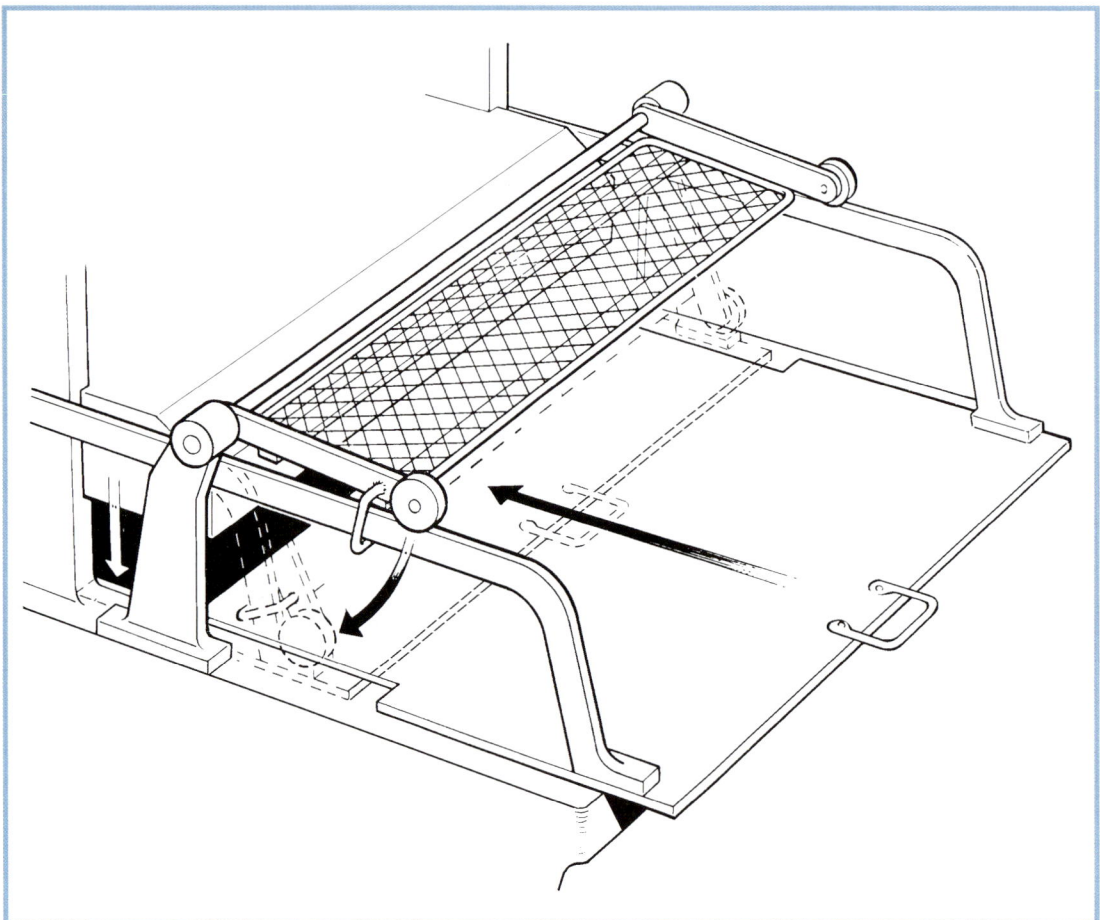

Figure 39 *Example of guarding a loose knife punching machine using a falling screen guard*

Flat-bed cutting and creasing machines

Cutting and creasing machines come in two forms:

- purpose-designed machines;

- converted printing presses. The Heidelberg Original Cylinder is a typical example of a converted machine.

The main risks are:

- moving components with associated crush or shear points. Cutting and creasing machines have an inherent oscillating motion, and movements may be sudden. Access (including direct or indirect, eg via the waste chute) to the moving parts should be prevented by means of guards or other devices that stop all dangerous motion before injury can result;

- weights of dies on larger machines;

- noise from larger machines, particularly those fitted with trimmings extraction systems;

- crush points at the outfeed of larger machines.

Purpose-designed machines

The feed-end of machines is similar to that of sheet-fed printing presses. Foot crushing risks from descending pallet tables should be avoided by having a manual system for the final 100 mm, or alternatively, hinged flaps that raise the operator's foot away from the trapping point. Transfer mechanisms from the product pile need to be adequately guarded to cover any in-running nips or shear points as in-feed devices oscillate.

The cutting/creasing and stripping areas must be guarded using either fixed or interlocked guards. If you need to be able to inch the machine with the guards open, then audible pre-start warnings must sound before the machine is moved, and the movement must be limited. It must not be possible to access the intermittently moving transport chains with the guards open.

Remove trimmings so that they do not accumulate. Vacuum extraction is often used, but the noise from the airflow and trimmings movement can exceed 85 dB(A) in many machines. Minimise the level to which the operators are exposed.

Delivery-end pallets can sometimes have poor access. It is often impractical to prevent access to this area but during normal operation it should not be necessary for personnel to enter the area where the pallet descends. Safe systems of work must be in place for the changeover of pallets or their carriage plates, stating that the machine must be isolated if access is required to the pallet descent area. Where machine parts or higher level platforms are positioned so that the operators may hit their heads during unloading operations, then these parts must be adequately padded. Housekeeping and neighbouring equipment must not cause an obstruction when removing product on pallet trucks.

When changing dies, appropriate equipment or systems of work must be provided to minimise the risk of injury through manual handling. Extending rails may be provided to enable the die to be removed from the machine and equipment or systems must address the movement to or from these rails.

Converted machines

Typical machines have the feed and delivery at the same end. Guards must be provided over the forme at the other end and these should be interlocked rather than fixed to facilitate changeover of dies. The risks from inking rollers are usually overcome by removing these with presses dedicated to cutting and creasing. The shear trap caused by the gap in the cylinder as it passes fixed machine parts must be guarded by either a fixed or interlocked guard. A common method of fixing such a guard is to use U-bolts or similar devices round the cross tie bar. Risks caused by oscillating delivery fingers must be controlled by ensuring that these are telescopic. Most presses were designed this way, but damage during use may have jammed the telescopic action.

Autoplatens

Automatic sheet-fed platens were not originally supplied with guards for the reciprocating platen or the inking rollers. At the very least, users need to ensure that fixed side and rear guards are provided and that, where still used, inking rollers are guarded. Safeguarding by means of interlocked gates or pressure-sensitive mats at the front of the machine should also be considered. It is particularly important that operators are properly trained and supervised.

Hand-fed platens used for cutting and creasing

Hand-fed platens have resulted in many serious accidents, including a number of fatalities. The main dangers are hand injury due to late feeding or taking out when the machine is in continuous (timer controlled dwell) operation, and body trapping due to accidental operation of the platen while making ready or clearing waste.

All electro-magnetic and electro-pneumatic machines should have:

- a U-shaped trip guard which closely surrounds the platen to within 12 mm on three sides;

- a trip bar or pressure-sensitive edge on the front edge of the moving platen;

- additional side guarding in the form of 1 m wide pressure-sensitive mats extending 250 mm beyond the back edge of the fixed platen or fixed/interlocked side tables;

- a control system and guarding circuits suitable for a high-risk application, eg dual-circuit cross-monitored.

A rise and fall guard may be provided on the front edge of older platen machines to ensure the minimum gap is maintained between the moving platen and the trip guard.

Where timer-controlled operation or a 'dwell' device is fitted, the 'dwell' period must not exceed 12 seconds. A maximum of 6 seconds dwell should be used for most operations.

The safe operation of hand-fed platens is critically dependent on their condition in use - deterioration of the safeguards will put the operator at significant risk. You need to ensure that regular inspections are carried out by a competent person at least annually to comply with regulation 6(2) of PUWER 98 (see Chapter 8).

Machines with mechanical (positive) clutches

These machines cannot be provided with all of the safeguards detailed under 'Hand-fed platens used for cutting and creasing' unless they are completely refurbished and provided with a suitable electro-magnetic clutch/brake unit. You should plan to upgrade or replace these old machines.

Some machines were fitted with a treadle conversion kit to disconnect the foot pedal from the clutch on operation of the U-shaped trip, preventing accidental operation. However, this measure was difficult to maintain and was not enough on its own.

Maintenance of hand-fed platen guards

The safeguards on all hand-fed platens need to be checked and tested on a daily or shift basis. Both of the tests outlined below should be carried out by properly trained operators to ensure that proper performance of the U-shaped trip is maintained.

Testing should also be done periodically by a member of management or an engineer. All tests should be recorded and all records held.

Test 1

The actual tripping point should be tested by turning the machine over by hand. (This may not be feasible on larger machines.) When operated, the trip device should ensure a gap of no less than 175 mm is maintained between the edge of the platen and the forme. On machines with a travel of less than 350 mm, tripping must occur not later than half way in the travel.

Test 2

Test 2 should be carried out when the machine is cold as well as when it is warmed up. The operator should carry out the tests but only following proper and careful instruction. A suitable test piece would be a 12 mm cardboard tube.

The stopping effect of the trip device should be tested with the machine running. The platen should come to rest no less than 90 mm from the forme, or on machines where the tripping distance may be less than 175 mm, no less than 65 mm.

Figure 40 *Testing a hand-fed platen*

ACCIDENTS

The operator of a Rabolini mechanical clutch hand-fed platen had his fingers from both hands amputated when he was clearing out stops. He inadvertently stood on the foot pedal, causing the machine to stroke and override the U-shaped trip.

Two brothers were seriously injured while removing the forme from a large Strumber platen. The U-shaped trip had been pushed into the rear position but the platen had not been isolated. Working on either side of the machine, the forme was supported with their hands between the platens while the securing screws were undone. Another employee then inadvertently operated the partially shrouded foot pedal, causing the platen to stroke. He immediately operated the sensitive edge but not before both brothers were trapped. Investigation revealed that the U-shaped trip had been provided with a single positively operating position switch which was ineffective because the grub screw securing the cam was loose. No side guards had been provided and no guard checking was being done.

Label punching machines

Where regular access is required for manual feeding, make sure that the feed opening for the material to be punched is safeguarded by an interlocked guard or photoelectric device.

Discharge openings should be designed in accordance with the reach distances specified in BS EN 294: 1992 *Safety of machinery. Safety distances to prevent danger zones being reached by the upper limbs.*

On new machines, when feeding the material requires regular and routine access to the danger point, the safety-related parts of the hydraulic/pneumatic control system should satisfy Category 3, and the safety-related parts of the electric/electronic system Category 4, of BS EN 954-1 *Safety of machinery. Safety related parts of control systems.* Electrosensitive protective devices should satisfy the requirements of Type 4 of BS EN 61496-1 and BS EN 61496-2 *Safety of machinery. Electro-sensitive protective equipment. General requirements and tests.*

Round cornering machines

Make sure that access to the trimming knife or saw is prevented by an adjustable transparent guard and that the cutting operation can only start once the material has been fed using a presence-sensing device. Operation of the cutters must be under the control of a hold-to-run device, which can be either hand- or foot-operated.

Fixed or interlocked guards should be provided at the rear and on both sides of the machine.

Folder gluer machines used in box making

This section covers smaller folder gluers used for cardboard box making; it does not cover corrugated carton manufacture. The main danger points on smaller machines are rotating shafts, in-running nips and traps caused by parts moving close to each other. Guarding may comprise individual fixed guards at each nip point, enclosing interlocked guards or photoelectric guards.

Power-driven shafts should be safeguarded by self-adjusting telescopic guards.

If automatic format setting is power-driven, hold-to-run control or a maximum setting speed of 0.5 m/min should be provided.

On modern machines, check with your supplier that the following standards have been achieved:

Feeder

- In-running nips at the feed/pull rolls should be safeguarded by fixed guards such as 'cheek plates'.

- The clearance between the lower edge of the moveable side lay and the feeding belt should be no more than 6 mm. Further movement of the side lay should not be possible unless residual pile monitoring is provided.

Folding and gluing section

- Safeguard in-running nips between the upper and lower roller tracks or folding belt by ensuring that the first roller allows 25 mm deflection and the remainder of the rollers have fixed guards on both sides.

- Raising and lowering of roller tracks under power should only be possible under hold-to-run control.

- Guard the traps created by folding hooks using fixed or interlocked guards.

- Make sure that the in-running nip between the glue applicator and blank is safeguarded; this is often achieved by the position of the gluing unit itself.

Folding belt

- The nips between this belt and pulleys should be guarded by fixed guards. The nips between the belt and hold-down rolls should be guarded by rolls which have a minimum 25 mm deflection, fixed or interlocking guards or photoelectric devices at least 850 mm from the trapping point.

Pressing section

- Safeguard the nip between the upper and lower pressing belt by limiting the pressing force to 500 newtons and ensuring a deflection of at least 120 mm by off-setting the upper and lower pulleys. Nips between the pressure rollers and the belt itself should be safeguarded by fixed guards or the rollers allowing a 120 mm deflection under a 100 newtons contact force.

Bindery

Handwork

Guards are required on edge-gumming machines with nipping rollers and on the in-feed belts of edge stripping machines. Some machines used in metal comb (spiro) binding work can be hazardous - guards on the powered bar or platen of the machines which close the comb must be properly adjusted and kept in position.

Adhesive (perfect) binding

The hazardous parts associated with the opening/closing and indexing of book clamps on adhesive binding machines should be guarded. This can often be achieved by all-enclosing interlocked guarding, though additional localised fixed and trip devices may be necessary at hand-feeding stations.

The milling cutter needs to be well guarded, typically by an interlocked all-enclosing guard and a self-adjusting/adjustable local guard. You can deal with cutter rundown time by using braked motors or guard locking. Minimise risks from hot melt adhesives by providing temperature control with limit monitoring together with suitable screens or covers and remote methods for refilling the adhesive. Provide extraction to control fume.

Machines using polyurethane hot melt glues should be provided with local exhaust ventilation to control isocyanate exposure (see Chapter 4).

Where the cover hopper is hand-fed, the separating elements should be designed to prevent traps and residual pile monitoring provided. Automatically fed machines should be provided with tunnel guards at least 550 mm long.

Access to traps caused by the movement of book carriages at the delivery should be prevented by tunnel guards at least 550 mm long.

Make-ready operations may require interlocked guards to be opened. Where this is necessary, a hold-to-run control should be provided at the slowest speed possible. Also, such operation should only be possible if the interlocked guards for danger zones outside the view of the operator are closed. If manual feeding is needed during set up, the hold-to-run speed of the binder must be limited to a maximum of 10 m/min whenever the interlocked guards are open.

Stand-alone stitching machines

Power-operated stitching machines should have a guard for the stitching head to prevent access when the work is in place. Guards designed for flat stitching are not effective during saddle stitching. Either two separate guards should be provided or, alternatively, reversible guards (often supplied by the manufacturer) should be used. Reversible guards are designed to be turned and secured in position depending on the type of stitching being carried out. Operators should be trained to use guards correctly.

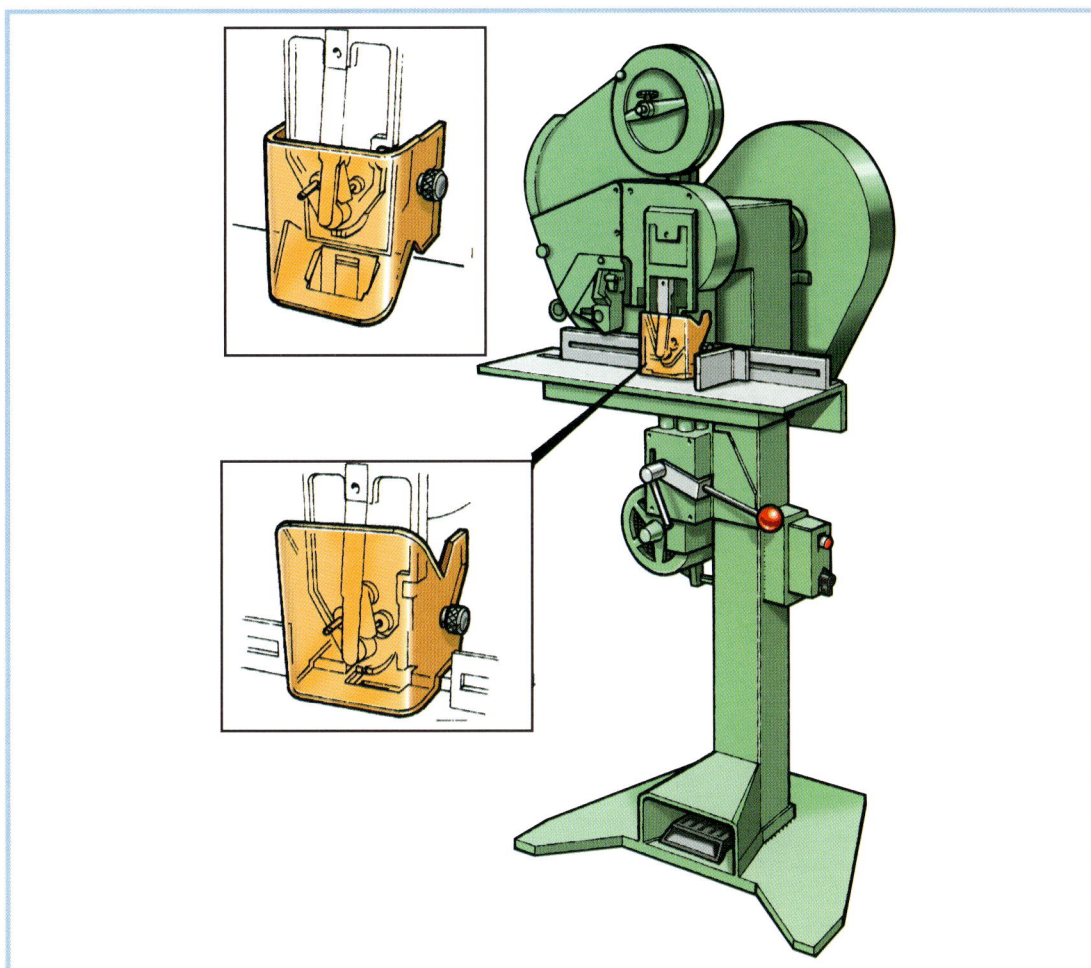

Figure 41 Guards for flat and saddle stitching

Gatherering, stitching and trimming

Serious accidents have resulted at gatherer-stitcher-trimmers (GSTs), collator-stitcher-trimmers and gang-stitcher-trimmers, particularly through contact with the trimmer knives and the incorrect operation of wander lead controls.

Gathering

Fixed and interlocked guards should be provided for hazardous parts of the gatherer/feed stations. Interlocked guards normally take the form of hinged perspex lift-up guards, either for individual feed stations, or as a single guard covering all the feed stations. Interlocking is normally achieved through the use of positively operating cam switches. Users need to carry out regular guard checks to ensure safety is maintained.

Under no circumstances should interlock switches be removed or defeated.

A single guard covering all feed stations can easily be rendered ineffective if only a single cam switch is provided and this moves out of alignment. It is then possible that the machine can be operated with the guard raised. In such circumstances, upgrading to provide a second cam switch operating in the opposite mode, mounted by the side of the original switch, would achieve a higher standard of safety.

Access should not be possible through or around guards to hazardous parts. BS EN 294: 1992 *Safety of machinery. Safety distances to prevent danger zones being reached by the upper limbs* should be applied.

Figure 42 *Fixed and interlocked guards should be provided for all dangerous parts of GSTs*

Stitching

Fixed and/or interlocked guards should be provided for hazardous parts associated with the stitcher section including the stitching heads and calliper roll. Guarding may take the form of a single hinged perspex guard fitted with a single cam-operated interlock switch. Any interlock switch should operate in the positive mode. Access should not be possible through or around guards to hazardous parts.

Trimming

Enclosing guards should be interlocked by means of positively acting interlock switches. The switches will normally be cam-operated. Care must be taken to ensure that the cams do not move out of adjustment - upgrading as outlined above may be appropriate. Regular guard checking is recommended. Opening of the guards while the blades are in motion must stop hazardous movement before a hand can reach a danger point.

Fixed guarding is usually not a suitable alternative to interlocked guards because of the need for frequent access.

Openings in the guards, including feed and delivery openings, should not allow access to hazardous parts. Where access is found to be possible through the delivery or other openings, guarding should be upgraded to prevent access.

Transmission machinery should be securely fenced. Standards for fixed or interlocked guarding should take account of the frequency of access. Machines should be designed so access is not required to hazardous transmission machinery on a frequent basis.

Precautions should be taken to prevent risks from lifting hinged guards falling under gravity.

Setting and adjustment of GSTs

Local two-hand hold-to-run controls or a two-hand hold-to-run wander lead can be provided which allow operation of the GST with one guard open. Single-button controls are not acceptable. Two-hand-controls should meet the following conditions:

- They should require simultaneous operation in line with BS EN 60204-1: 1993 *Safety of machinery. Electrical equipment of machines. Specification for general requirements* and be suitably positioned to prevent spanning by one hand. Controls that fail to meet this standard should be upgraded.

- With the gatherer/feeder station or the stitcher guard open (but not the trimmer guard) the machine may, in exceptional circumstances, run at speeds of more than 10 m/min although the speed should be set as low as possible.

- Setting, maintenance and knife change operations with the trimmer guards open should be a one-person operation carried out by a trained operator who should be in control of any inch or pendant controls. Accidents have occurred when two operators have been working together and one has operated the wander lead while the other has had their hands in the trimmer section (see 'Three knife trimmers' earlier in this chapter).

Book sewing

Automatic/semi-automatic machines should be provided with a combination of fixed and interlocked guards to prevent access to hazardous parts. Fit hand-fed machines with adequate trip guards to guard the sewing heads. These guards should be effective during threading up and normal running.

Signature presses

Make sure that the trap between the moving press plate and material supply and the intermediate plate are safeguarded using a hold-to-run control.

Book presses

Safeguard any trap between the moveable and fixed pressing plates or the forming bar with a trip device. The movement of the trip should be greater than the stopping distance of the pressing plate.

On presses where several pressing plates can be moved independently, a guard should be provided between the plates to prevent a shear trap.

The gap between the guard and the pressing plate should not exceed 6 mm.

Backlining and headbanding

Where book signatures are transported between vertically mounted conveyors, guard feed-side in-running nips with tunnel guards of at least 550 mm. Glue rollers and any hot melt parts should be safeguarded with interlocked guards and warning signs affixed. The gauze cutting knife should be safeguarded by fixed guards and the in-running nips of the gauze unwinding section by fixed nip bars. Access to hazardous parts at the head banding section and counter pressure sections should be prevented by fixed or interlocking guards.

Book nipping (smashing)

Safety on hand-fed book nipping or smashing machines can only be achieved by providing guarding and safe systems of work. You need to fit adjustable access-limiting guards.

On horizontally moving platens where the book is fed from the top, a spring-loaded guard can be used where the back of the book displaces the guard so that it covers the gap between the book and the platen. Alternatively, letterbox-type guards which have a slot opening of the same dimensions as the book can be used, but the platen side of the guard must overlap the front edge of the platen.

On vertically moving platen machines, adjustable plates should be fitted which are adjusted to the book size for each production run. These will prevent operators from leaving their fingers on the upper surface of the book. The outside edge of the plate should extend beyond the platen edge to prevent a secondary trap.

Rounding and backing

Automatic machines should be provided with a combination of fixed and interlocked guards to prevent access to hazardous parts such as in-running nips on the feed and delivery belts, traps on the tipping section, traps and hot parts on the preheater section, and traps and shear points on the preforming, rounding and backing section.

On hand-fed machines, access is required to feed the book to the feed/rounding rollers but must be prevented during powered movement. You can prevent access to the shear trap by using sequential two-hand controls and interlock guarding.

Case making and casing-in

On most types of case-making and casing-in machines, the hazardous parts can be adequately guarded by providing all-enclosing guards interlocked to the machine's drive. The feed and discharge parts of the machines should be outside the guarded area, with openings designed to meet the reach distance requirements of BS EN 294: 1992 *Safety of machinery. Safety distances to prevent danger zones being reached by the upper limbs*.

Access to in-running nips and traps between fixed and moving parts need to be prevented on case making machines, especially the traps between the rotating picker head and adjacent fixed parts on older machines. For these machines, a combination of fixed and interlocked guards fitted to the outside edge of the machine frame are suitable. Where cover cloth is hand-fed to a cylinder, any in-running nips should be guarded.

On casing-in machines, hazardous parts include in-running nips at the cover bending section, crushing and nip points and hot machine parts at the heated forming section, crushing points at the casing-in section, in-running nips at the gluing section and in-running nips at the counter-pressure section. Pictograms warning of hot parts should be provided in the vicinity of heated book-cover crease-forming devices which are accessible once the interlocking guards have been opened.

At the book signature feed and delivery points, tunnel guards at least 550 mm long should be provided to prevent contact with traps between the book transport fingers and fixed parts of the machine.

Traps on the book cover feeder caused by separating elements and transport devices should be prevented by design or where blanks are fed from the bottom of the pile, safeguarding can be achieved by residual pile monitoring.

Chapter 5

· ·

Process safety

Blocking machines

The trap between the closing platens (one of which is often heated) on foil blocking machines is very hazardous and must be guarded. On automatic machines this can be achieved by the provision of all-enclosing interlocked guards.

On hand-fed up-stroking or down-stroking machines, the rear and sides of the platens can be guarded by fixed/interlocked guards. The front feed table should be provided with an adjustable (often rod type) pivoting guard, which trips if the bottom of the guard is pushed in, or a trip device and simultaneous two-hand hold-to-run controls.

Book production lines

Make sure that the in-running nips on the feed and delivery conveyor belts are safeguarded using in-fill blocks.

Traps created by separating elements on the book cover feeder should be safeguarded.

Check that fixed or interlocked guards have been provided to prevent access to hazardous parts at:

- the preheater. Interlocked guards should be supplemented by suitable pictograms warning of hot parts. Once interlocked guards are opened, the preheater should only operate under hold-to-run control;

- the back rounding and pressing sections;

- the glue sections. Glue replenishment should be possible during the production run without the need to open guards. Hot melt pans should have temperature control and limit temperature monitoring;

- the knife and gauze clamps. Nip bars should be fitted at any remaining in-running nips at gauze unwinding rollers once the interlocked guard has been opened;

- the head banding and backlining section. Nip bars should be fitted at any remaining in-running nips at head banding unwinding rollers once the interlocked guard has been opened;

- the cover bending and rounding sections;

- the casing-in section.

After opening any interlocked guards, it should only be possible to operate the line with a limited inch of 75 mm or a hold-to-run maximum crawl speed of 5 m/min. If a higher crawl speed is required, this should only be possible using a combination of two-hand control and ensuring:

- all other interlocking guards are closed;

- a selector switch for this operation has been provided; and

- the hold-to-run speed is the slowest possible and does not exceed a maximum of 20 m/min.

Check that emergency stop buttons are provided at least on each main control panel. Where overall vision of the production line is restricted, make sure a pre-start warning device has been provided.

Paper drills

The stroke of manually fed paper drills should be under hold-to-run control and a workpiece support provided. When the hold-to-run control is released, the drill or workpiece should return to its start position.

Make sure the shatter and trapping hazards on drills and chuck jaws are safeguarded by a fixed or interlocked guard.

Multi-drill machines should have fixed or interlocking guards to prevent contact with the rotating chuck jaws. Make sure the distance between the workpiece support or guard and chuck jaw is at least 25 mm.

ACCIDENTS

Book sewing

An experienced operator crushed their index finger between the bottom platen and the book as the top platen compressed the book. No guarding had been provided.

An operator amputated the tips of two fingers while pushing books through the continuously stroking press.

ACCIDENTS

Rounding and backing machines

An employee crushed his hand between the rounding rollers and backing jaw when he inadvertently started the machine cycle.

An operator bruised and lacerated his finger in the pressing plate of a rounding machine. A guard was provided but not used.

Finishing machines

Coaters

Check:

- with your supplier, where routine and regular access is required to danger points, that the safeguards are of the right integrity (the safety-related parts of the hydraulic/pneumatic control system satisfy at least Category 3 of BS EN 954-1: 1997 *Safety of machinery. Safety related parts of control systems*, and the safety-related parts of the electric/electronic control system satisfy at least Category 4);

- where overall vision of the coater is restricted, a pre-start warning device has been provided;

- web-threading devices are provided for webbing up.

Reel unwinding and rewinding units need to be safeguarded (see 'Reel unwinds and rewinds' earlier in this chapter).

Ensure that the following in-running nips are safeguarded:

- between the guide rollers and guide rollers/fixed machine parts by ensuring a minimum separation of 120 mm, or with fixed/interlocked guards or nip bars;

- at the dosing gap with fixed/interlocked guards or nip bars;

- between the coating roller and cooling roller/coating roller with fixed/interlocked guards;

- at the Teflon belt (where hot melt polyethylene is being used) with fixed/interlocked guards.

Prevent contact with parts associated with hot melt material using fixed guards.

The traversing movement of the coating rollers or coating roller and cooling roller should be safeguarded by means of a hold-to-run speed of 5 m/min or interlocked guards.

Accessible in-running nips between the coated, tear-resistant web and guide rollers where there is a wrapping angle of 45° or more should be protected by fixed guards.

For precautions relating to fire risk on coaters, see earlier in this chapter.

Continuous flow dryers

Check with your supplier that the dryer meets the requirements of BS EN 1539: 2000 *Dryers and ovens in which flammable substances are released. Safety requirements* if the coating material you use generates flammable substances.

It is important that the trap created when closing the upper and lower parts of the dryer is safeguarded using a hold-to-run control. Automatic closing should only be possible for the last 300 mm of movement and safeguarded by trip bars.

Ignition of the web in the dryer should be prevented using an air wiper/cushioned curtain to keep the web at an adequate distance from the heat source.

If hydraulic or pneumatic cylinders are provided for opening the dryer, make sure these have safety-rated check valves which can be overridden. In addition, a mechanical scotch should be inserted during inspection work.

Ensure emergency stop buttons are provided at each operator position.

Laminators with adhesive foil

Reel unwinding and rewinding units need to be safeguarded (see 'Reel unwinds and rewinds' earlier in this chapter).

Make sure the following in-running nips are safeguarded:

- at feed and delivery belts by infilling between the belt and roller;

- between guide rollers and guide rollers/fixed machine parts by ensuring a minimum separation of 120 mm, or with fixed/interlocked guards or nip bars;

- accessible nips between the laminated, tear-resistant web and guide rollers where there is a wrapping angle of 45° or more by fixed or interlocked guards;

- at the laminating roller using fixed or interlocked guards. If the material thickness exceeds 18 mm, the opening should not be more than 30 mm and the safety distance at least 200 mm.

The traversing movement of the laminating rollers for make-ready and cleaning should be safeguarded by means of a hold-to-run speed of 5 m/min or interlocked guards.

In hot foiling work, prevent contact with the lamination rollers by using fixed guards.

Ensure cutting devices are safeguarded by interlocking guards.

Check that emergency stop buttons are provided at least on each main control panel.

Laminators with glue application

Where isocyanate-containing adhesives are used, control of employees' exposure is crucial. See Chapter 4 'Use of isocyanates' and the booklet *Safe use of isocyanates in printing and laminating*.

On new machines, where routine and regular access is required to danger points, check with your supplier that the safety-related parts of the hydraulic/pneumatic control system satisfy at least Category 3 of BS EN 954-1: 1997 *Safety of machinery. Safety related parts of control systems*, and the safety-related parts of the electric/electronic control system satisfy at least Category 4.

Where overall vision of the laminator is restricted, make sure a pre-start warning device has been provided.

Web-threading devices should be provided for webbing up.

Reel unwinding and rewinding units need to be safeguarded (see 'Reel unwinds and rewinds' earlier in this chapter).

The feeder and delivery units need to be properly designed and safeguarded (see 'Pile lifting and lowering devices' earlier in this chapter).

Check that the following in-running nips have been safeguarded:

- on belts using fixed or interlocked guards;

- between guide rollers and guide rollers/fixed machine parts by ensuring a minimum separation of 120 mm, or with fixed/interlocked guards or nip bars;

- accessible nips between the laminated, tear-resistant web and guide rollers where there is a wrapping angle of 45° or more by fixed or interlocked guards;

- on the sheet feed rolls by ensuring that the rolls have a displacement of at least 25 mm or roller contact is by their own weight;

- at the glue rollers and on the dosing gap using interlocked guards;

- between the laminating rollers using fixed or interlocked guards. If the material thickness exceeds 18 mm, the opening should not be more than 30 mm and the safety distance at least 200 mm;

- between pressing rollers and guide rollers and pressing belt by fixed guards, or by ensuring rollers are held in position by their own weight and have a displacement of at least 120 mm;

- between the upper and lower pressing belts at the infeed point. Use either fixed or interlocked guards with a safety distance of at least 850 mm from an opening aperture of at least 120 mm to the point where there is at least 10 mm between the belts, or pressing rollers capable of displacement to create a gap of 120 mm and with a maximum pressing force of 200 newtons at the 850 mm point.

Make sure rotary knives are fully enclosed using fixed guards which preferably do not have to be removed for tool change.

Check that the opening and closing movement of the laminating rollers is safeguarded if the travel path is more than 6 mm by means of hold-to-run control not exceeding 5 m/min or interlocking guards.

Check that danger points on the sheeter are not accessible by means of interlocked or fixed guards.

Make sure that the crushing point between the package stop and transport belt is safeguarded with interlocked or fixed guards if the maximum closing force exceeds 200 newtons.

Ensure that shearing points between the turning belt and transport belts are safeguarded with fixed guards.

See Chapter 7 for fire precautions relating to laminators.

Baling machines

Machines used for baling waste paper and board have caused fatal accidents and amputation injuries. Large machines typically consist of a horizontal or vertical baling chamber which is conveyor fed. These machines will have an automatic or semi-automatic bale wiring mechanism, incorporating wiring needles that pass through slots in the face of the baling ram.

Fatal accidents have occurred when people have fallen from the conveyor into the chamber while the baler is in operation, for example when following an unsafe system of work for clearing blockages, and when they have gained access to the area behind the ram in its forward position for running repairs, and the ram has retracted.

Amputation injuries have been caused by people gaining access to traps created by moving parts such as the ram, wire tying mechanism or wiring needles. On large machines, distributors may also constitute a danger.

At small compactors there may not be a high risk of fatality, but precautions will be needed

to prevent amputations, crushing and similar major injuries.

A high standard of initial safeguarding is needed at all machines, combined with regular checks on the operation of the safety devices and maintenance. Follow safe systems of work to deal with occurrences such as blockages, and maintenance activities. Such systems should include lock-off isolation procedures for both conveyor and baler.

Initial safeguards will include a high standard of fixed and interlocked guarding, emergency stops and trip wires, fixed ladders (with hoops as appropriate) and working platforms for access to high levels of the machine.

Waste is usually loaded onto the conveyor using vehicles. Guard the edge of the conveyor or pit as far as possible and make the exposed area for loading clearly identifiable, for example by using robust overhead indicators.

Access onto conveyors should be strictly controlled by a safe system of work incorporating an effective isolation procedure. The means of electrical isolation should be readily accessible and lockable. It must isolate both the conveyor and the baling machine.

Fit conveyors with emergency stop devices which stop both the conveyor and the baling mechanism. Emergency stop buttons should be readily accessible from all operating stations. Emergency stop buttons or trip wires should also be provided on the inclined section of the conveyor. They can either be fitted to run up the side (preferably on both sides) or they can be positioned like goal-posts horizontally across the conveyor and hung with vertical cords for ease of operation. Personal detection systems can be used as well as but not as an alternative to safeguards.

If frequent blockages occur in the hopper above the baler then a permanent platform (at least 1.1 m below the top of the hopper) with a fixed access ladder should be provided. If it is not possible to provide a fixed access platform, harnesses with anchorage points may be necessary in addition to the safe system of work and isolation procedure described above.

*F**igure 43** An unacceptable baling press*

ACCIDENTS

An operator was attempting to clear a blockage in a baler. Paper was fed automatically from the shredder to the baler. When the paper level reached a magic eye the ram operated. The operator had climbed into the chute bolted to the baler. When the baler operated, his foot was badly crushed by the ram.

An employee was crushed to death when he became trapped by the returning ram of a large horizontal paper baling machine. He had gained access to the baling chamber via the rear of the ejector ram when the ram was in the forward position. The machine had not been isolated and the ram retracted.

An employee was killed when he fell into the baling chamber and covered the magic eye which activated the ram. The employee had been clearing a blockage at the top end of the conveyor. The machine had not been isolated.

Effectively guard all openings (even small ones allowing hand access) in the vicinity of the baling chamber and the compactor/ejector ram. Access panels may be fixed in position if infrequent access is required and this should be made through a permit-to-work system incorporating an isolation procedure.

Where access is required more frequently, an interlocked guard should be provided. The standard of the interlocking required depends on the nature of the risk. If head or body access is possible then interlocking to a high standard will be required, for example, guard-inhibited power interlocking or a key exchange system. Alternatively, use a dual-channel system with interlocks and cross-monitoring.

On hydraulic machines, dual-channel interlocking can use a different control medium for each channel, ie one hydraulic and one electric. Where whole-body access is possible, provide protection to prevent inadvertent closing of the guard panel/door while a person is inside the machine. Key exchange systems provide this protection. An equivalent standard of protection will be needed if other types of interlocking are used. Where head or body access is not possible, interlocking by means of a single positively interlocked switch may be acceptable as long as it is properly maintained.

Access to the moving parts of the needles and wire-tying mechanism should be prevented by using fixed or interlocked guarding according to the principles described in the previous paragraphs. Needles will often pass vertically through the bale, with an access pit under the machine, but they may also be horizontal. If people have to work under the needles during maintenance, mechanical scotches should be provided to hold the needles in a safe position.

Maintenance is very important because of the heavy duty environment. Not only is it essential to ensure that safety switches/devices are regularly checked, but preventive maintenance on the equipment is important to reduce the need for operator intervention.

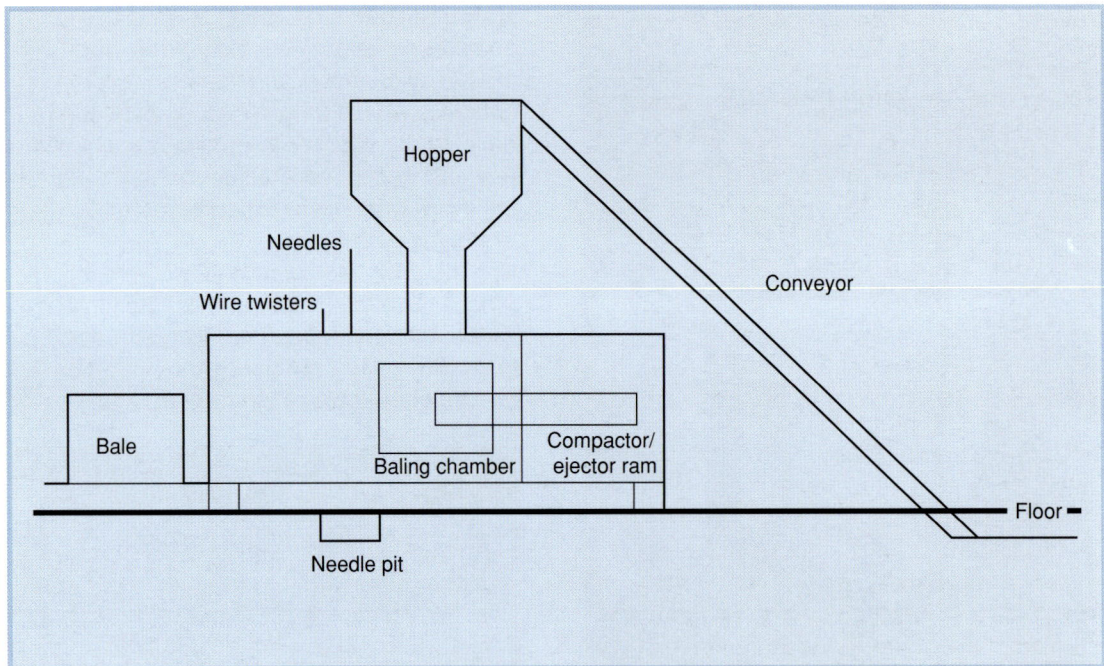

Figure 44 *Simplified diagram of a baling machine*

Shredders

Machines can be hand-fed either on vertical or horizontal planes. Horizontally fed machines may have short feed-side conveyors to aid the transfer of material to the cutters. Some machines may have a second conveyor to deliver the shreddings at the outrun.

Feed-side access to rotary cutters

Access to the cutting rollers should be prevented by suitable distance guarding in line with BS EN 294: 1992 *Safety of machinery. Safety distances to prevent danger zones being reached by the upper limbs.*

For the smallest office-based machines, this can be done by using narrow feed slots (typically narrowing to no more than 4 to 6 mm). The slots should not be in a direct vertical line with the in-running nip created by the contra-rotating cutters because of entanglement hazards to operators' hair, jewellery or clothing. Where residual risks remain, suitable warning labels should be placed in prominent positions to alert operators of the potential hazard.

Where waste paper etc is fed into a shredder via a top-feed chute, the chute should extend far enough to prevent the operator's hand or arm accessing the rotating cutters through the chute. You can also use hinged interlocked flaps fitted with single positively operating cam switches. Opening of the flaps while the cutters are in motion should stop hazardous movement before a hand can reach the hazardous parts.

Feed chutes should be fixed in position or interlocked using positively operating switches which stop movement of the cutters before access can be gained. The type and method of interlocking should take account of cutter rundown times where applicable. Consider guard locking for machines with long cutter rundown times.

Where machines are fed horizontally using feed tables (often fitted with small integral feed conveyors), the feed table should act as a distance guard. Suitable side panelling and/or fixed or interlocked tunnel guarding should be provided to prevent access to hazardous parts from the sides of the feed table. Safety reach distances should comply with BS EN 294: 1992. Where hinged sections are provided in the guarding arrangements, these should be interlocked using positively operating interlock switches.

Outrun access to rotary cutters

Shredding machines are usually provided with a reversing drive for the rotary cutters to aid blockage removal. The reverse facility results in the otherwise out-running nips at the delivery side of the cutters becoming hazardous in-running nips. Access to these hazardous parts while they are in motion should be prevented by means of localised fixed guarding (found on some smaller machines, particularly vertically fed machines); suitable tunnel guards (fixed or interlocked); or interlocked guards. Localised fixed guards or tunnel guards should comply with BS EN 294: 1992 safety reach distances.

In exceptional circumstances reversal by means of a two-hand hold-to-run control placed out of reach of hazardous parts may be acceptable for strictly solo operating practices. Such controls should be designed to provide limited inch movement only. The controls should require simultaneous operation and comply with BS EN 60204: 1993 *Safety of machinery. Electrical equipment of machines. Specification for general requirements*.

Two-hand-controls are not considered acceptable if the cutters are capable of automatic reverse running. Some machines may be fitted with over current sensors which automatically reverse the direction of the cutters (and of the feed table conveyor) if the machine is electrically overloaded. After about five seconds of reverse motion, the machine switches itself off. Provide fixed or interlocked guarding where there is a possibility of automatic reversal.

Where there are hazards after interruption of the power supply, consider interlocking methods incorporating braking and/or guard locking, for example where cutters or other hazardous parts have long rundown times. Systems should be designed to incorporate a device to either cause the hazard to be eliminated as the guard is opened (by applying a brake), or prevent the guard from being opened until the risk of injury from the hazard has passed (guard locking).

Where shredders are combined with integral baling mechanisms, any access door provided at the rear of the shredder/top of the baler should be interlocked using at least one positively operating interlock switch which prevents movement of both the shredding cutters and the baling ram as soon as the access door is opened. Hydraulic or pneumatic operated baling rams should block and dump their supply on operation of the interlock.

Provide a trip mechanism in the form of tripped access flaps or a full-length trip bar as well as distance guarding where there is any possibility of an operator becoming entangled and dragged towards the cutter blade.

ACCIDENTS

An operator was feeding a paper shredder with old newspapers when her finger touched blades through an opening in the machine. The feed opening had not been restricted.

An operator severed the tip of an index finger in the cutters of a paper shredder while checking for a fault. A fixed guard had been removed from over the cutting head. Closing the electrically interlocked door of the waste sack bin had activated the cutters.

An operator lost parts of three fingers when they were sheared off by one of the compacting rams on a shredder baler machine which makes shredded newspaper into bales for animal bedding. Blockages on the machine were a regular occurrence and were frequently cleared by inserting an arm through a slot in the machinery housing while the rams were in motion. No fixed or interlocked guard was in place before the accident.

Acquiring machinery and other work equipment

The law

Supply of Machinery (Safety) Regulations 1992 (amended 1994)

These Regulations impose duties on the manufacturers, suppliers and importers of new machinery and are intended to provide protection for the users of the equipment as machinery which complies with these Regulations should be safe.

The requirements of the Regulations were voluntary for new and second-hand machines from 1 January 1993 until 1 January 1995 (if they were not followed the machinery still needed to comply with the health and safety provisions in force in the United Kingdom). The requirements of the Regulations became compulsory from 1 January 1995.

Duties on manufacturers or their responsible persons

- Ensuring that the machinery or safety component satisfies the relevant essential health and safety requirements (EHSRs).

- Ensuring that an appropriate conformity assessment procedure has been carried out in accordance with the Regulations.

- Ensuring that the machinery or safety component has been issued with either a Declaration of Conformity or a Declaration of Incorporation.

- Ensuring that the machinery or safety component has been 'CE' marked to show that it satisfies the EHSRs (unless it is has a Declaration of Incorporation and is going to be incorporated into a machine or assembly of machines that will be 'CE' marked as a whole).

- Ensuring that the machinery or safety component is safe.

- Carrying out research and testing to determine that the machinery is capable of being erected and put into service safely.

Duties on suppliers (where the supplier is not the manufacturer or the manufacturer's appointed responsible person)

- Ensuring that the relevant machinery or safety component is safe.

Duties on users

- If you directly import any machinery (second-hand or new) from outside the European Economic Area, then the Regulations regard you as supplying the machinery to yourself and impose the duties of a supplier under the Regulations.

Examples of matters covered by the essential health and safety requirements include: principles of safety integrity; lighting; design of machinery to facilitate handling; safety and reliability of control systems; prevention of risks related to moving parts; requirements for guards and protective devices; protection from hazards (including temperature, electricity supply, static electricity, fire, explosion, noise, vibration, radiation and dusts); markings; and instructions.

Provision and Use of Work Equipment Regulations 1998 (PUWER 98)

Duties on users/employers

These Regulations apply to buying or hiring machinery. As an employer you must ensure that the work equipment you provide is suitable and safe for use.

These Regulations also require you to check that any equipment you acquire conforms to the relevant Community Directives, eg the Supply of Machinery Regulations.

For practical purposes, you can start by ensuring that:

- machinery supplied from 1 January 1995 comes with a copy of the manufacturer's Declaration of Conformity which states the manufacturer's name and address, the machine model and type etc;

- the machine complies with the essential health and safety requirements (EHSRs);

- the machine is accompanied by instructions for use and is 'CE' marked. Sometimes, if the machinery is going to be incorporated into other relevant machinery, eg at newspaper presses, it will come without CE marking and a Declaration of Conformity, in which case you should ask to see the manufacturer's Declaration of Incorporation. Once the equipment is assembled, the assembly as a whole will need to meet the EHSRs to be CE marked and you or the person assembling the plant will need to draw up a Declaration of Conformity.

Health and Safety at Work etc Act 1974, section 6

This section of the Act places duties on designers, manufacturers, importers and suppliers to ensure, so far as is reasonably practicable, that any articles for use at work are safe and without risks to health and are accompanied by adequate information for use.

Word of caution

When purchasing or hiring new or second-hand machinery and work equipment, take special care to ensure that any associated risks have been assessed and that you are complying with the law. You should check that any contract deals with health and safety and that there is no misunderstanding about the condition of the machine and its guards.

The law applies not only to guarding, but to other aspects which may affect health and safety, such as noise generated by machinery, solvent vapour emission, and protection against fire and explosion.

Situations may arise where 'CE' marked equipment is not entirely safe as the marking and declaration process is a self-certifying one and manufacturers or suppliers may have failed to fulfil their obligations under the Regulations.

It is your duty as an employer to make sure that machinery is safe before it is brought into use. Employers are obliged by law to carry out and act upon their own assessments of health and safety risks (see 'Planning and risk assessment' in Chapter 1). Assess both new and existing machinery and bring them up to required standards.

Chapter 6

ELECTRICITY
. . . .

See the 'References' section at the back of the book for details of publications which relate to ELECTRICITY

Relevant legislation

The Electricity at Work Regulations 1989 require precautions to be taken against the risk of death or injury from electricity at work. *The memorandum of guidance on the Electricity at Work Regulations 1989* (HSR25) has further information.

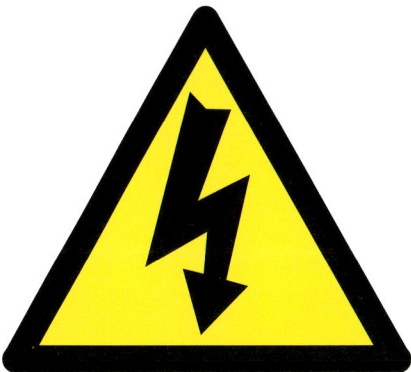

Electricity can kill, at normal mains voltage of 230 V ac and even at voltages considerably less than this. Each year about 1000 accidents at work involving electric shock or burns are reported to HSE, around 30 of which are fatal. Fires started by poor electrical installations can cause deaths and injuries. Explosions can be caused by electrical apparatus or static electricity igniting flammable vapours or dust.

General hazards and precautions

Check that:

- all electrical wiring is installed to a suitable standard by a competent person such as a qualified electrician. Poor workmanship can be dangerous and dangerous installations are illegal. (All new electrical work should be inspected and tested before being put into use.) BS 7671: 1992 *Requirements for electrical installations* gives guidance on suitable standards;

- power cables to machines are insulated and protected, eg sheathed and armoured or installed in conduit. All connections should be in good condition. Switches, fuses and circuit-breakers should be labelled to identify the circuits they serve;

- there is a switch or isolator near each (fixed) machine to cut off power in an emergency;

- plugs, sockets and fittings are adequately protected and suitable for the working environment;

- whenever practicable, flexible cables and wires do not trail on the floor. They are more liable to damage, and may cause a tripping hazard;

- flexible cables have a suitable plug with the flex firmly clamped to stop the wires (particularly the earth) pulling out of the terminals;

- wherever reasonably practicable, enough socket outlets should be provided for the number of appliances to be used at any one time. When this is not possible a fused extension lead with a multiway socket block can be used in appropriate locations;

- frayed and damaged cables are replaced completely. Join lengths in good condition only by using proper connectors or cable couplers - 'chocolate-block' connectors do not provide the strength or protection required for a joint in a cable and are not suitable for this purpose;

- access is prevented to electrical danger, eg by keeping isolator and fuse box covers closed, secured and, it is strongly recommended, locked, with the key held by a responsible person;

- fuses, circuit-breakers and other devices are correctly rated for the circuit they protect;

- home appliances such as fires, radios and kettles are not brought in for use at work;

- there are no overhead cables that could be accidentally struck in areas where lift trucks operate.

Particular hazards and precautions for printing

Some precautions relate to the special conditions to be found in printing. These include:

- not using portable fan heaters or hair dryers in dark rooms or in wet conditions - they are not designed for use in such environments and can cause electric shocks;

- making sure that the power to high-pressure water-jet machines is supplied through a 30 mA residual current circuit-breaker which is regularly tested by operation of its test button. This precaution will provide added protection against electrical shock;

- ensuring electrical equipment is of suitable explosion-protected construction if it is to be used in a potentially explosive atmosphere. Potentially explosive atmospheres may, for example, arise in solvent storage areas and in some process areas such as in the

vicinity of flexographic and gravure presses, and ink mixing areas. You may need specialist advice to choose the correct equipment. Low voltage equipment, eg 12 V, gives no protection against the risk of ignition in such environments.

Static electricity can also be a source of ignition in such environments. This is a particular problem in flexographic and gravure printing. Important precautions include:

- the use by operators of anti-static footwear to prevent the build-up of electrostatic charges which might cause a spark. Where this is a hazard, operators also need to avoid wearing clothing made of man-made fibre (this can have the additional advantage of reducing the severity of burns in the event of a fire);

- the use of closed metal containers when carrying flammable liquids such as solvents;

- the bonding and earthing of metalwork as necessary to prevent accumulation of static where flammable liquids such as solvents are transferred by pipe or poured.

See Chapter 7 for further advice on fire and explosion.

Inspection and maintenance

All electrical equipment, wiring installations (including battery sets), their connections (including fixed items of machinery) and portable electric tools must be maintained so far as is reasonably practicable to prevent danger. You will need to carry out inspection and testing to check the condition of the equipment, and follow this up with repair or replacement where necessary. The frequency of the inspection and testing will depend on the equipment you use and where you use it. You may find it helpful to keep records of inspection and testing.

Take suspect or faulty equipment out of use, label it 'DO NOT USE' and, where appropriate, remove the plug and keep the equipment secure until a competent person confirms that it is, or has been made safe to use. Make sure your employees know how to report any damage or defects they discover and who they should tell.

Don't overlook hired or borrowed electrical equipment or equpment such as floor polishers which may be used after the premises have closed. Check to ensure that any electrical equipment that contractors bring onto site is safe to use.

Check that residual current circuit-breakers work by operating the test button regularly, in accordance with the manufacturer's advice.

Anyone carrying out electrical work must be competent to do it safely. This may mean bringing in outside contractors. If you do need to use electrical contractors you should use those who belong to a recognised trade organisation which checks their work such as the National Inspection Council for Electrical Installation Contracting (NICEIC). Your own staff must also be competent if you do the work in-house.

If you do use electrical equipment in flammable atmospheres, make sure that special maintenance requirements for explosion-protected equipment have been written down and that someone with enough training is responsible for carrying out the work, and records that they have done so. The manufacturer of the equipment should be able to give you advice on this.

No one should be allowed to work on or near exposed live equipment. In exceptional circumstances live working may be permissible, but only if this can be done in full compliance with regulation 14 of the Electricity at Work Regulations 1989 and the person doing the work is competent to undertake the specific task(s) involved. If in doubt, ask your health and safety inspector or enforcing authority for advice.

Electric shock

Would you know what to do if someone received an electric shock? Knowing what to do should be part of your emergency procedures and first-aid arrangements. Think about displaying a copy of the 'Electric shock placard' which shows you what to do.

ACCIDENTS

A minder received an electric shock when he touched a metal table beside his machine. A damaged cable running along the floor was in contact with the table, making it electrically live. The man was off work for one week, but the accident could have had far more serious consequences.

A manager was killed while using a pressure washer. An electrical fault on the washer made its frame and lance live at 240 V. Earthing was inadequate and no residual current device was fitted in the supply.

A 16-year-old trainee printer received a 240 V electric shock and burns to his fingers when he touched a switch, the cover to which had been removed and not replaced.

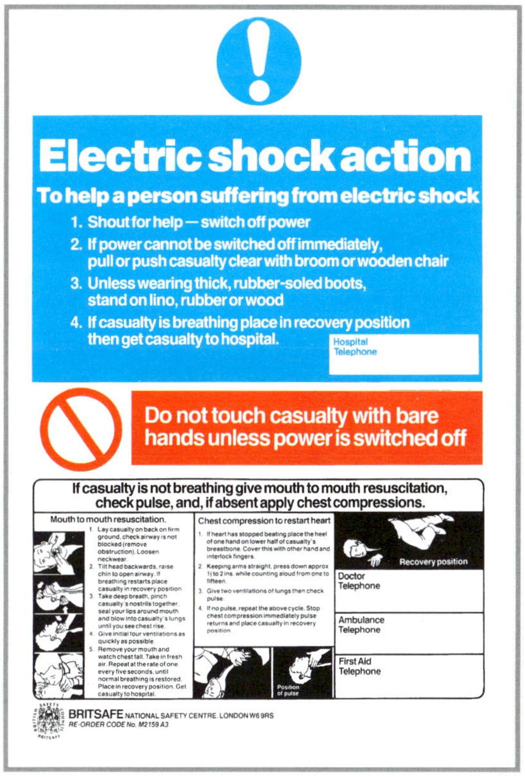

Figure 45 Electric shock placard

Chapter 7

FIRE AND EXPLOSION

See the 'References' section at the back of the book for details of publications which relate to FIRE AND EXPLOSION

Relevant legislation

Requirements to assess and control fire and explosion risks can be found in the following pieces of legislation:

- Health and Safety at Work etc Act 1974 (HSW Act)

- Management of Health and Safety at Work Regulations 1999

- Workplace (Health, Safety and Welfare) Regulations 1992

- Provision and Use of Work Equipment Regulations 1998 (PUWER 98)

- Supply of Machinery (Safety) Regulations 1992 (as amended)

- Chemicals (Hazard Information and Packaging for Supply) Regulations 1994 (CHIP)

- Highly Flammable Liquids and Liquefied Petroleum Gases Regulations 1972 (HFL&LPG) (to be replaced by Dangerous Substances and Explosive Atmospheres Regulations (DSEAR))

- Equipment and Protective Systems for Use in Potentially Explosive Atmospheres Regulations 1996

- Electricity at Work Regulations 1989

- Petroleum (Consolidation) Act 1928 (to be amended by DSEAR)

- Fire Precautions (Workplace) Regulations 1997 (as amended) (FPWR)

- Fire Precautions Act 1971

Several hundred fires occur every year in the printing industry. There have also been a number of explosions. In some incidents people have been killed or injured; in many others there has been extensive damage to buildings, equipment and materials.

Explosions can occur at dryers used in association with flexographic presses and when blanket washing on heat-set web offset presses (see BS EN 1539: 2000 *Dryers and ovens in which flammable substances are*

released - Safety requirements and pr EN 12753 *Thermal cleaning systems for exhaust gas from surface treatment equipment - Safety requirements)*. They occur when flammable substances, such as solvents, blanket wash etc are used or stored incorrectly, and the vapour forms an explosive mixture with air.

Risk assessment

The Management of Health and Safety at Work Regulations 1999 and The Fire

Precautions (Workplace) Regulations 1997 contain explicit risk assessment requirements in relation to fire safety covering both general fire precautions and process fire precautions.

Fire risk management

Management arrangements are needed to ensure that fire risks are adequately controlled. These should include arrangements to ensure that:

- the risk of fire occurring is reduced to the absolute minimum;

- the risk of fire spreading is minimised;

- adequate fire-detection and warning systems are in place;

- everyone is able to escape from the building quickly and safely.

It might be appropriate to designate a senior member of the management team to have specific responsibility for fire-risk management and staff training.

A thorough fire survey is likely to be necessary to properly assess the fire risks from materials and processes, the actions necessary to reduce the risk of fire occurring and arrangements that are needed in the event of fire breaking out. The action plan in Figure 47 deals with both identification and follow-up action. An example is given in Figure 46.

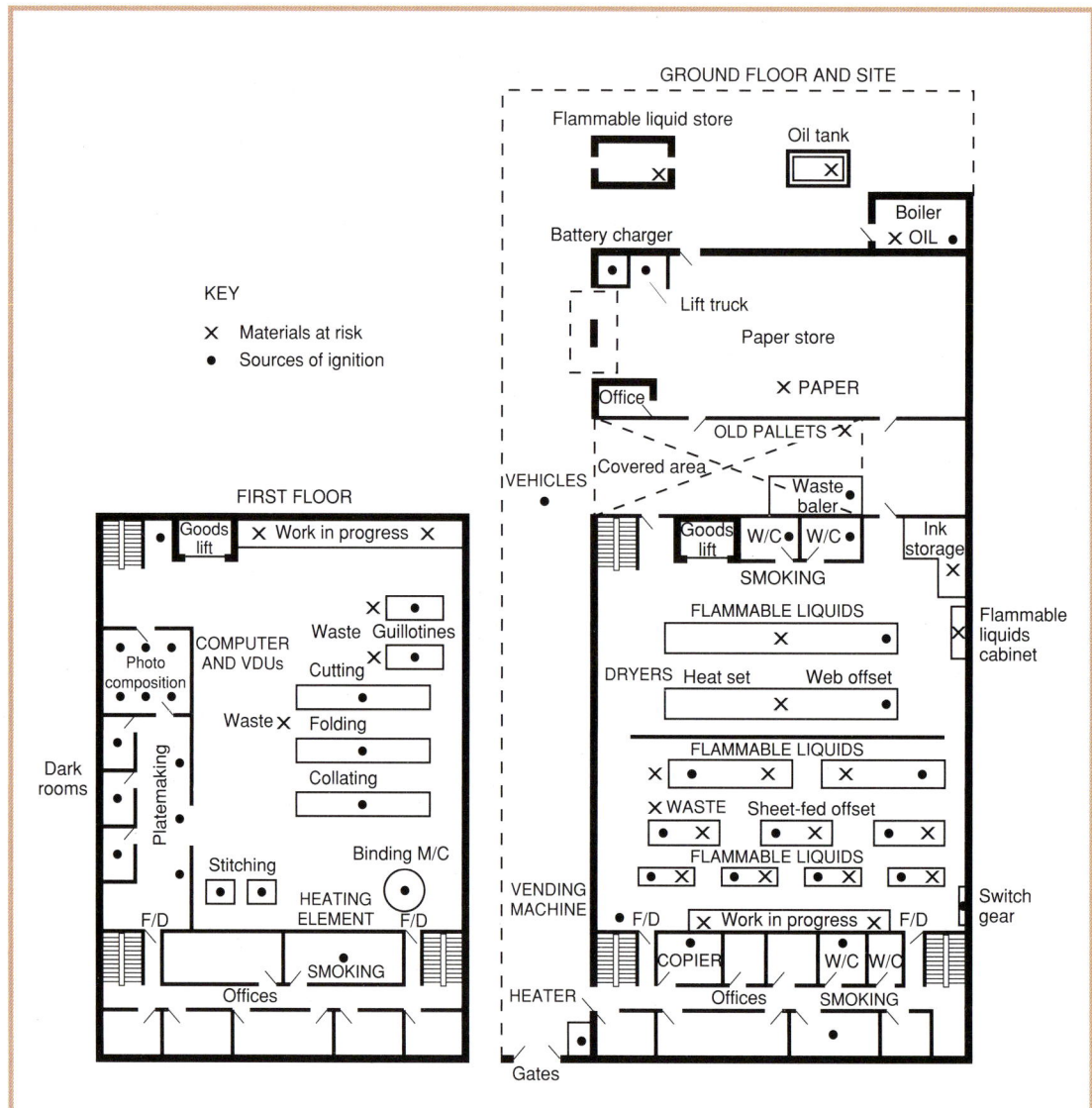

Figure 46 *Example of a plan prepared during a fire assessment*

Action plan for fire risk management

Managing Director decides to minimise fire risks

Senior Manager appointed to consider improvements needed to reduce fire risks
Involve company safety representatives in all stages of the programme

Assessment and control programme initiated

General fire precautions

Process fire precautions

Arrangements in the event of fire assessed and identified

Combustible/flammable materials identified

Adequate fire precautions provided

Ignition sources identified including arson

Staff instructed and trained in fire evacuation drills

Fire risks from materials and processes assessed and improvements identified

Fire evacuation drills held at regular intervals

Control measures implemented

Standards monitored by management inspections, inspections by safety representatives and thorough investigation of any incidents - corrective action taken

Report at defined intervals to senior management and review

FIRE RISKS CONTROLLED

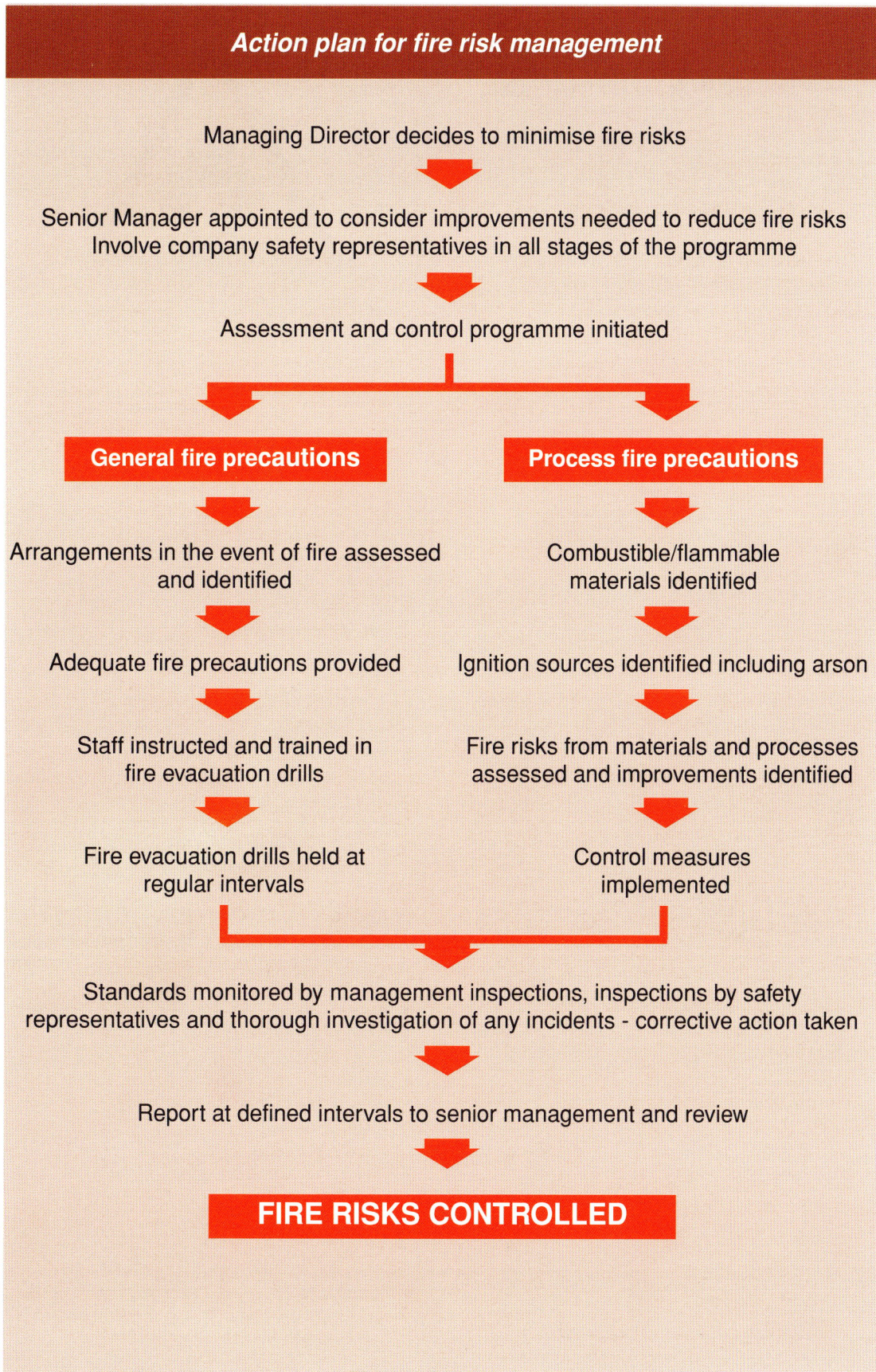

Figure 47 Action plan for fire risk management

General fire precautions

These are intended to facilitate the unaided evacuation of premises in the event of an escalating fire, eg fire-alarm systems, signage, means of escape and fire-fighting equipment.

The Fire Precautions (Workplace) Regulations 1997 (FPWR) require employers to take account of general fire precautions including fire-fighting, fire detection, emergency routes and exits and their maintenance. The FPWR also introduce requirements for competent assistance to deal with general fire safety risks, provision of information to employees, co-operation and co-ordination with others and provision of comprehensive information on fire provisions to outside employers (eg the emergency services). See *Fire safety: An employer's guide* in the 'References' section.

Your local fire authority, rather than HSE, will give you advice on this. You may need a fire certificate for your building - this will depend on the kind of business you run and the number of people employed in your building. The main pieces of legislation are the Fire Precautions Act 1971 and the Fire Precautions (Workplace) Regulations 1997 (as amended).

A fire certificate issued by the appropriate enforcing authority is generally required if more than 20 people are at work in the premises at any one time or if more than ten people are at work at any one time elsewhere than on the ground floor. It details the general fire precautions required at the premises. A fire certificate may also be required if explosive or highly flammable materials are stored or used either in, on or under the premises.

Fire certificates are tailored specifically to individual premises. They may demand requirements for maintaining the means of escape and associated fire precautions, training the workforce, limiting the number of people who might be in the premises at any one time and other precautions that have to be observed. Normally the occupier of the premises is responsible for ensuring all requirements of a fire certificate are met. The law states that fire certificates are kept on the premises to which they relate and are available for reference or inspection at all times. If any of the following are proposed, the fire authority should be informed in advance:

- you intend to undertake structural alterations to the building;

- you intend to reorganise the internal arrangements of the premises, eg move internal walls and/or doors;

- you intend to store, use or increase explosive or highly flammable materials on site.

You need to check that:

- everyone knows what to do in case of fire. Display clear instructions and have a fire drill periodically;

- people know how to raise the alarm and use the extinguishers where appropriate;

- arrangements are in place for calling and meeting the fire brigade following any suspected outbreak of fire;

- enough exits are provided for everyone to get out easily;

- fire doors and escape routes are provided which are clearly marked and unobstructed;

- fire escape doors can be opened easily from the inside whenever anyone is on the premises - don't forget 'out of hours' working;

- fire doors are never wedged open - they are there to stop smoke and flames spreading;

- if a wall is meant to be fire-resisting, it has no holes or gaps (eg around pipework)

and the wall continues above any false ceiling;

- fire alarms are checked regularly and work. Can they be heard everywhere over normal background noise?

- enough fire extinguishers are provided and they are of the right type (and properly serviced) to deal promptly with small outbreaks.

Process fire precautions

These are intended to prevent a fire starting. They relate to special precautions in connection with any work process, including the use and storage of material connected with that process, to prevent or reduce the likelihood of fire breaking out and control its intensity.

Main fire hazards

The main fire hazards are:

- poor housekeeping/accumulation of waste material;

- handling/storage of flammable liquids, solids and gases, eg solvents in litho and letterpress printing;

- heating and drying equipment, eg ultraviolet curing units, gravure dryers;

- poorly maintained or unsuitable electrical equipment;

- frictional heat, eg from hot bearings;

- frictional sparks, eg from using tools;

- electrostatic sparks;

- welding and cutting;

The Fire Triangle

Each point of the triangle represents one of the three elements essential for fire: fuel, oxygen and a source of ignition. Fire can be prevented by avoiding all three of these elements existing simultaneously.

For example, it is important to ensure that combustible materials such as paper, board and inks do not come into contact with potential sources of ignition, eg hot surfaces, static electricity, cigarettes, battery chargers.

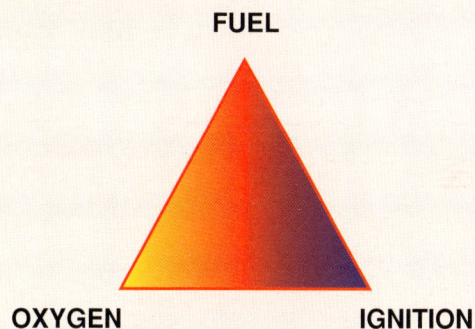

Figure 48 Fire triangle

- smoking materials;

- arson and horseplay

Storage and use of flammable liquids

Flammable liquids in this context include those materials defined by the CHIP Regulations as 'Extremely Flammable', 'Highly Flammable' and 'Flammable' (see HSG51 *The storage of flammable liquids in containers* and HSG140 *Safe use and handling of flammable liquids* for definitions).

The main hazard in the storage of flammable liquids is fire involving either the bulk liquid or escaping liquid or vapour. Most vapours are heavier than air and can travel over a large distance. Ignition can occur for as long as the vapour concentration exceeds the lower explosion limit (LEL). This is the concentration (percentage, by volume, of the material in air) below which the mixture is too lean to undergo combustion.

Figure 49 Flammable liquid stores should be secure and have suitable markings, ventilation and spillage retention

Some flammable liquids can be eliminated or substituted by substances that are less flammable or non-flammable and do not require the same specialist storage arrangements. Where this cannot be achieved, flammable liquids should be kept in suitable containers in:

- a safe position in the open air (where necessary, protected from direct sunlight); or

- a storeroom that is in a safe position; or

- a fire-resisting store; or

- if the total quantity is less than 50 litres, in the workroom in a suitable fire-resisting cupboard or bin.

All storerooms, cupboards or bins should be marked to indicate the nature of their contents, eg 'highly flammable'. Storerooms should also have adequate ventilation. All storage facilities should have spillage retention, eg bunding.

Further guidance on the storage of flammable liquids can be found in HSG51 *Storage of flammable liquids in containers* and HSG176 *Storage of flammable liquid in tanks*.

Some of the key steps for the safe use and control of flammable liquids are to:

- minimise the amount kept at the workplace;

- dispense and use them in a safe place with adequate natural or mechanical ventilation;

- keep containers closed, eg always replace the cap after use or use safety containers with self-closing lids;

- contain spillages, eg by dispensing over a tray and having absorbent material handy;

- provide a safe procedure for dealing with spillages should they occur;

- ensure that all electrical equipment installed or brought into areas where flammable liquids are stored or used is suitable, eg intrinsically safe or flameproof where appropriate;

- control ignition sources, eg naked flames and sparks, and make sure that 'no smoking' rules are obeyed;

- minimise the potential for ignition by static electricity by earth bonding where appropriate and introduce regular bonding efficiency checks;

- keep contaminated material, eg rags containing isopropyl alcohol (IPA) in a suitably labelled, lidded, metal bin. This should be emptied regularly and the contents disposed of in a safe manner;

- prevent the accumulation of combustible materials such as waste paper in areas in

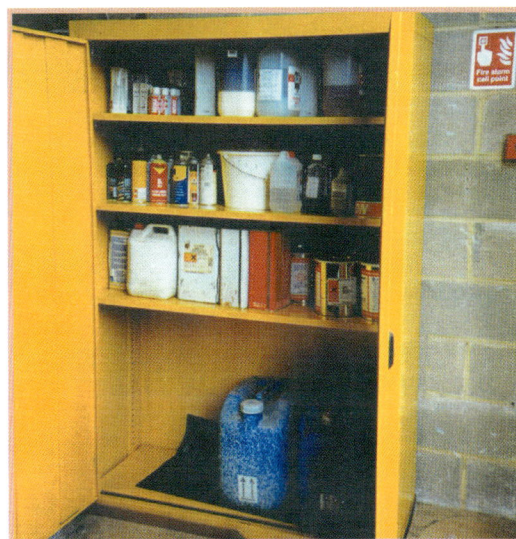

Figure 50 *Flammable liquid storage containers need to be maintained, correctly sited and protected from vehicle damage to remain effective*

which highly flammable and flammable liquids are kept or used;

- dispose of waste safely, using previously agreed safe working procedures, eg burn rubbish in a suitable container well away from buildings and flammable materials. Have fire extinguishers on hand. Never burn aerosol cans or 'brighten' fires with flammable liquids.

Further guidance can be found in HSG140 *Safe use and handling of flammable liquids*.

Storage of paper reels

A small fire in a paper reel store can rapidly escalate into a serious fire as the vertical reels are able to unwrap quickly to fuel the growing fire. The chimney effect of the vertical reels creates a draught which also exacerbates the fire.

- Ensure that loose paper such as wrappers and ends are disposed of and that damaged reels are wrapped or taped on delivery.

- Minimise the chimney effect between adjacent reels stacked on end by reducing stack height and the space between stacks to less than 25 mm, and staggering the reels.

- Where this cannot be achieved without risk of dislodging reels in adjacent stacks, increase the space to 1.1 m.

- Ensure sprinkler systems are designed to deal with fires within stacked reels.

- Provide a means of automatic smoke venting.

- Rigorously control sources of ignition.

- Ensure that there is a means of escape from inner rooms. If people work in an inner room, provide a vision panel and an alternative means of escape (ie not through the reel store) if necessary (see *Fire safety: An employer's guide*).

- Avoid storing vertically stacked paper reels beneath an occupied floor or basement.

- Check that stacked reels do not adversely affect the audibility of the fire-alarm system.

- Ensure adequate fire separation (at least 1/2 hour fire resistance) between storage and production areas.

Charging electrically operated lift trucks

- To prevent accidental short circuit of the cell terminals and ignition of hydrogen vapour, always use insulated tools and remove metallic jewellery from the neck, hands and wrist.

- Always carry out charging in an area intended for the purpose which has a high level of ventilation (see BS 6133: 1995 *Code of practice for safe operation of lead-acid stationary batteries* which includes a formula for calculating ventilation rates for battery charging rooms).

- Ensure that light and other electrical fittings are positioned away from the immediate charging area.

- Prohibit smoking and naked lights from the area.

- Always ensure that the charger is switched off before making or breaking the plug and socket connection.

- Maintain all vent plugs in position during charging.

- Before disconnecting battery terminal connections, switch off all electrical circuits including the charger and ensure that the terminal connected to the vehicle body is disconnected first and reconnected last.

- Keep suitable fire-fighting equipment available in the area.

Lithographic printing

- Observe the general process fire precautions described earlier in this chapter.

- Avoid the use of blanket washes, ink strippers, blanket revivers etc with low flashpoints, eg methyl ethyl ketone (MEK).

- Substitute low flashpoint products with high flashpoint preparations such as blends containing vegetable cleaning agents (VCA).

- Where infrared dryers and ultraviolet curing units are used, provide automatic systems to shut off the heat/light source if paper remains under the drying/curing unit for an extended period.

Explosion risks in blanket wash systems

Serious explosions have occurred at blanket wash systems at heat-set web offset printing. Explosions have occurred in dryers on web offset printing lines when the web has transferred blanket wash solvent into the dryer and the concentration of solvent vapour in the dryer has exceeded the lower explosion limit (LEL) (See 'Precautions for dryers' later in this chapter).

The design and operation of heat-set dryers are such that ignition of solvent vapour is almost inevitable if a concentration above the lower explosion limit is formed within the dryers. Standards have been devised to ensure the safe operation of this type of plant. You will need to check that your equipment has been designed with safety in mind.

New dryers and, where fitted, thermal oxidisers should be designed according to BS EN 1539: 2000 and prEN 12753, which detail the measures to prevent and mitigate fire and explosion hazards in dryers and ovens in which flammable substances are released. You will need to ensure that the safety features are understood and that the oven and associated coating equipment are operated and maintained in accordance with the manufacturer's instructions.

The lower explosion limit of flammable liquids is temperature dependent - an important factor which needs to be considered when determining process operating conditions. The standards also give information on how the lower explosion limit is affected by operating temperature.

For dryers installed before the publication of BS EN 1539 you will need to check that they have:

- suitable gas safety features on gas-fired dryers, including safety shut-off valves, ignition systems, flame failure devices and purging arrangements. Equivalent safety features should be included on oil-fired systems where appropriate;

- adequate explosion-relief doors or panels on the dryer. This protection is critical if the damage caused by an explosion is to be minimised. The area and weight of explosion relief panels need to be carefully calculated, so that they are effective if there is an explosion;

- enough exhaust ventilation from the dryer, so that under all operating conditions the concentration of solvent in the dryer does not exceed the lower explosion limit. To ensure this, dryers should be designed so that under normal operating conditions the solvent levels are maintained at less than 25% of the lower explosion limit. As failure of the exhaust system may have critical effects, it should be monitored so that any reduction in the air flow below pre-determined levels will automatically and safely shut down the fuel supply to the dryer, the blanket wash system and the printed web. It should also activate a visible and audible alarm;

- an annual check to confirm that solvent vapour levels in the dryer remain within design parameters for all operating conditions.

Check the automatic blanket wash systems for the following:

- the monitoring and control devices automatically ensure that in all circumstances the overall solvent concentration in the dryer does not exceed 25% of the lower explosion limit;

- the system is not used for the first time until it has been commissioned and safe operating limits established. This should include measurement of the maximum concentration of solvent within the dryer, both above and below the web, as solvent application is progressively introduced at additional print units;

- commissioning tests use the maximum web width and all paper types. Where necessary, to maintain solvent concentrations within the dryer to below 25% of the lower explosion limit, an automatic time delay operates after completion of one blanket wash cycle before another starts;

- there are measurement checks of solvent levels in the dryer annually, and after any change to operating conditions, plant or blanket wash to ensure that vapour levels in the dryer remain within design parameters for all operating conditions;

- the solvent or ink used in the system is the same as that which was used when the system was commissioned. Different solvents may have different explosion limits, and a change of solvent may result in dangerous conditions. Check with the supplier of the system before making any changes;

- the blanket wash supplier has provided information about the lower explosion limit for the solvent used, in relation to the typical dryer operating temperatures (160-260°C);

- the quantity of solvent applied to the blanket cylinders is metered, and is the minimum necessary. This volume will have been set during commissioning. Check that unauthorised access to the controlling mechanism is prevented;

- the manual application of additional solvent is strictly prohibited. Safety will be compromised if the amount of solvent reaching the dryer is greater than that expected by the designer of the system;

- if blanket wash drip-trays are used, care is taken so that they do not overflow and allow the web to take excess solvent into the dryer;

- adequate written information has been provided by the supplier about the conditions under which the system has been commissioned, operational limitations, the safety devices, the results of commissioning and necessary maintenance requirements. Where applicable, the supplier should have provided an EC Declaration of Conformity;

- managers, operators and assistants are adequately trained in the explosion hazard associated with blanket washing and in the necessary precautionary measures.

In addition, when blanket washing by hand, remember that it is important to:

- remove or break the web before the dryer, and don't use it as a wiper;

- keep the quantity of solvent applied to a minimum.

FIRES IN THE PRINTING INDUSTRY

Fire in reel store

Three employees died in a fire in the reel store of a printing factory. The fire started in some reels of paper at one end of the reel store in the single-storey factory. There was no fire separation between the reel storage area and the production area. Shortly after the fire was first discovered there was a sudden rapid spread of fire (flashover) across the top of reels of paper and the whole building rapidly filled with smoke. The roof collapsed within minutes.

Horseplay with flammable thinners

A 17-year-old apprentice died of extensive burns after an initiation ceremony in which 2 litres of flammable thinners were poured on his clothing. The victim was changing his soaked clothing in a toilet cubicle when some matches were lit. The apprentice was engulfed in flames and died three weeks later of burns which covered 80% of his body.

Arson

On arriving at a warehouse just after midnight, the fire brigade found a timber tea chest or pallet on fire outside double timber doors in an alleyway adjacent to the seven-storey building. The doors were burning and fire was spreading under the doors into a stairwell. The first and second floors were also alight. Fire spread was rapid due to the type of storage and unprotected stairways in the warehouse areas. The entire seven-storey warehouse was severely damaged.

Ignition of toluene vapour

A printer was off work for six weeks after receiving severe burns to his right hand when a static discharge occurred as he was using a toluene-soaked rag to clean the doctor blade of a gravure printing press. It is thought that an earlier modification to a cover at the doctor blade had reduced the extraction system's ability to remove vapours given off by the printing ink. Anti-static footwear was not in use.

Smoking near flammable solvent

An employee sustained burns to his face and hair as he cleaned a roller washing machine with flammable solvent while smoking. After the incident all staff were instructed not to smoke in the room where the machine was located and 'no smoking' signs were posted up.

Explosion risks in flexographic and gravure

These processes often use flammable inks which create significant fire and explosion risks. Consider substitution with water-based inks. Where this cannot be achieved:

- segregate printing areas from storage areas and other parts of the building with half-hour fire-resistant partitioning;

- mix inks within a dedicated fire-resisting room provided with spillage retention and mechanical ventilation, which is separate from the storage area;

- drums and handling equipment should be earth bonded;

- provide local exhaust ventilation at print units to prevent flammable vapour entering the workroom and reduce employees' exposure. See HSG37 *An introduction to local exhaust ventilation* and HSG54 *Maintenance, examination and testing of local exhaust ventilation* (Chapter 4 references);

- ensure the workroom itself is adequately ventilated;

- minimise the amount of solvent vapour released into the air by covering ink ducts and keeping supply containers closed when not in use. Pump ink to presses and return to storage using an enclosed system;

- where connections are frequently broken and re-made, use a sealed end coupling;

- make sure pipework and fittings are to a suitable standard (such as ANSI B 31.3) and make arrangements for planned preventive maintenance;

- use inks and coatings at as low a temperature as possible to reduce the amount of vapour produced;

- ensure that any electrical equipment on the press or in the immediate area, including portable equipment, is suitable for use in potentially explosive atmospheres;

- the fan motor of extraction equipment should not be located in the path of the vapour, eg within the trunking. The trunking should be of fire-resisting construction and fumes should be expelled to a safe location, preferably at high level, and not local to air intakes for equipment or ventilation systems etc;

- provide fixed fire-detection and extinguishing systems such as CO_2, designed for both manual and automatic operation. Further solvent should be prevented from entering dryers/extract ducting on operation of the system and dampers should shut to stop the loss of the extinguishing medium;

- where there is a solvent recovery unit, provide a damper to isolate it from any fire on the press or in the ducting;

- where vapour detection equipment is not provided inside print units, take regular measurements to ensure that the atmosphere is maintained below 25% of the lower explosion limit;

- clean rollers, cylinders and ancillary equipment using highly flammable liquids only in a contained solvent-cleaning machine with exhaust ventilation or in a ventilated purpose-designed booth;

- avoid the generation of static electricity which can ignite flammable vapour by taking the following precautions:

  - limit the flow speed of piped flammable liquids to 1 m/second where water could be present or to 7 m/second where there is no possibility of this;

- use anti-static additives to increase the conductivity of the liquid;
- use conductive, bonded and earthed containers, pipework and hoses;
- regularly check the resistance to earth of all metal parts of fixed plant;
- equip personnel with anti-static footwear and protective clothing made from natural fibres and instruct them not to remove items of outer clothing in areas where flammable vapour may be present;
- avoid flooring materials that are highly insulating;
- provide electrostatic eliminators constructed to an explosion-protected standard where insulating web material is being printed on.

Precautions for dryers

New dryers should be designed according to BS EN 1539: 2000 which details measures to prevent or mitigate fire and explosion hazards. For dryers installed before the publication of this standard it is necessary to check that certain safety features are incorporated. (See 'Lithographic printing' and 'Explosion risks in blanket wash systems' earlier in this chapter).

Dryers should be designed with enough air flow to keep the solvent concentration below 25% of the lower explosion limit - check at commissioning. Air flow should be monitored so that the printing process and means of heating is stopped if the air flow is inadequate.

Provide an emergency stop button on the dryer which shuts down the means of heating but not the exhaust ventilation.

Continuous monitoring of the solvent concentration should be provided where in exceptional circumstances dryers have been designed to operate between 25% and 50% of the lower explosion limit and vapour concentrations change slowly relative to detection and activation of shut-down systems. Such detection equipment should:

- be suitable for the solvent type;

- be suitably calibrated for the conditions of use (eg operating temperature), tested and maintained;

- sample at the highest vapour concentration points;

- operate an audible and visual alarm;

- have two independent means of measuring concentration, each capable of shutting down the printing process and heat source before the 50% lower explosion limit is reached;

- be arranged to fully open dampers if there is a malfunction in the monitoring system;

- monitor the progression of the solvent vapour concentration.

Note *A detailed risk assessment should be carried out to identify additional control measures which may be necessary to prevent and mitigate hazardous conditions arising, eg explosion relief. Further information is given in BS EN 1539.*

Precautions for coating machines

Make sure that fans exhausting potentially explosive atmospheres or combustible dusts are explosion protected. Ducting used for exhausting these materials should be of fire-resisting construction, conductive and electrostatically grounded. The fan motor should not be located within the duct, ie in the path of the vapour. Fumes should be exhausted to a safe location, preferably at high level, away from air intakes for other equipment or ventilation systems.

Explosion-protected electrical equipment will only be required on the coater where there is a risk of generating an explosive atmosphere, for example when using a highly flammable liquid

or heating a flammable liquid, such as the electric drive motor on the recirculation pumps and switches (where these are mounted on the pump). Make sure that the distance between the drive motor and the outer flange of the lantern agitator for viscosity control is at least 50 mm and a disc is mounted on the shaft to increase the preventive effect.

Precautions for laminators with glue application

As for coating machines, any fans exhausting potentially explosive atmospheres or combustible dusts should be explosion-protected, and the ducting used for exhausting these materials should be made of fire-resisting material, conductive and electrostatically grounded. The fan motor should not be located within the duct, ie in the path of the vapour. Fumes should be exhausted to a safe location, preferably at high level, away from air intakes for other equipment or ventilation systems.

Explosion-protected electrical equipment will only be required on the laminator where there is a risk of generating an explosive atmosphere, for example when using a highly flammable liquid or heating a flammable liquid.

The electric drive motor on laminating material recirculating pumps should have explosion protection in accordance with the relevant standard, currently BS EN 50018: 2000 *Electrical apparatus for potentially explosive atmospheres. Flameproof enclosure 'd',* or BS EN 50019: 2000 *Electrical apparatus for potentially explosive atmospheres. Increased safety 'e'.*

Chapter 8

MAINTENANCE

■ ■ ■ ■ ■ ■ ■ ■ ■ ■ ■

See the 'References' section at the back of the book for details of publications which relate to MAINTENANCE

Relevant legislation

- Provision and Use of Work Equipment Regulations 1998 (PUWER 98)

- Workplace (Health, Safety and Welfare) Regulations 1992

- Health and Safety at Work etc Act 1974 (HSW Act)

- Control of Substances Hazardous to Health Regulations 1999 (COSHH)

- Pressure Systems Safety Regulations 2000

- Electricity at Work Regulations 1989

- Lifting Operations and Lifting Equipment Regulations 1998 (LOLER)

What needs maintenance?

All buildings, equipment and plant need to be maintained in good working order and in good repair to prevent any dangerous situations.

Statutory testing and thorough examination

The law contains some specific requirements for maintenance such as periodic testing and/or thorough examination. For example:

- lifting chains and ropes - generally every six months (although this will be dependent on the findings of an appropriate risk assessment);

- lifts and hoists - generally every six months (although this will be dependent on the findings of an appropriate risk assessment);

- cranes - generally every 12 months (although this will be dependent on the findings of an appropriate risk assessment);

- steam boilers/air receivers and pressure systems - in accordance with your competent person's written scheme for examination of pressure vessels;

- local exhaust ventilation - minimum every 14 months (see the General Approved Code of Practice for the Control of Substances Hazardous to Health Regulations 1999, listed in the 'References' section for Chapter 4).

Periodic tests such as these need to be carried out by a competent person - this may be your insurance engineer.

Other examples of required and industry recommended inspections and checks include:

- inspection of personal protective equipment, eg hearing protection;

- weekly inspection of scaffolds;

- monthly examination of breathing apparatus/rescue equipment;

- regular visual inspections of electrical equipment at appropriate intervals. Practical experience/manufacturer's guidance will help to determine the frequency at which inspection and test by a competent person is necessary (eg quarterly/annually), and this should be backed up with more frequent checks by the users. Keeping records will help to determine the frequencies. Guidance is contained in HSG107 *Maintaining portable and transportable electrical equipment.*

Routine lubrication, service and overhaul activities might include:

- cleaning of floors and machinery access platforms/walkways (eg flexographic presses);

- annual servicing of fire extinguishers.

Be guided by the manufacturer's recommendations when working out your own maintenance schedules for items such as vehicles, lift trucks, ventilation plant, ladders, portable electrical equipment, protective clothing and equipment and machine guards. Check the legal requirements, especially for examinations by a competent person.

Maintenance and inspection required by PUWER 98

Maintenance frequency

Equipment may need to be checked frequently to make sure that safety-related features are working properly. Some faults in safety-critical systems could remain undetected unless appropriate checks are made. The frequency of maintenance checks should be determined by factors such as the operating environment, the intensity of use, the variety of operations the equipment is used for, and the risk to health and safety from malfunction or failure.

Maintenance management

Powered equipment should be accompanied by a maintenance manual, which details the manufacturer's recommendations either for keeping the equipment in working order or for safety reasons. Maintenance management techniques include planned preventive maintenance, condition-based maintenance and breakdown maintenance. Where you have safety-critical parts which could fail and render guards or other protection devices inoperable, you will need a formal system of planned preventive maintenance or condition-based maintenance.

A good example of the maintenance checks required under PUWER 98 is the daily check of guards and safety mechanisms by machine operators. It is recommended that you keep a maintenance log to record these checks, which may comprise a series of completed guard checklists. This is particularly important in the case of high-risk equipment such as power-operated guillotines and hand-fed platens, but also applies to press and other machinery guarding. Where you have a log, you need to keep it up to date.

Inspection

Under PUWER 98, where risk assessment identifies that a major injury or worse could occur because of incorrect installation or re-installation, deterioration or exceptional circumstances affecting the safe operation of work equipment, inspection is necessary. The purpose of inspection is to identify whether the equipment can be used safely and to detect any deterioration before it causes unacceptable risk.

Inspection will vary from simple external examination to comprehensive internal examination including dismantling and testing. It should always include safety-related parts. Individuals carrying out the inspection will determine its nature and should have the necessary knowledge and experience.

Examples where inspection is needed because equipment operation is critically dependent on its condition in use and deterioration would lead to a significant risk to the operator include:

- daily/monthly/six-monthly testing of guillotine safety devices (see the PIAC booklet *The guide to safe use of power-operated paper-cutting guillotines)*;

- daily/annual testing of hand-fed platens (see Chapter 5);

- daily/weekly testing of trip nip bars on sheet-fed offset presses where the slow crawl safe system of work for cleaning is being used (see Chapter 5).

Safety during maintenance work

During maintenance work, conditions are very different from those normally encountered, and new hazards may be introduced. It is essential that everyone concerned is aware of the hazards and of the correct precautions.

Additional personal protective equipment may be needed during maintenance activities, eg overalls, protective footwear and headwear. Don't forget gloves for handling inky machine parts, eg changing ink rollers on a litho press using UV inks.

Safety during maintenance activities can be achieved by using isolation, lock-off and permit-to-work procedures. Generally speaking, simple isolation procedures may be suitable for minor maintenance work and formal lock-off procedures for more major maintenance work.

Permits to work

A permit-to-work system is a formal written system used to control certain types of potentially hazardous work. The permit details the work to be done and the necessary precautions to be taken, and forms an essential part of many safe systems of work for maintenance activities, for example allowing work to start only after effective isolation has been achieved. Permits will always be needed when normal safeguards cannot be used or when new hazards are introduced by the work, for example hot work or work where someone has to enter a confined space.

It is essential that those asked to do the work understand that they cannot start until the person in control of issuing a permit has fully explained the precautions to be taken and is satisfied that they have been complied with.

This may include provision of effective isolation and lock-off. Permits should be formalised by means of a written handover procedure, which includes the signatures of those people issuing a permit and those doing the work.

Permits should contain the following:

- clear and unambiguous information and instruction;

- exact details of the item of plant on which the work is required, the nature of the work, and the precautions needed to ensure the safety of all personnel;

- the start and expiry time and any conditions under which work should cease should be detailed;

- a place for the permit issuer to sign that they have satisfied themselves by personal inspection that all the necessary action for work to commence has been taken before a start is made;

- a place for the permit issuer to sign that they have checked completion of the work before signing the permit off.

Make sure that the issuer has enough technical knowledge of the hazards and precautions to be taken as well as the authority to require other responsible people to make recommendations where they have special knowledge, and to co-ordinate the duties of all concerned.

Permit-to-work procedures will normally be needed for activities such as the following:

- entry into vessels, confined spaces or machines;

- hot work which could cause explosion or fire;

- building, maintenance or installation work by contractors, especially where this interfaces with normal activities;

- mechanical or electrical work requiring isolation of the power source, eg before working inside large machines;

- work on plant, mixers, boilers etc which must be cut off from the possible entry of fumes, gas, liquids or steam.

Isolation and lock-off procedures

Isolation procedures usually comprise the following:

- switch off;

- disconnect plug or switch off at isolator;

- tag isolator.

In addition to the above, lock-off procedures usually involve the following steps:

- isolate the machine from the main supply by locking off the power;

- use a safety lock with only one key which is kept by the person doing the work;

- use a multiple hasp where several people are working so each can fit their own lock;

- put a warning notice on the isolator.

ACCIDENTS

An experienced guillotine operator lost four fingers on one hand when a repeat stroke occurred. The machine had not been maintained, its brake was worn and oily and the automatic sweepaway guard did not operate to its full extent. PIAC-recommended examinations would have identified these faults early enough to prevent an accident.

A machine operator had his right index finger severely crushed while cleaning the ink rollers of a bag printing machine. The interlock for the hinged guard had worked loose and he inadvertently depressed the start button. Daily checking and maintenance of the safety device would have prevented the accident. Shrouding of the start button would have prevented accidental operation of the button.

The operator of a three-knife trimmer received an electric shock while picking up a knife from the floor and resting one hand on the machine. Investigation by an electrician revealed a faulty earth connection. Regular planned maintenance would have identified this defect.

An experienced fitter was killed while working at the feed end of a paper cutting and creasing machine when the operator, who did not see him, started up the machine. There was no safe system for maintenance work and the machine had not been isolated.

Appendix 1

SAFEGUARDING TERMS

Audible pre-start warning device - a device (normally automatic on depression of a start or slow crawl control on larger machinery) that delivers a clearly audible signal before start-up of the machine. (See guidance and diagrams under 'Machine controls' in the 'Safety hazards by process section' of Chapter 5.)

Contra-rotating rollers/cylinders - rollers/cylinders that rotate towards each other.

Crawl - slow speed, where machines can run at crawl speeds with guards open they should be capable of running at slow crawl only (see 'Slow crawl'). Where machines run at crawl speeds with guards in position/closed, the crawl speeds can be in excess of those set out for slow crawl as the crawl in this context is not designed to be a safety feature.

Electrosensitive safety system - electrosensitive protective equipment, eg photoelectric safety system.

Emergency stop device - readily accessible stop controls intended to effect a rapid response to a potentially dangerous situation. Not designed for use as a stop during normal day-to-day operation. Common types include mushroom-headed buttons, push bars, pull wire and kick plates.

Fail to danger - any failure of the machinery, its associated safeguards, controls or power supply that leaves a machine in a dangerous or unsafe condition.

Fail to safety/fail-safe - any failure of the machinery, its associated safeguards, controls or power supply that leaves the machine in a safe condition.

Fixed guard - guards that require a tool for removal, eg an Allen key or spanner. Wing nuts or similar are not acceptable. Openings in fixed guards are permissible provided safety reach distances are maintained in accordance with BS EN 294 (see 'Machinery standards' in the References section).

Gap covers - usually curved metal sections designed to be fitted in the gaps of plate and blanket cylinders to create a cylinder of smooth circumference.

Guard - a physical barrier that prevents or reduces access to a danger point or area.

Guard locking - an additional safety feature of certain interlocked guarding for machines with long rundown times which prevents the guards from being opened until dangerous movement within the guarded area has stopped.

Hickey picking - removal of hickeys (pieces of fluff or other foreign bodies), usually from the surface of printing cylinders.

Hold-to-run controls (dead man's control) - permit movement of a machine only on continued activation of a control. Hold-to-run control devices should be designed to allow movement limited to a maximum of 25 mm or with a maximum operating speed of 1 m/min or where this would reduce the ability of the machine to perform its function and there would be no substantial increase in hazard movement limited to a maximum of 75 mm or with a maximum operating speed of 5 m/min.

Inch - limited movement. Movement should be limited to 25 mm, or 75 mm where this is not possible and does not increase the hazards substantially. Inching is not continuous motion under hold-to-run control.

In-running nip - trapping and drawing-in hazard created by rotating rollers or cylinders. Can occur between two contra-rotating rollers (powered or non-powered); one rotating roller and a stationary roller or adjacent fixed part of the machine; rollers rotating in the same direction but with different peripheral speeds or surface properties (friction); guide rollers and driving belts, conveyor belts and possibly the web.

Integrity - the ability of devices, systems and procedures to perform their function without failure or defeat.

Interlock - a safety device that interconnects a guard with the control system or the power system of the machine.

Interlocked guard - a guard that when opened operates an interlock to stop movement of dangerous parts before they can be reached by an operator or other person.

Isolate - the removal of all sources of energy in a secure manner, ie by ensuring that inadvertent reconnection is not possible.

Lift out/pop out rollers - rollers that are not fixed in position and are light enough to lift out of position if a blockage or entanglement occurs without causing injury.

Multi-operator presses - presses designed to be operated by more than one person.

Nip bar - fixed section, normally metal, either round or angled, running along the length of rollers or cylinders situated no more than 6 mm from the cylinder or roller surface designed to minimise the risk of entanglement by the nip created by contra-rotating rollers.

Safe by position - out of reach. See also safety reach distances in BS EN 294 (see 'Machinery standards' in the References section).

Safe system of work or safe working practice - a method of working that eliminates or reduces the risk of injury.

Safety device/protective device - a device other than a guard that eliminates or reduces danger.

Safety reach distance - safety distance that should prevent dangerous parts from being reached by operators or others.

Slow crawl - safety-related restricted operating speed. As a rule, the slow crawl speed should be set at a maximum operating speed of 1 m/min, or 5 m/min where this is not possible because it would reduce the ability of the machine to perform its function and where there would be no substantial increase in hazard.

Slow speed - production crawl (with guards in position) - see also 'Crawl'.

Trip devices - devices which bring dangerous parts of machinery to rest when activated (eg knocked) by operators or other people.

Trip nip bar - similar to a fixed nip bar but when deflected acts to cut the power supply to the motor, causing the press to come to a rapid but controlled stop. The withdrawal path/deflection of the trip bar should be longer than the stopping path of the hazardous movement.

Tunnel guard - fixed or interlocked guard that prevents access to dangerous parts using the principles of safety reach distances in construction of the guard, often using a tunnel shape.

Two-hand control - controls designed so that simultaneous operation of the controls (within approximately 0.5 seconds) is required before the machine will operate. Operation of the machine by such controls should usually allow limited movement, eg a single stroke of a guillotine, or movement at slow crawl speeds only. Hazardous movement should stop when either actuator/control is released.

Wander lead control/pendant control - portable control panel usually on flexible armoured cable lead allowing operation of the machine from different positions. If the control allows operation of the machine with guards open it should operate as a two-hand control (see 'Two-hand control').

Web-driven rollers - non-powered rollers that act as if powered due to the driving force of the web.

Zoning - each control only allows operation of a limited press or associated area with a guard open when guards elsewhere that are not clearly visible are closed, eg at print units of larger presses.

Appendix 2

EXAMPLE RISK ASSESSMENT FORM

RISK ASSESSMENT		NO	
Site		Area	
Operations covered by the assessment			
Maximum number of people exposed:			
Frequency and duration of exposure:			
Hazards			
Action already taken to reduce risk		Residual risk	
		Likelihood	Severity
Hazards still outstanding			
Assessment of residual risk: low/medium/high			
Further actions required:		Person responsible	Date completed
Signed: Position:	Date	Review date	
Responsible Director's approval		Date	

This is a suggested risk assessment form. You do not have to use this - it is merely an example of the sort of form you may use

Appendix 3

ASSESSING HAZARDS IN A SMALL PRINT WORKS

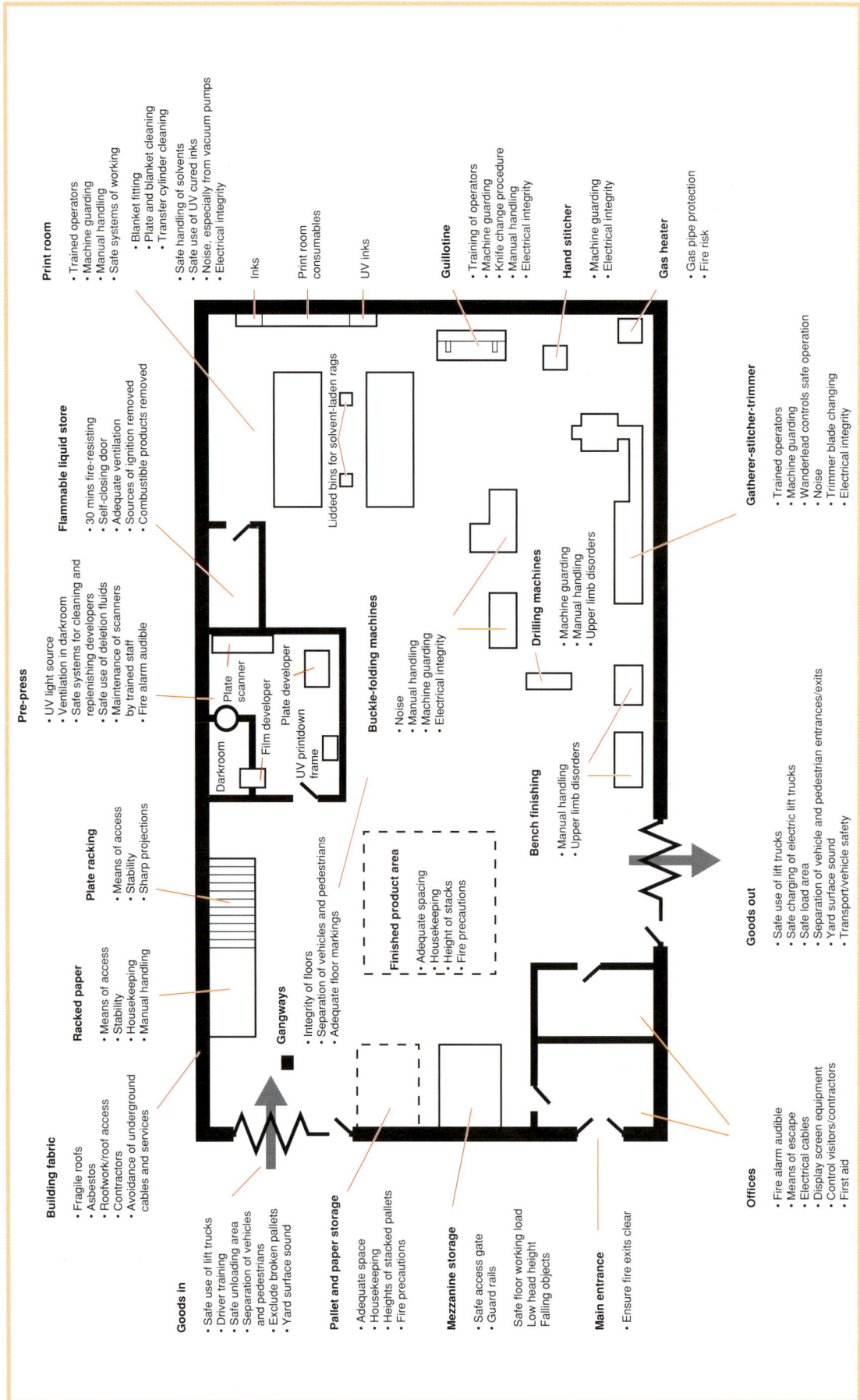

Building fabric
- Fragile roofs
- Asbestos
- Roofwork/roof access
- Contractors
- Avoidance of underground cables and services

Goods in
- Safe use of lift trucks
- Driver training
- Safe unloading area
- Separation of vehicles and pedestrians
- Exclude broken pallets
- Yard surface sound

Pallet and paper storage
- Adequate space
- Housekeeping
- Heights of stacked pallets
- Fire precautions

Mezzanine storage
- Safe access gate
- Guard rails
- Safe floor working load
- Low head height
- Falling objects

Main entrance
- Ensure fire exits clear

Offices
- Fire alarm audible
- Means of escape
- Electrical cables
- Display screen equipment
- Control visitors/contractors
- First aid

Racked paper
- Means of access
- Stability
- Housekeeping
- Manual handling

Plate racking
- Means of access
- Stability
- Sharp projections

Gangways
- Integrity of floors
- Separation of vehicles and pedestrians
- Adequate floor markings

Finished product area
- Adequate spacing
- Housekeeping
- Height of stacks
- Fire precautions

Pre-press
- UV light source
- Ventilation in darkroom
- Safe systems for cleaning and replenishing developers
- Safe use of deletion fluids
- Maintenance of scanners by trained staff
- Fire alarm audible

Darkroom
Plate scanner
Film developer
Plate developer
UV printdown frame

Buckle-folding machines
- Noise
- Manual handling
- Machine guarding
- Electrical integrity

Bench finishing
- Manual handling
- Upper limb disorders

Drilling machines
- Machine guarding
- Manual handling
- Upper limb disorders

Flammable liquid store
- 30 mins fire-resisting
- Self-closing door
- Adequate ventilation
- Sources of ignition removed
- Combustible products removed

Lidded bins for solvent-laden rags

Print room
- Trained operators
- Machine guarding
- Manual handling
- Safe systems of working
  - Blanket litting
  - Plate and blanket cleaning
  - Transfer cylinder cleaning
- Safe handling of solvents
- Safe use of UV cured inks
- Noise, especially from vacuum pumps
- Electrical integrity

Inks
Print room consumables
UV inks

Guillotine
- Training of operators
- Machine guarding
- Knife change procedure
- Manual handling
- Electrical integrity

Hand stitcher
- Machine guarding
- Electrical integrity

Gas heater
- Gas pipe protection
- Fire risk

Gatherer-stitcher-trimmer
- Trained operators
- Machine guarding
- Wanderlead controls safe operation
- Noise
- Trimmer blade changing
- Electrical integrity

Goods out
- Safe use of lift trucks
- Safe charging of electric lift trucks
- Safe load area
- Separation of vehicle and pedestrian entrances/exits
- Yard surface sound
- Transport/vehicle safety

REFERENCES

CHAPTER 1 - MANAGING HEALTH AND SAFETY

Management of health and safety at work. Management of Health and Safety at Work Regulations 1999. Approved Code of Practice and guidance L21 (Second edition) HSE Books 2000 ISBN 0 7176 2488 9

Homeworking: Guidance for employers and employees on health and safety Leaflet INDG226 HSE Books 1996 (single copy free or priced packs of 15 ISBN 0 7176 1204 X)

Working alone in safety: Controlling the risks of solitary work Leaflet INDG73(rev) HSE Books 1998 (single copy free or priced packs of 15 ISBN 0 7176 1507 3)

RIDDOR explained: Reporting of Injuries, Diseases and Dangerous Occurrences Regulations Leaflet HSE31(rev1) HSE Books 1999 (single copy free or priced packs of 10 ISBN 0 7176 2441 2)

A guide to the Reporting of Injuries, Diseases and Dangerous Occurrences Regulations 1995 L73 (Second edition) HSE Books 1999 ISBN 0 7176 2431 5

RIDDOR reporting: Information about the new incident centre Leaflet MISC310 HSE Books 2001

First aid at work. The Health and Safety (First Aid) Regulations 1981. Approved Code of Practice and guidance L74 HSE Books 1997 ISBN 0 7176 1050 0

First aid at work: Your questions answered Leaflet INDG214 HSE Books 1997 (single copy free or priced packs of 15 ISBN 0 7176 1074 8)

Basic advice on first aid at work Leaflet INDG215(rev2) HSE Books 1999 (single copy free or priced packs of 20 ISBN 0 7176 2423 4)

Health and safety in construction. Construction (Design and Management) Regulations 1994. Approved Code of Practice HSG150 HSE Books 2001 ISBN 0 7176 2106 5

Having construction work done? Duties of clients under the Construction (Design and Management) Regulations 1994 Leaflet MISC193 HSE Books 1999

A guide to the Construction (Health, Safety and Welfare) Regulations 1996 Leaflet INDG220 HSE Books 1996 (single copy free or priced packs of 10 ISBN 0 7176 1161 2)

Consulting employees on health and safety: A guide to the law Leaflet INDG232 HSE Books 1996 (single copy free or priced packs of 15 ISBN 0 7176 1615 0)

A guide to the Health and Safety (Consultation with Employees) Regulations 1996. Guidance on Regulations L95 HSE Books 1996 ISBN 0 7176 1234 1

Safety representatives and safety committees L87 (Third edition) HSE Books 1996 ISBN 0 7176 1220 1

Essentials of health and safety at work
HSE Books 1994 ISBN 0 7176 0716 X

Health and safety law: What you should know Leaflet HSE Books 1999 (priced packs of 25 ISBN 0 7176 1702 5)

Successful health and safety management HSG65 (Second edition) HSE Books 1997 ISBN 0 7176 1276 7

Five steps to risk assessment Leaflet INDG163(rev1) HSE Books 1998 (single copy free or priced packs of 10 ISBN 0 7176 1565 0)

A guide to risk assessment requirements: Common provisions in health and safety law Leaflet INDG218 HSE Books 1996 (single copy free or priced packs of 5 ISBN 0 7176 1211 2)

Working together: Guidance on health and safety for contractors and suppliers Leaflet INDG268 HSE Books 1998 (single copy free or priced packs of 10 ISBN 0 7176 1548 0)

Managing health and safety: Five steps to success Leaflet INDG275 HSE Books 1998

CHAPTER 2 - TRAINING

PUWER 1998: Provision and Use of Work Equipment Regulations 1998. Open learning guidance HSE Books 1999 ISBN 0 7176 2459 5

LOLER 1998: Lifting Operations and Lifting Equipment Regulations 1998. Open learning guidance HSE Books 1999 ISBN 0 7176 2464 1

Managing health and safety: An open learning workbook for managers and trainers HSE Books 1997 ISBN 0 7176 1153 1

The training of first aid at work: A guide to gaining and maintaining HSE approval HSG212 (Second edition) HSE Books 2000 ISBN 0 7176 1896 X

Five steps to information, instruction and training Leaflet INDG213 HSE Books 1996 (single copy free or priced packs of 10 ISBN 0 7176 1235 X)

Printing industry: Health and safety training package. An open learning package PIAC/HSE Books 1998 ISBN 0 7176 1481 6

CHAPTER 3 - WORKPLACE AND TRANSPORT SAFETY

Workplace health and safety

Workplace health, safety and welfare. Workplace (Health, Safety and Welfare) Regulations 1992. Approved Code of Practice L24 HSE Books 1992 ISBN 0 7176 0413 6

Workplace health, safety and welfare: A short guide for managers Leaflet INDG244 HSE Books 1997 (single copy free or priced packs of 10 ISBN 0 7176 1328 3)

Lighting at work HSG38 (Second edition) HSE Books 1997 ISBN 0 7176 1232 5

Display screen equipment work. Health and Safety (Display Screen Equipment) Regulations 1992. Guidance on Regulations L26 HSE Books 1992 ISBN 0 7176 0410 1

Working with VDUs Leaflet INDG36(rev1) HSE Books 1998 (single copy free or priced packs of 10 ISBN 0 7176 1504 9)

Seating at work HSG57 (Second edition) HSE Books 1997 ISBN 0 7176 1231 7

Young people at work: A guide for employers HSG165 (Second edition) HSE Books 2000 ISBN 0 7176 1889 7

Thermal comfort in the workplace: Guidance for employers HSG194 HSE Books 1999 ISBN 0 7176 2468 4

Slips and trips: Guidance for employers on identifying hazards and controlling risks HSG155 HSE Books 1996 ISBN 0 7176 1145 0

Preventing slips, trips and falls at work Leaflet INDG225 HSE Books 1996 (single copy free or priced packs of 15 ISBN 0 7176 1183 3)

Safe movement of vehicles

Managing vehicle safety at the workplace: A short guide for employers Leaflet INDG199 HSE Books 1995 (single copy free or priced packs of 10 ISBN 0 7176 0982 0)

Rider-operated lift trucks. Operator training. Approved Code of Practice and guidance L117 HSE Books 1999 ISBN 0 7176 2455 2

Safety in working with lift trucks HSG6 (Third edition) HSE Books 2000 ISBN 0 7176 1781 5

Safe use of lifting equipment. Lifting Operations and Lifting Equipment Regulations 1998. Approved Code of Practice and guidance L113 HSE Books 1998 ISBN 0 7176 1628 2

Workplace transport safety: Guidance for employers HSG136 HSE Books 1995 ISBN 0 7176 0935 9

Reversing vehicles Leaflet INDG148 HSE Books 1993 (single copy free or priced packs of 15 ISBN 0 7176 1063 2)

Asbestos

Managing asbestos in premises Leaflet INDG223(rev2) HSE Books 2001 (single copy free or priced packs of 10 ISBN 0 7176 2092 1)

CHAPTER 4 - HEALTH RISKS

Need help on health and safety? Guidance for employers on when and how to get advice on health and safety Leaflet INDG322 HSE Books 2000 (single copy free or priced packs of 10 ISBN 0 7176 1790 4)

Health surveillance at work HSG61 (Second edition) HSE Books 1999 ISBN 0 7176 1705 X

Understanding health surveillance at work: An introduction for employers Leaflet INDG304 HSE Books 1999 (single copy free or priced packs of 15 ISBN 0 7176 1712 2)

Hazardous substances

General COSHH ACOP (Control of substances hazardous to health) and Carcinogens ACOP (Control of carcinogenic substances) and Biological agents ACOP (Control of biological agents). Control of Substances Hazardous to Health Regulations 1999. Approved Codes of Practice L5 (Third edition) HSE Books 1999 ISBN 0 7176 1670 3

COSHH a brief guide to the regulations: What you need to know about the Control of Substances Hazardous to Health Regulations 1999 (COSHH) Leaflet INDG136(rev1) HSE Books 1999 (single copy free or priced packs of 10 ISBN 0 7176 2444 7)

Control of chemicals in printing: COSHH essentials for printers PIAC/HSE Books 2000 ISBN 0 7176 1835 8

COSHH essentials: Easy steps to control chemicals. Control of Substances Hazardous to Health Regulations HSG193 HSE Books 1999 ISBN 0 7176 2421 8

Safe use of printing chemicals: COSHH and substitution Video HSE Books 1998 ISBN 0 7176 1858 7

A step by step guide to COSHH assessment HSG97 HSE Books 1993 ISBN 0 7176 1446 8

Seven steps to successful substitution of hazardous substances HSG110 HSE Books 1994 ISBN 0 7176 0695 3

Why do I need a safety data sheet? Leaflet INDG182 HSE Books 1994 (single copy free or priced packs of 10 ISBN 0 7176 0895 6)

Working safely with solvents: A guide to safe working practices Leaflet INDG273 HSE Books 1998

Health risk management: A guide to working with solvents HSG188 HSE Books 1998 ISBN 0 7176 1664 9

Occupational exposure limits 2002 Guidance Note EH40 HSE Books 2002 ISBN 0 7176 2083 2

Specific process health hazards

Safety in the use of inks, varnishes and lacquers cured by ultraviolet light or electron beam techniques PIAC/HSE Books 1993 ISBN 0 11 882045 1

Ozone: Health hazards and precautionary measures Guidance Note EH38(rev) HSE Books 1996 ISBN 07176 1206 6

Electrical risks from steam/water pressure cleaners Guidance Note PM29 (Second edition) HSE Books 1995 ISBN 0 7176 0813 1

Monitoring strategies for toxic substances HSG173 HSE Books 1997 ISBN 0 7176 1411 5

Organic isocyanates in air MDHS25/3 HSE Books 1999 ISBN 0 7176 1668 1

Isocyanates: Health hazards and precautionary measures Guidance Note EH16 (Fourth edition) HSE Books 1999 ISBN 0 7176 1701 7

Safe use of isocyanates in printing and laminating PIAC/HSE Books 1997 ISBN 0 7176 1312 7

Noise

Reducing noise at work. Guidance on the Noise at Work Regulations 1989 L108 HSE Books 1998 ISBN 0 7176 1511 1

Noise at work: A guide for employees Leaflet INDG99(rev) HSE Books 1991 (single copy free or priced packs of 20 ISBN 0 7176 0962 6)

Ear protection: Employers' duties explained Leaflet INDG298 HSE Books 1999 (single copy free or priced packs of 5 plus 5 posters MISC185 and 30 pocket cards INDG299 ISBN 0 7176 2484 6)

Protect your hearing Pocket card INDG299 HSE Books 1999 (single copy free or priced packs of 25 ISBN 0 7176 1924 9 or priced pack of 30 plus 5 posters MISC185 and 5 leaflets INDG298 ISBN 0 7176 2484 6)

Noise reduction at buckle folding machines PIAC/HSE Books 1986 ISBN 0 11 883849 0

Noise reduction at web-fed presses PIAC/HSE Books 1988 ISBN 0 11 883972 1

Health surveillance in noisy industries: Advice for employers Leaflet INDG193 HSE Books 1995 (single copy free or priced packs of 10 ISBN 0 7176 0933 2)

A guide to audiometric testing programmes Guidance Note MS26 HSE Books 1995 ISBN 0 7176 0942 1

Introducing the Noise at Work Regulations: A brief guide to the requirements for controlling noise at work Leaflet INDG75(rev) HSE Books 1989 (single copy free or priced packs of 15 ISBN 0 7176 0961 8)

Keep the noise down: Advice for purchasers of workplace machinery Leaflet INDG263 HSE Books 1997 (single copy free or priced packs of 15 ISBN 0 7176 1480 8)

Manual handling

Manual handling. Manual Handling Operations Regulations 1992. Guidance on Regulations L23 (Second edition) HSE Books 1998 ISBN 0 7176 2415 3

Handling the news: Advice for employers on manual handling of bundles PIAC Leaflet IACL105 HSE Books 1999

Handling the news: Advice for newsagents and employees on safe handling of bundles PIAC Leaflet IACL106 HSE Books 1999

What the papers weigh: Safe handling of bundles Video HSE Books 1999 ISBN 0 7176 1948 6

Back in work: Managing back pain in the workplace - A leaflet for employers and workers in small businesses Leaflet INDG333 HSE Books 2000

Work-related upper limb disorders in the printing industry Leaflet IACL91 HSE Books 1994

Work related upper limb disorders: A guide to prevention HSG60 HSE Books 1990 ISBN 0 7176 0475 6

Manual handling: Solutions you can handle HSG115 HSE Books 1994 ISBN 0 7176 0693 7

Getting to grips with manual handling: A short guide for employers Leaflet INDG143(rev1) HSE Books 2000 (single copy free or priced packs of 15 ISBN 0 7176 1754 8)

Radiation

Laser safety in printing HSE Books 1990 ISBN 0 11 885436 4

BS EN 60825-1: 1994, IEC 60825-1:1993 *Safety of laser products. Equipment classification, requirements and user's guide* British Standards Institution

Skin disease

Assessing and managing risks at work from skin exposure to chemical agents: Guidance for employers and health and safety specialists HSG205 HSE Books 2001 ISBN 0 7176 1826 9

Choice of skin care products for the workplace: Guidance for employers and health and safety specialists HSG207 HSE Books 2001 ISBN 0 7176 1825 0

Preventing dermatitis at work: Advice for employers and employees Leaflet INDG233 HSE Books 1996 (single copy free or priced packs of 15 ISBN 0 7176 1246 5)

Skin problems in the printing industry PIAC Leaflet IACL101(rev1) HSE Books 2002

Other health issues

Tackling work-related stress: A managers' guide to improving and maintaining employee health and well-being HSG218 HSE Books 2001 ISBN 0 7176 2050 6

Work-related stress: A short guide Leaflet INDG281(rev1) HSE Books 2001 (single copy free or priced packs of 10 ISBN 0 7176 2112 X)

Stress at work: A guide for employers HSG116 HSE Books 1995 ISBN 0 7176 0733 X

New and expectant mothers at work: A guide for employers HSG122 HSE Books 1994 ISBN 0 7176 0826 3

Drug misuse at work: A guide for employers Leaflet INDG91(rev2) HSE Books 1998 (single copy free or priced packs of 10 ISBN 0 7176 2402 1)

Don't mix it: A guide for employers on alcohol at work Leaflet INDG240 HSE Books 1996 (single copy free or priced packs of 10 ISBN 0 7176 1291 0)

Passive smoking at work Leaflet INDG63(rev1) HSE Books 1992 (single copy free or priced packs of 10 ISBN 0 7176 0882 4)

Legionnaires' disease. The control of legionella bacteria in water systems. Approved Code of Practice and guidance L8 (Second edition) HSE Books 2000 ISBN 0 7176 1772 6

Legionnaires' disease: A guide for employers Leaflet IAC27(rev2) HSE Books 2001 (single copy free or priced packs of 15 ISBN 0 7176 1773 4)

A guide to the Asbestos (Licensing) Regulations 1983 as amended. The Asbestos (Licensing) Regulations 1983. Guidance on Regulations L11 (Second edition) HSE Books 1999 ISBN 0 7176 2435 8

The control of asbestos at work. Control of Asbestos at Work Regulations 1987. Approved Code of Practice L27 (Third edition) HSE Books 1999 ISBN 0 7176 1673 8

Work with asbestos insulation, asbestos coating and asbestos insulating board. Control of Asbestos at Work Regulations 1987. Approved Code of Practice L28 (Third edition) HSE Books 1999 ISBN 0 7176 1674 6

Local exhaust ventilation

An introduction to local exhaust ventilation HSG37 (Second edition) HSE Books 1993 ISBN 0 7176 1001 2

Maintenance, examination and testing of local exhaust ventilation HSG54 (Second edition) HSE Books 1998 ISBN 0 7176 1485 9

Personal protective equipment

Personal protective equipment at work. Personal Protective Equipment at Work Regulations 1992. Guidance on Regulations L25 HSE Books 1992 ISBN 0 7176 0415 2

Cost and effectiveness of chemical protective gloves for the workplace: Guidance for employers and health and safety specialists HSG206 HSE Books 2001 ISBN 0 7176 1828 5

Selecting protective gloves for work with chemicals: Guidance for employers and health and safety specialists Leaflet INDG330 HSE Books 2000 (single copy free or priced packs of 15 ISBN 0 7176 1827 7)

Preventing asthma at work. How to control respiratory sensitisers L55 HSE Books 1994 ISBN 0 7176 0661 9

Respiratory sensitisers and COSHH: Breathe freely - An employers' leaflet on preventing occupational asthma Leaflet INDG95(rev2) HSE Books 1995 (single copy free or priced packs of 15 ISBN 0 7176 0914 6)

BS EN 166: 1996 *Personal eye-protection. Specifications* British Standards Institution

BS EN 345-1: 1993 *Safety footwear for professional use. Specification* British Standards Institution

BS EN 345-2: 1997 *Safety footwear for professional use. Additional specifications* British Standards Institution

BS EN 346-1: 1993 *Protective footwear for professional use. Specification* British Standards Institution

BS EN 346-2: 1997 *Protective footwear for professional use. Additional specifications* British Standards Institution

BS EN 352-1: 1993 *Hearing protectors. Safety requirements and testing. Ear-muffs* British Standards Institution

BS EN 352-2: 1993 *Hearing protectors. Safety requirements and testing. Ear-plugs* British Standards Institution

BS EN 352-3: 1997 *Hearing protectors. Safety requirements and testing. Ear-muffs attached to an industrial safety helmet* British Standards Institution

CHAPTER - 5 PROCESS SAFETY

Safe use of work equipment. Provision and Use of Work Equipment Regulations 1998. Approved Code of Practice and guidance L22 (Second edition) HSE Books 1998 ISBN 0 7176 1626 6

The Supply of Machinery (Safety) Regulations 1992 SI 1992/3073 The Stationery Office 1992 ISBN 0 11 025719 7

The Supply of Machinery (Safety) (Amendment) Regulations 1994 SI 1994/2063 The Stationery Office 1994 ISBN 0 11 045063 9

VDUs: An easy guide to the regulations HSG90 HSE Books 1994 ISBN 0 7176 0735 6

The guide to safe use of power-operated paper-cutting guillotines (Second edition) PIAC/HSE Books 1999 ISBN 0 7176 1707 6

Application of electro-sensitive protective equipment using light curtains and light beam devices to machinery HSG180 HSE Books 1999 ISBN 0 7176 1550 2

Pressure systems: Safety and you Leaflet INDG261(rev1) HSE Books 2001 (single copy free or priced packs of 15 ISBN 0 7176 1562 6)

Supplying new machinery: A short guide to the law and some information on what to do for anyone supplying machinery for use at work Leaflet INDG270 HSE Books 1998 (single copy free or priced packs of 15 ISBN 0 7176 1560 X)

Buying new machinery: A short guide to the law and some information on what to do for anyone buying new machinery for use at work Leaflet INDG271 HSE Books 1998 (single copy free or priced packs of 15 ISBN 0 7176 1559 6)

Using work equipment safely Leaflet INDG229 HSE Books 1997 (single copy free or priced packs of 5 ISBN 0 7176 1326 7)

Safe systems of work for cleaning sheet-fed offset lithographic printing presses Printing Information Sheet PIS1 HSE Books 2000

Safe systems of work for cleaning web-fed offset lithographic printing presses Printing Information Sheet PIS2 HSE Books 2000

Safe systems of work for cleaning flexographic, rotary letterpress and gravure printing presses Printing Information Sheet PIS3 HSE Books 2000

Safety at power-operated paper cutting guillotines: Your responsibilities PIAC Leaflet INDG282 HSE Books 1998

Machinery standards

The current EN Standards give specifications for new machines. However, some of the precautions may be relevant to existing machines when it is reasonably practicable to fit them.

BS EN 292-1: 1991 *Safety of machinery. Basic concepts, general principles for design. Basic terminology, methodology* British Standards Institution

BS EN 292-2: 1991 *Safety of machinery. Basic concepts, general principles for design. Technical principles and specifications* British Standards Institution

BS EN 294: 1992 *Safety of machinery. Safety distances to prevent danger zones being reached by the upper limbs* British Standards Institution

BS EN 349: 1993 *Safety of machinery. Minimum gaps to avoid crushing of parts of the human body* British Standards Institution

BS EN 811: 1997 *Safety of machinery. Safety distances to prevent danger zones being reached by the lower limbs* British Standards Institution

BS EN 953: 1998 *Safety of machinery. Guards. General requirements for the design and construction of fixed and movable guards* British Standards Institution

BS EN 954-1: 1997 *Safety of machinery. Safety related parts of control systems. General principles for design* British Standards Institution

prEN 1010: 1998 *(Draft) Safety of machinery: Safety requirements for the design and construction of printing and paper converting machinery*

BS EN 1050: 1997 *Safety of machinery. Principles for risk assessment* British Standards Institution

BS EN 1088: 1996 S*afety of machinery. Interlocking devices associated with guards. Principles for design and selection* British Standards Institution

BS EN 1539: 2000 *Dryers and ovens in which flammable substances are released. Safety requirements* British Standards Institution

BS EN 60204-1: 1993 *Safety of machinery. Electrical equipment of machines. Specification for general requirements* British Standards Institution

BS EN 61496-1: 1998, IEC 61496-1:1997 *Safety of machinery. Electro-sensitive protective equipment. General requirements and tests* British Standards Institution

CHAPTER 6 - ELECTRICITY

Memorandum of guidance on the Electricity at Work Regulations 1989. Guidance on Regulations HSR25 HSE Books 1989 ISBN 0 7176 1602 9

Your guide to the essentials of electrical safety CD ROM HSE Books 2000 ISBN 0 7176 1714 9

Do you use a steam/water pressure cleaner? You could be in for a shock! Leaflet INDG68(rev) HSE Books 1997

Electricity at work: Safe working practices HSG85 HSE Books 1993 ISBN 0 7176 0442 X

Electric storage batteries: Safe charging and use Leaflet INDG139 HSE Books 1993

Electrical safety and you Leaflet INDG231 HSE Books 1996 (single copy free or priced packs of 15 ISBN 0 7176 1207 4)

Maintaining portable electrical equipment in offices and other low-risk environments Leaflet INDG236 HSE Books 1996 (single copy free or priced packs of 10 ISBN 0 7176 1272 4)

BS 7671: 1992 *Requirements for electrical installations. IEE Wiring Regulations. Sixteenth edition* British Standards Institution

CHAPTER 7 - FIRE AND EXPLOSION

Fire safety: An employer's guide HSE Books 1999 ISBN 0 11 341229 0

The storage of flammable liquids in containers HSG51 (Second edition) HSE Books 1998 ISBN 0 7176 1471 9

Safe use and handling of flammable liquids HSG140 HSE Books 1996 ISBN 0 7176 0967 7

Safe working with flammable substances Leaflet INDG227 HSE Books 1996 (single copy free or priced packs of 15 ISBN 0 7176 1154 X)

The storage of flammable liquids in tanks HSG176 HSE Books 1998 ISBN 0 7176 1470 0

Control of fire in the printing industry PIAC/HSE Books 1992 ISBN 0 11 886375 4

BS EN 1539: 2000 *Dryers and ovens in which flammable substances are released. Safety requirements* British Standards Institution

BS 6133: 1995 *Code of practice for safe operation of lead-acid stationary batteries* British Standards Institution

PrEN 12753 *(Draft) Thermal cleaning systems for exhaust gas from surface treatment equipment - Safety requirements* British Standards Institution

BS EN 50018: 2000 *Electrical apparatus for potentially explosive atmospheres. Flameproof enclosure 'd'* British Standards Institution

BS EN 50019: 2000 *Electrical apparatus for potentially explosive atmospheres. Increased safety 'e'* British Standards Institution

BS EN 50021: 1999 *Electrical apparatus for potentially explosive atmospheres. Type of protection 'n'* British Standards Institution

CHAPTER 8 - MAINTENANCE

Maintaining portable and transportable electrical equipment HSG107 HSE Books 1994 ISBN 0 7176 0715 1

Improving maintenance: A guide to reducing human error HSE Books 2000 ISBN 0 7176 1818 8

Permit-to-work systems Leaflet INDG98(rev3) HSE Books 1997 (single copy free or priced packs of 15 ISBN 0 7176 1331 3)

While every effort has been made to ensure the accuracy of the references listed in this publication, their future availability cannot be guaranteed.

See the 'Further Information' section for details of how to obtain publications.

FURTHER INFORMATION

How to obtain publications

HSE publications

HSE priced and free publications (including many PIAC publications) are available by mail order from:

HSE Books
PO Box 1999
Sudbury
Suffolk CO10 2WA
Tel: 01787 881165
Fax: 01787 313995
Website: www.hsebooks.co.uk
(HSE priced publications are also available from bookshops.)

British Standards

British Standards are available from:

BSI Customer Services
389 Chiswick High Road
London W4 4AL
Tel: 020 8996 9001
Fax: 020 8996 7001
Website: www.bsi-global.com

Stationery Office (formerly HMSO) publications

Copies of the Acts, Regulations and other Stationery Office (formerly HMSO) publications mentioned in this guide are available from:

The Publications Centre
PO Box 276
London SW8 5DT
Tel: 0870 600 5522
Fax: 0870 600 5533
Website: www.clicktso.com
(They are also available from bookshops.)

Other useful addresses

Printing Industry Advisory Committee (PIAC)

The Secretary
PIAC
Health and Safety Executive
3 East Grinstead House
London Road
East Grinstead
West Sussex RH19 1RR
Tel: 01342 334200
Fax: 01342 334222

Graphical, Paper and Media Union

Graphical, Paper and Media Union
Keys House
63/67 Bromham Road
Bedford MK40 2AG
Tel: 01234 351521
Fax: 01234 270580
Website: www.gpmu.org.uk

British Printing Industries Federation

British Printing Industries Federation
Farringdon Point
29-35 Farringdon Road
London EC1M 3JF
Tel: 020 7915 8300
Fax: 020 7405 7784
Website: www.bpif.org.uk

Institute of Occupational Health and Safety (IOSH)

IOSH
The Grange
Highfield Drive
Wigston
Leicestershire LE18 1NN
Tel: 0116 257 3100
Fax: 0116 257 3101
Website: www.iosh.co.uk

Royal Society for the Prevention of Accidents (RoSPA)

RoSPA
Edgbaston Park
353 Bristol Road
Edgbaston
Birmingham B5 7ST
Tel: 0121 248 2000
Fax: 0121 248 2001
Website: www.rospa.co.uk

British Safety Council

British Safety Council
70 Chancellors Road
London W6 9RS
Tel: 020 8741 1231
Fax: 020 8741 4555
Website: www.britishsafetycouncil.org

INDEX

Printed and published by the Health and Safety Executive   C75   03/02